SARA WHEELER

Sara Wheeler's travel books include *Terra Incognita: Travels in Antarctica* ('I cannot believe there will ever be a better book about the Antarctic' – *Telegraph*), *The Magnetic North: Travels in the Arctic* ('Exceptional' – *New York Times Book Review*) and *Access All Areas: Selected Writings 1990–2010*. She has also written biographies of Apsley Cherry-Garrard ('Superb' – *Guardian*) and Denys Finch Hatton ('Magnificent' – *Sunday Times*); and *O My America!* ('Unforgettable' – *Sunday Telegraph*).

Praise for Sara Wheeler:

'Spirited, humorous and highly intelligent, she is also a writer of rare talent'
Observer

'Sara Wheeler is an eloquent and intrepid guide'
Elizabeth Kolbert

'Wheeler's sense of place, science, self and story is exceptional'
New York Times Book Review

'A pleasure to read'

SARA WHEELER

Mud and Stars

Travels in Russia

VINTAGE

1 3 5 7 9 10 8 6 4 2

Vintage
20 Vauxhall Bridge Road,
London SW1V 2SA

Vintage is part of the Penguin Random House group
of companies whose addresses can be found
at global.penguinrandomhouse.com

 Penguin
Random House
UK

First published by Vintage in 2020
First published in the UK by Jonathan Cape in 2019

penguin.co.uk/vintage

A CIP catalogue record for this book is available
from the British Library

ISBN 9780099584131

Printed and bound in Great Britain by Clays Ltd, Elcograf S.p.A.

Penguin Random House is committed to a sustainable future for
our business, our readers and our planet. This book is made
from Forest Stewardship Council® certified paper.

In Memoriam
Gillon Reid Aitken
1938–2016

We sit in the mud, my friend, and reach for the stars.

Turgenev, *Fathers and Sons*

Contents

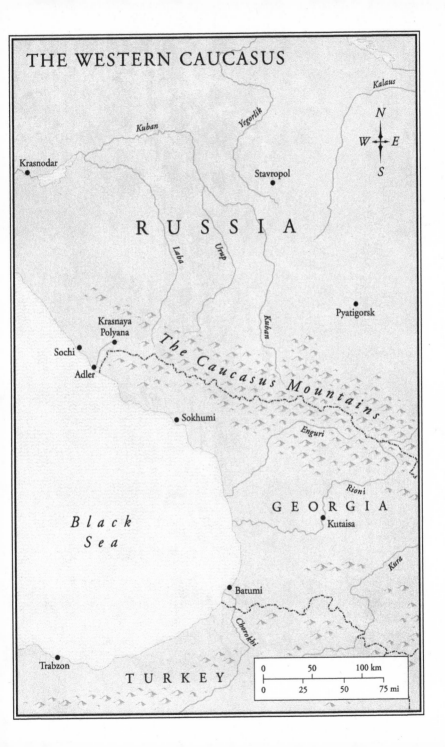

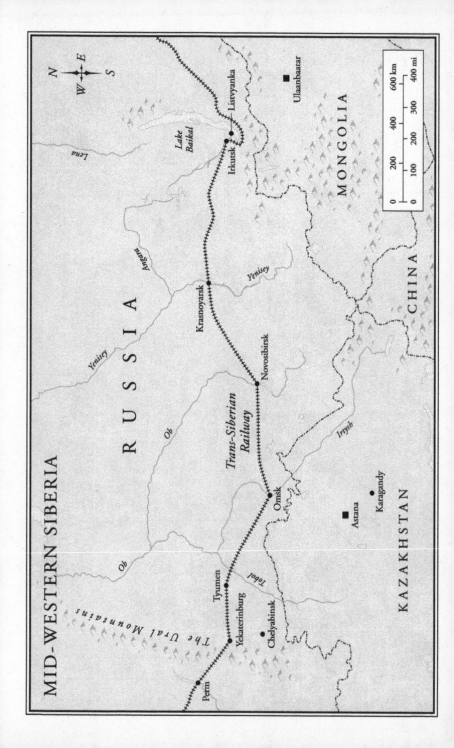

Introduction

I travelled across eight time zones, from rinsed north-western beet-root fields to Far Eastern Arctic tundra where Chukchi still hunt walrus in a region the size of France that has no roads. I paddled through the cauldron of ethnic soup that is the Caucasus, where flashing-epauletted Lermontov died in the aromatic air, and where sheaves of corn still stand like soldiers on a blazing afternoon, just like they do in Gogol's stories. I sunbathed fully clothed, even wearing a woolly hat, on the shore of fabled Lake Baikal eating 'caviar' with my fingers from a tub purchased at the fish market for 300 roubles (about £4). I went to writers' homes – one of a few things Russia does well (preserving them, I mean). I was at Turgenev's forest-buried estate of Spasskoye-Lutovinovo in spring, when the scent of dog rose hung on the breeze, bougainvillea tubercular on walls. Turgenev complained in a letter that spring in Europe lacked the explosiveness of that season in Russia. I took the Trans-Siberian Railway in winter, crunching across snowy platforms to buy table tennis bats of dried fish from *babushki*, and sailed the Black Sea in summer where dolphins leapt in front of violet Abkhazian peaks. I was searching for a Russia not in the news – a Russia of common humanity and daily struggles – and my guides were writers of the Golden Age.

Russia was the first foreign country I ever visited. I was eleven. I
have been looking over my shoulder at it ever since. Like many, I am
in thrall to these writers, roughly Pushkin to Tolstoy, who continue
to dominate world literature. It helped, getting through them all, to
have spent a lot of time in the polar regions: Tolstoy's doorstops
were made for whiteouts. I read *War and Peace* for the first time at
the South Pole, looking through the plastic porthole of a tent at
hundreds of kilometres of shimmering flat ice as a thousand horses
galloped over the plain at Borodino. The second time, many years
later, I was stranded in another tent, on the Greenland ice-cap, and
again Tolstoy's genius filled bright night whiteness. My aim in this
book is to show how the best writers of the Golden Age, which I
define, broadly, as the period between 1800 and 1910,* represent their
country, then and now. I followed nineteenth-century footsteps in
order to make connections.

The writers here are not a homogeneous group. One scholar says
Tolstoy tells us to give away our money; Dostoyevsky tells us to go
to church; Chekhov says 'I'm sorry, there's nothing I can do'; Gogol
says 'To hell with it'. But they all deal with a fumbling search for
certainties with which we all engage. And they are failures in one sense
or another, as we all are. Tolstoy was obsessed with truth, but only
told it in his novels. Dostoyevsky, obsessed not with truth but with
God, was a compulsive gambler. He pawned his watch so many times
that his saintly second wife said she never knew what time it was.
While each chapter of *Mud and Stars* is centred on a particular writer,
or in two cases, a couple of writers, I have aimed at a flowing whole,
not discrete essays. There are biographical pages – I always like to
know about a writer's life, though I am not particularly interested in
tracing connections between life and work. Biography has no bearing

---

* Authors mainly active from about 1890 to 1934 are generally thought to belong
to the Silver Age, but as they don't feature in this book, I've stuck to the old-
fashioned definition of the Golden Age: 1800–1910.

on a reader's appreciation of books. It doesn't matter how much or how little you know about a life.

Moscow and Petersburg are so unrepresentative of Russia that I avoided them as much as possible. They always have been unrepresentative. Alexander Sergeyevich Pushkin was born into the nobility in 1799, when French was the language of the cultured classes. Tens of millions of Russians outside the two main cities, however, knew nothing of European influences, just as 140 million today know nothing of oligarchical bling. Their lives were and are consumed with the generally dreadful business of being Russian. I cherish the old-fashioned ideal that government can play a role enhancing the lives of its citizens without threatening civil liberties, allowing individuals the maximum space to live and flourish as they choose. I saw nothing of this in Russia.

Mostly, on my travels, I used homestays. I spent many months in fourth-floor 1950s apartments with windowless bathrooms, sprawled on sofas with my hosts, watching television, my new friends bent over devices moaning about Ukraine. I remember lifting the curtain and peeping from a sofabed in Irkutsk in Siberia at six in the morning to see people scurrying to work through snow in darkness illuminated by the annunciatory glow of the few streetlamps that worked, heads down, shoulders hunched.

I wrote this book at a time of deteriorating relations between the West and Russia. Nationalism had besieged the country. People I stayed with or met on trains had no illusions about the kleptocracy under which they lived, but as we watched flickering images of Putin bending a piece of metal with his bare hands or spearing an emperor-sized fish, the prevailing attitude was 'Yes, he's a monster. But he's our monster.' Almost everyone felt that the West was out to get them, and in the light of that, at least Putin was batting for Russia. The country's GDP at that time was approximately equal to that of Italy, a country with just over a third of the population of Russia and under a fiftieth of the landmass.

Russia emerged as an increasingly shocking country. It is in the grip of a murderous dictatorship. The leadership stinks, at every level, if people can stink at levels, which I think they can. But what about the ones who aren't leaders or rich or powerful? I resolved to give them a voice, in my small way. You'll hear them in these pages. I wrote about what I saw and heard, or tried to.

Along the way I learned Russian, at least well enough to read a Chekhov story in the original (and indeed read the master's underappreciated travel writing: 'At the inn where I was staying the maid, when giving me a spoon, wiped it against her backside'). But I never dreamed in Russian. I've learned a few languages, and that's when you know you've got it. I also pursued some topics for fun, and I include them here for the same reason. I tried to learn to cook Russian dishes, for example, and went to concert halls to hear Russian songs. I hope that besides the fun, these themes contribute to an amateur's sketch of a country which is lovable despite it all.

There is no such thing as the Russian soul, or perhaps even Russian culture – it's too big a country: one-sixth of the earth's landmass, and it's too diverse and too socially divided. (Catherine the Great said it was too big to govern, or so they say she said.) Once I'd been in the polar north and the Caucasian south I saw that for myself. The books discussed in these pages engage not with that chimera, but with the complexity of human experience. There is a Russian literal landscape, and its emotional counterpart.

*

I worked on the project with great pleasure for two years, until a crisis overtook my personal life. I became a former writer. When I eventually roused myself – after a couple more years – and decided life might be worth living, I returned to my Russian notes, of which I had hundreds and hundreds of pages, and my shelves of annotated books. Rereading it all, I met myself coming back. These pages give form to the vanished years. I was in the mud, and my writers were the stars. Books have been kinder to me than life. I have attempted to show how I have appropriated the volumes mentioned in these pages into my own life. All literature is a dialectic. The same goes for my stabs at cooking Russian food and so on. I was trying to absorb as much as I could.

The writers you'll find between these covers made wonderful companions. They kept me pretty cheerful. When I was writing about Dostoyevsky I told one of my Russian teachers that I found him and his work a balm. She raised an eyebrow at such a description of that messianic, tortured xenophobe and genius. But Dostoyevsky wrote about human mutuality, and about taking responsibility. I felt he would have understood my trauma better than anyone.

When I started this project I was worried that scholars of Russian would heap scorn on a work that attempted only a superficial glance at a rich and broad culture. But after what happened to me in that two-year hiatus, I felt that nothing could ever frighten me again. And in any case I have faced the fear of experts with every book I have ever written, as I am by nature that most unfashionable thing, a generalist. Someone has to be one. I am neither an expert nor an academic and I only touched on everything here with butterfly wings, but from a personal point of view that was better than not touching it at all.

I

The People Stay Silent

The people stay silent (*Narod bezmolvstvuyet*)

Pushkin, *Boris Godunov*

Alexander Sergeyevich Pushkin was a lubricious, bawdy, impetuous, whoring gambler who seldom missed an opportunity to pick a fight. He never had a proper job, even though he was for a while nominally at the Ministry of Foreign Affairs, a department of the Chancery. He lived mostly off his father. He had a tortured relationship with both the civil service and the authorities. The government of Alexander I, the tsar who had defeated Napoleon and was by European standards a medieval figure, was becoming increasingly reactionary, and an incontinent loudmouth like Pushkin had no chance. One prince, a high-level civil servant, recorded in his diary after a dinner in January 1822, 'Listened to Pushkin at table … he tries to convince everyone he meets … that only a scoundrel would not wish a change of government in Russia. His favourite conversation is based on abuse and sarcasm and even when he tries to be polite there is a sardonic smile on his lips.' Pushkin was opposed to landowners, supported the abolition of serfdom, and indeed when he got going – according to the princely dinner companion – 'began to pour abuse on all classes of the population'. He announced 'that all noblemen should be hanged, and that he would tighten the noose round their necks with pleasure'. It is a testament to the respect in which literature was held that the government didn't kill him. Of course, three generations later Pushkin's dream of an egalitarian world came true in Russia. But they shot writers then.

Pushkin chose to write poems in Russian. Literary Russian had only evolved in the eighteenth century, stimulating a new school of poets from which Pushkin emerged. He turned to prose later. In his short story 'The Queen of Spades' ('*Pikovaya dama*'), when the countess asks her grandson if he will bring her a novel, he replies with a question: would she like a Russian one? 'Are there any Russian novels?' the countess queries. (As a young woman in the middle of the eighteenth century she only read in French.) Pushkin produced the first major Russian work in almost every literary genre. Just as Peter the Great, standing on the banks of the Neva, founded St Petersburg 'to open a window onto Europe', so Pushkin both Russified literary Russian and made his nation's books into something of Europe. And he is contemporary for all time.

The young Pushkin, 'Sasha', grew up with household serfs and then attended the prestigious Imperial Lycée, where pupils were not permitted to leave during their six-year term. They studied the humanities, following the English public school system, and cultivated the worship of male friendship. ('My friends, this brotherhood of ours will live. | United, like the soul, it cannot perish.') Parents could visit on Sundays and feast days, but for two years, as a young teenager, Pushkin never saw his mother. While he was a pupil, Napoleon entered Moscow and for four days the city burned. This was the defining trauma of Pushkin's generation. His uncle was one of many who lost everything. The man fled the city with only the clothes he stood up in.

In the summer of 1824 the tsar dismissed the poet from the civil service (besides his political leanings, Pushkin was having an affair with his boss' wife, which can't have helped). Alexander exiled him first to the south, and then to his ancestral estate in the north-west, where he remained under civil and church surveillance in the company of the serf Nikita Timofeyevich Kozlov, who had brought him up. Whenever a friend visited from Petersburg, the pair would hear the sleighbells of the abbot from the local monastery. The old man would shuffle in for a glass of rum, the three would drink and mumble in the candlelit room, and the abbot would ride off again to compose his report.

*

Through an open window, linden boughs traced lines in smalt blue. A branch bent inside the room, jewelled pods trembling, and sunlight glinted off a champagne cooler. Silhouette cut-outs were fashionable in the 1820s, and the young women of the house had stuck a dozen to the music room walls, an indoor version of linden branches against the sky. I had gone to find Pushkin in the north-west. When, in 1824 – already the most famous poet in Russia – the tsar exiled him to his mother's ancestral land for writing anti-royalist verses, the prisoner visited this neighbouring house on the Trigorskoye estate (the name means 'three hills') every day, walking or riding from his own, contiguous, land. In a letter to a friend, he referred to Trigorskoye's owner, a 43-year-old widow, as 'an elderly lady'. But in exile, elderly ladies have their charms.

Irina, my guide in Pushkin country, was a true apostle, and reluctant to admit that the great man had affairs not only with the widow, but with the five daughters of the house, and with his serfs too. Pushkin was a heroic shagger who only had time to write when he had a sexually transmitted disease. A friend once told a mutual acquaintance, '[Pushkin] is finishing the fourth canto of his poem. Two or three more doses of the clap and it'll be done.'

Alexander Sergeyevich was short – five foot three (160 centimetres) – with darkish wavy hair. One girlfriend wrote of 'dreadful side whiskers, dishevelled hair, nails like claws, small stature, affected manners, and an arrogant attitude towards the women he chose to love'. Who could resist? Like many great artists, Pushkin lacked something in the human department. A contemporary described him as 'our immortal bard, who in spite of his great talent, is an extremely vain, bad-tempered man, spoilt by the admiration of his contemporaries'. His reputation declined in his last years, and subsided further after his death, historical revisionism being as unavoidable as the grave. It took a generation or two for him to come back, then the Bolsheviks put the boot in; Lenin's wife, Nadezhda Krupskaya, led a special campaign to have the class enemy Pushkin's books banned from public libraries. But by the centenary of the poet's death in 1937 the Soviets decided Pushkin was acceptable after all, and might as well be co-opted into the flagging cause. The country went berserk with festivities for this anniversary: plays, films, pilgrimages, factory study groups, carnivals on collective farms, hundreds of streets renamed. Tens of millions subscribed to a new *Collected Works*. *Pravda* declared the poet a 'semi-divine being', and the Central Committee claimed he was 'the Father of Communism'. Stalin was at that time zealously murdering writers who made the mistake of being alive. Of the 700 authors who attended the First Writers' Congress in 1934, 650 were dead by the time the second came around. The vaunted *Collected Works* appeared twelve years late because the institute responsible had repeatedly lost staff to the purges.

Trigorskoye nestles on the western rim of Russia, close to the Estonian border and a couple of hours' motoring from Pskov, an ancient city on the Velikaya River. That waterway joins the Baltic via a network of lakes and once-navigable channels which formed one of the earliest Russian trade routes. So it's a kind of border itself: Putin went to Pskov in 2000 and said 'Russia starts here', meaning both geographically and historically. Many people repeated this phrase to me. It gave them a purchase on the nationalism besieging twenty-first-century Russia. The country was too big to be anything but itself – too powerful to need alliances, too badly governed to go to the good, too corrupt to build from the base. Putin was at that time energetically blocking UN resolutions to end the fighting in Syria.

The widow and her five daughters and one stepdaughter had lived in the former flag factory I stood in, a single-storey dwelling with rooms off a broad central corridor. A veranda looked over the lake beyond the trees. It was a house of chaste simplicity – champagne cooler notwithstanding – with polished wood floors that still smelled of cedar and ceiling-height stoves whose blue-and-white tiles reflected lacy patterns of light.

When the weather was fine, the occupants danced in an outdoor ballroom next to the teal-green lake. Sometimes the young women of the house – in addition to the daughters, nieces came to visit – sent a serf over to Pushkin's house with cut flowers, even though roses bloomed around his place too. Pushkin said his heart stayed in Trigorskoye.

The state has preserved the house and opened it to the public. Russians revere the role of the writer – he or she occupies a kind of vatic position – and their record on such matters as the preservation of writers' houses is commendable. It's an easy thing to do if you're controlling all artistic output and locking up harmless pop stars. At Trigorskoye Irina and I were the only visitors. A female employee sat in each room. Their job was to close the door after me. Irina reckoned these attendants earn about 7,000 roubles a month (£62). They looked at me hatchet-faced. A veil of Soviet suspicion still hung over proceedings, and often I was asked, in some deserted museum, to show my ticket six or seven times.

Looking out on such a serene house and a landscape of dips and rivers, lakes, blooms and small wooden bridges, I didn't wonder that Pushkin had loved this place. Yet he was the least serene human being to have lived. I mentioned this to Irina. 'But he had a heart,' she said, squeezing her lips together. She had dyed her hair the colour of cornflakes, a shade popular with Russian women, but she also had a glass eye. This seemed to suit a Pushkinian guide perfectly. His genius lay in his ability to observe with a sea eagle's eye, but he refracted what he saw through the medium of formal poetry. As we moved into the bedrooms Irina broke into a poem – she did this every five minutes.

> *In alien lands devoutly clinging*
> *To age-old rites of Russian earth,*
> *I let a captive bird go winging*
> *To greet the radiant spring's rebirth.*

Pushkin is part of the Russian national consciousness. Some years ago I was researching in the Far Eastern region of Chukotka, the sepulchral back end of Siberia over 6,000 kilometres from the lindens that bent through the Trigorskoye windows. The territory was closed to foreigners (I had inveigled myself onto a multinational but small science project). Forbidden zones were familiar to the point of institutionalisation in the Soviet system, but more than forty 'sensitive' cities remain shut off. I was billeted in the regional capital in a homestay apartment on the fourth floor of a *khrushchevka*, the Soviet blocks that are as Russian as cucumber. As is often the case in northern Russia, a coal-fired power plant maintained a tropical temperature in the sub-Arctic, and my landlords, Sasha and Marina, a couple in their sixties, patrolled the apartment in shorts and vests. One day we hunched over their small kitchen table extracting eggs from the roe of an unidentified fish by rubbing beige lumps over the strings of a badminton racquet. Conversation drifted along, punctuated by long periods of silence. Suddenly, apparently without thinking, and almost as fluently as cornflake-haired Irina, Sasha began declaiming the opening lines of Pushkin's *The Bronze Horseman*. They describe Peter the Great, six feet eight inches (200 centimetres) tall, looking out over the Neva on the spot that became St Petersburg:

> *On the shore of desolate waves*
> *He stood, full of lofty thoughts,*
> *And gazed afar.*

Continuing through the poem, skipping verses here and there and not minding about forgotten half-lines – *Where swamp and forest stood da da da da* – Sasha recounted how an eagle flew over Peter's head before settling at the top of two birch trees that formed an arch, at which Peter said, 'Here shall be a town.' My host's voice rose and fell like the Neva tide, and the three of us instinctively began rubbing the roe in time with Pushkin's four-iamb lines (iambic tetrameters), possibly the first time this had ever occurred. There were no books in the flat and we were eight time zones from Petersburg. I had thought about those minutes in the kitchen many times in the intervening years. It was my introduction to the significance of Pushkin. Above all, I wondered, what framework lay beneath his place in the inner life of Russia?

*

Many of Pushkin's friends in Moscow and St Petersburg were members of secret societies, and while he was in exile they plotted rebellion and revolution. In December 1825, the poet was larking in the Trigorskoye music room when a courier brought news that one of these groups of liberal noblemen had taken action (they became known as Decembrists). Confusion over the succession following Alexander I's sudden death in Taganrog provoked the December revolt (although the perpetrators had been on the lookout for an opportunity to act). Alexander's legitimate children had predeceased him, and his younger brother Constantine had renounced his claim in favour of the other brother, Nicholas – except the latter didn't know of Constantine's renunciation. Confusion swirled around Petersburg barracks, especially when Nicholas forced soldiers to swear allegiance to Constantine. New oaths echoed around the military courtyards when the truth emerged, and in the chaos the Decembrists sowed disorder. Nicholas began his reign, which was to be autocratic even by imperial standards, by crushing the rebellion. Besides a desire to overthrow the tsar, the Decembrists wanted to establish a common national language. The issue was linked to notions of a civil society (though these notions varied widely), and was similar to the arguments of the previous century over what constituted a Russian literary language. The zealous rebels aimed to expunge foreign words and replace them with Russian ones. Many of the rebels believed that Peter the Great's Europeanisation had steered Russia away from her national destiny. Pushkin launched a debate on whether Peter's reforms were a good thing.

When the news came that the Decembrists had acted, Pushkin shouted orders for a sleigh, and set out to join the revolution. But a hare crossed his path – bad luck – and he turned the horses back. (During the years of Soviet rehabilitation the authorities played up Pushkin's anti-tsar activities.) He was always impetuous. Folklore and superstition were real to him – he had absorbed them from his serf nanny, and as part of his concept of essential Russianness they informed his imagination. When he incorporated folklore in his early work, critics blamed him for using material they considered unworthy of the poetic muse. They said it was like introducing a bearded peasant into the drawing room. Some time after the running hare episode, Pushkin received news that the Decembrist uprising had failed. Five of the leaders were hanged, and the tsar banished the rest. Alexander Sergeyevich clung to his ideals, trying to achieve that impossible compromise between criticism and criminality.

We walked, as he had done so many hundreds of times, from the low walls of Trigorskoye across to the Pushkin estate, called Mikhailovskoye. A shower had greened the beetroot fields, and storks swooped in from the river to pick frogs from a tractor's wake. Outbuildings appeared, the first a large birch-and-pine *banya* (Russian sauna) with a mossy roof. Inside, bunches of birch twigs dangled from the stove. Russians claim the *banya* as their first doctor, vodka being the second and raw garlic the third.

We stopped in a glade next to the riverbank. Wisps of cirrostratus drifted across the sky. 'This', said Irina, pointing ahead, 'is Tatiana's Bench.' I kicked through undergrowth and sat down on a plain wooden seat in dappled shadows. This, then, inspired the famous moonlit scene in *Eugene Onegin* (pronounced *An-YE-ghin*), the first Russian novel, albeit in verse. Tatiana confesses to her nurse:

> *'I am in love,' again she whispered*
> *To the old woman mournfully.*
> *'You are unwell,' her nurse persisted.*
> *'I am in love. Go. Let me be.'*

Pushkin often returned to the pathology of love.

He had arrived at Mikhailovskoye with three cantos of *Onegin* in his writing case. Pushkin had invented a special fourteen-line stanza form of iambic tetrameters and a sequence of rhymes; the formality, he hoped, would enable him to smuggle in themes otherwise

unacceptable to the tsar.* His parents and siblings were in residence
when he got there, but they soon left, and he was alone. He finished
Onegin at Mikhailovskoye, writing with bitten-off bits of quill, some
so small he could barely hold them in his fingers. When the bits reached
the end of their useful lives he tossed them on the floor, so the area
around his desk resembled a spiny carpet.

It's a book-length poem about everyday things – tweezers and
toothbrushes, bedbugs, lingonberry juice, tulle mobcaps, coping with
rejection, looking back with regret, floundering around in the mass of
doubts and dreams that separate us from animals. To a Russian the
verse-novel is made up entirely of quotations.

And it's funny. Picture the scene when Onegin arrives at the theatre:

> *Applause all round. Onegin enters,*
> *Treading on toes at every stall,*
> *Askew, his double eyeglass centres*
> *On ladies whom he can't recall.*

Pushkin captures a scene in a few brushstrokes. Here is Onegin rushing
to a ball:

> *Through sleeping streets, past houses darkened*
> *Twin carriage lamps pour out a jocund*
> *Illumination row on row,*
> *Projecting rainbows on the snow.*

---

* Stanley Mitchell, whose translations I have mostly used in this chapter (because
they are the best in accuracy, in fluency and above all in tone), explains the form
thus: 'The iambic tetrameter is an octosyllabic line with a weak and a strong beat
repeated four times (as in, *The boy stood on the burning deck*). This is the so-called
masculine line, which has a strong stress on the final syllable. The feminine line adds
an unstressed syllable (*The boy stood on the burning vessel*). The *Onegin* stanza is made
up of eight masculine lines and six feminine.'

Onegin is a dandy ('At least three hours he spent preparing | In front of mirrors in his lair') and suffers *khandra*, that special kind of melancholy boredom the French call *ennui* and Anglo-Saxons don't acknowledge ('Naught touched Onegin to the core | He noticed nothing any more'). He befriends his country neighbour Vladimir Lensky and his fiancée Olga, whose dreamy, bookish sister Tatiana falls in love with him. Onegin is indifferent to Tatiana, and flirts instead with Olga. Lensky, 'with hatred blazing', needlessly challenges Onegin to a duel, and, starting at thirty-two paces, Onegin shoots his friendly neighbour dead. He then sets off on a three-year wander. I imagined the poet absorbed in the composition of those passages at Mikhailovskoye, close to the samovar, lonely for his friends. Onegin returns to Petersburg and meets Tatiana again. But she has married a stodgy military man ('A certain general of substance | Won't take his eyes off her at all') and lives as a princess. She rejects Onegin, choosing duty and fidelity ('"But I am someone else's wife, | To him I shall be true for life."') The poet conveys the tension between Tatiana's sense of duty and her acknowledgment of past feelings. The action covers five and a half years, and Pushkin reckoned it had taken him longer than that to write the book.

As for Mikhailovskoye, Empress Elizabeth had given the estate and its forty-one villages to Pushkin's great-grandfather Abram Gannibal, along with 800 serfs. Gannibal was a black man. Slavers had plucked him from Africa when he was eight; he was probably from Logone-Birni, in what is now Cameroon, though Eritrea also claims him, and not long ago, in another example of the importance of Pushkin in Russia, a scholar was mugged on the streets of Moscow by what he called 'the Eritrean mafia' for uncovering the Cameroon link. The kidnappers shipped Gannibal to the Ottoman court in Constantinople where the Russian ambassador bought him as a present for Peter the Great, a tsar with a taste for the exotic. He became Peter's protégé, and an accomplished military engineer. What did the Mikhailovskoye serfs make of the new master? They had never seen a black man before. Pushkin inherited his thick curly hair.

*

We began our tour, floorboards creaking confidentially as sentries sat mute. Stopping in front of a portrait of one of the poet's brothers, Irina said, 'Lev had many gambling debts which Alexander Sergeyevich paid off.'

'Alexander Sergeyevich was a gambler too, wasn't he?' I asked.

'This is a chair he must have sat in,' said Irina, squeezing her lips together again. He often lost everything he possessed. I found the reverential attitude touching.

Butterflies described circles in lindens, and a woodpecker worked on a hollow trunk. Not far from the house, a sign indicated ALLEYA KERN, Kern Avenue. The beauty Anna Petrovna Kern was one of the widow's nieces. Pushkin wrote the most famous love poem in the Russian language to her.

> *That moment comes to me again:*
> *You passed before my eyes,*
> *A fleeting vision of pure beauty,*
> *A spirit from the skies.*

I was standing in the chequered light with Irina. 'He had a love affair with her, didn't he?'

'No. She was married.'

After divorcing her elderly husband, Kern married her sixteen-year-old cousin. She sold Pushkin's letters.

The tsar granted Pushkin conditional freedom in 1826, and when the poet appeared in Moscow theatre stalls on returning from exile, everyone turned to look at him. Men he had never met came up to say how pleased they were that he had come back. At a ball, he met Natalya Goncharova, a teenager in a white chiffon dress with a gold circlet on her head. Two years later, he married her, writing to a friend to say that she was his 113th love. In an earlier expression of misgivings about the institution of marriage he had said that 'lawful cunt castrates the mind'. On his engagement, his father gave him 200 serfs. The marriage was like an ocean voyage in a non-ocean-going boat. Natalya was beautiful and popular at court. Pushkin hated the way she lapped up the niceties of high society, and wrote her sacks of letters asking her to stop flirting. She spent too much on frocks. They had four children.

Still pursued by censors, Pushkin wrote in exasperation to a friend to say that when he used the word 'tree' it was interpreted to mean 'constitution', and 'arrow' was supposed to mean 'autocracy'. In addition, he had financial difficulties – he complained at one point of the damnable expense of changing cooks. The court meanwhile roiled in affairs and liaisons, intrigue and gambling. How anything ever got done remains a mystery. Pushkin wanted to move back to Mikhailovskoye as he hated the protocol and expense. 'Moscow is a city of nonentities,' he wrote to a friend. 'On its gates is written, "Abandon all intelligence, O ye who enter here."'

The tsar was Asiatic Russia incarnate: a prominent writer described him as Genghis Khan with a telegraph (Stalin, others said later, was Genghis with a telephone; somebody must be saying now that Putin is Genghis with the internet). Nicholas would not let Pushkin leave, not least because he, the tsar, was enjoying a flirtatious relationship with Natalya. He appointed Pushkin to a relatively low rank at court, lent him money and awarded him a salary for historical research. Nicholas found the company of his national poet congenial, and in public lavished favours on him. But in private he was determined to keep free speech in chains. This public/private polarity characterised the Golden Age. And so it goes on. Not long ago Mikhail Prokhorov, Russia's third richest man and a banking and mining titan who ran against Putin in 2012 for the presidency, remembered his Soviet youth when his parents and their friends gathered in their flat (Prokhorov was born in 1965). 'At work,' he remembered, 'everyone was a strict Communist, but in the kitchen everyone was a dissident.'

Pushkin became depressed. His mother died. He grew tired of playing both ends (court and liberal writers) against the middle. He was angry all the time. Friends perished. He worked, but, like Prospero, every third thought was of the grave.

The poet of the human heart had staggered into a marriage that was to kill him. Convinced he was a cuckold, in 1837 Pushkin challenged French guardsman Georges-Charles d'Anthès to a duel. So life was imitating art. Was Pushkin show-boating, for all his repugnance for the niceties of court? Probably. The duel took place beyond the Chernaya River. The day was clear and sunny, and Petersburgers were tobogganing in the hills. D'Anthès wounded his aggressor, and Pushkin died on a couch at home two days later. He was thirty-seven. The tsar paid off his debts and granted his children a generous sum.

They took him, in a covered wagon, up to his ancestral estate in the north-west, changing horses at the post stations. Nikita Kozlov, the dead man's childhood servant, sat next to the coffin the whole way. They buried him at the Svyatogorsky Monastery, where the old abbot who used to spy on Pushkin had also entered the soil. Two serfs hacked a hole in the frozen ground. They lowered the coffin and covered it with snow. He was next to his mother, and there he remains, surrounded by iron railings garlanded with bouquets in cellophane wrapping.

The young Mikhail Lermontov mourned Pushkin, in verse, and the tsar exiled him to the Caucasus for irreverence. So the baton was passed from poet to poet.

*

On the spring day of my visit, Pushkin pilgrims milled around the courtyard taking photographs of the modest stone obelisk on an arched plinth. Someone had put an apple in there. The bell tolled for worship, and monks flew out of the side buildings like starlings and flapped towards the plain cream church. People were buying plastic beakers of a honey drink.

'Let's have some!' I said.

'It's horrible,' said Irina, slicing the air with a forefinger in the direction of the drink stand. She was unyielding in all matters. But then she said, almost under her breath, '*Narod bezmolvstvuyet.*' She was looking over a sea of visitors, many there for religious purposes rather than for Pushkin, many old, most decrepit, and all poor. '*Narod bezmolvstvuyet*' is the final stage direction in the revised version of Pushkin's *Boris Godunov*. It means 'The people stay silent', and it has become the most famous line in the play. Russians quote it when collectively obliged to acquiesce in their leaders' actions.

*

My hotel, the Arina R., on the outskirts of a village not far from the Pushkins' ancestral home, was named after Pushkin's serf nanny, Arina Rodionovna Yakovleva. He called her 'Mother'; his real mother was cold. It was common for young noblemen to revere their nannies. ('My friend in days devoid of good … you still await me with your love,' Pushkin wrote when Arina Rodionovna died.) The Arina R. consisted of low-level wooden chalets in undulating countryside. Regulations in Russia bar guides from trespassing on one another's territory, so at the monastery Irina had arranged to pick up a local colleague. Here, as at every hotel I stayed, the whole team hurried in to inspect my room: guide, local guide, driver, passers-by. Once they had left, I took a shower – a rusty tap ran a shattering stream of cold water – and settled on the terrace of the simple, two-storey main building and ordered *pelmeni*, filled parcels of dough usually translated as 'dumplings' but more like ravioli, or wontons. Siberian women used to make sacks of them at the onset of winter, and hang supplies out to freeze. Mine arrived in a clay dish, stuffed with mushrooms and served with chives and *smetana* (sour cream). Pushkin loved small baked potatoes prepared in this way and wrote to his wife when they were apart to say he ate them like a peasant, together with soft-boiled eggs, which he consumed like Louis XVIII.

I settled with a bilingual *Eugene Onegin* on the terrace. The light was still golden at 11.15 p.m., filtering obliquely through the trees. As I was thinking about a retreat to my room, a man in plastic sandals and a toupee approached carrying a carafe of vodka and sat at my table without asking. A television in the corner was showing footage of Putin on a horse. I pointed at the screen. 'What do you think of that?' I asked my companion.

He said something I didn't understand, the tone indicating that it might mean 'Bollocks'. The fellow snorted sourly before pulling a smartphone from his pocket and stabbing at the keyboard, knocking the glass onto the tiled floor as he did so. When he reached the required site, he handed me the phone. It was showing a YouTube clip of Putin attempting, on national television, to bend a frying pan with his bare hands. The president's near monopoly of the television networks facilitated this crude construction of a celebrity cult (though crucially, he didn't control the web. Not yet anyway).

Television relentlessly promotes Putin as the embodiment of Russian statehood. And even in the internet era, more than eighty per cent of Russians get their news from television. (That said, Putin has ushered his nation into the digital age. The Soviets did not connect to the internet until 1990.*) The day after I wrote the lines about the toupee man in my notebook, I read about the president's performance in a high-profile all-star ice hockey match. His team thrashed the opposition 18–6, with the leader, then aged sixty-two, firing in eight of the eighteen. You couldn't make it up. You don't have to now.

---

* The internet famously drove wide-scale Russian intervention in the 2016 US presidential election. Putin loathed Obama, and therefore Democrats in general, in part because of sanctions imposed post-Crimea. (Moscow-controlled television had branded Obama 'a eunuch'.) Two weeks before Trump's inauguration in January 2017, Washington's director of national intelligence, testifying before the Senate, described a complex Russian operation that hacked into Democratic Party emails and publicised its discoveries via WikiLeaks. Many hundreds of Russian tech experts have left commercial firms to work for state cyber teams, and military ads show a soldier putting down a rifle and turning to a keyboard. Of course, the US has for decades funded media outlets and civil-society groups that poke their noses into Russian affairs.

Television was Putin's priority when he became president in 2000, and total control his goal. Wherever I stayed, across 9,000 kilometres, beams of lies illuminated the gloom of shabbily identical flats. Peter Pomerantsev, the son of Russian political exiles, returned to work in Moscow in the television industry. In his book *Nothing Is True and Everything Is Possible* he reports the words of a top political TV presenter:

> We all know there will be no real politics [on television]. But we still have to give our viewers the sense that something is happening. They need to be kept entertained. So what should we play with? Shall we attack oligarchs? Who's the enemy this week? Politics has got to feel like ... like a movie!

Pomerantsev comments, 'It was television through which the Kremlin decided which politicians it would "allow" as its puppet opposition, what the country's history and fears and consciousness should be. And the new Kremlin won't make the same mistake the old Soviet Union did: it will never let TV become dull.'

The Duma was sitting when news broke that Trump had won. Applause erupted. Their man was in. Vladimir Zhirinovsky, head of the Liberal Democratic Party of Russia (more nationalist than liberal), bought 132 bottles of champagne for parliamentarians and staff. Zhirinovsky expressed the opinion of many when he said, publicly, that Trump would assist Russia's strategic aims, often by default. 'What's Crimea to him? He doesn't even know where it is.'

The media followed suit. Russians had for years been fed a diet of propaganda about the evils of America's unfair democratic process. This had intensified as Clinton looked set to win. But suddenly, with Trump in the White House, America was a model of functioning democracy. The networks linked Trump's victory with Corbyn and Brexit, all, as they saw it, welcome triumphs of populism overcoming the liberal establishment.

'I don't care about politics,' said my new friend, now slugging vodka straight from the carafe. 'We are individuals here.' The toupee went up and down like the lid of a pedal bin.

The notion of an apolitical atomisation of society drifted through my travels like a Greek chorus. Nobody believed anybody and only the individual was real. Yet when Ukraine kicked off, I noticed an appearance, in ordinary kiosks in non-tourist parts of the country (which is most of them), of key-rings and other trinkets bearing Putin's face or – more often – his torso as he posed semi-naked. Once I spotted a boxing ring in which Putin was sparring with Obama. I wondered about this anomaly. Again and again, people in drab *khrush-chevki* told me they had lost faith in the political system and trusted no politician. They had all seen their healthcare and education systems fatally eroded. Yet there was something about Putin; something that represented Mother Russia, despite everything. And they could not turn away from it, not even this apolitical vodka slugger. Something of the genius Pushkin's crude nationalism lingered. Here's a quote from a piece in the *New Yorker* published in March 2017:

> When Putin returned to the Presidency for a third term, in 2012, he felt the need to develop a Russian ideology of his own, and called on currents that run deep in Russian political culture: nationalism, xenophobia, and social conservatism. When, four years ago, Putin endorsed anti-gay legislation, for instance, he was playing to entrenched conservative prejudices that predate Soviet Communism – perhaps not for Western-orientated intellectuals and the urban middle class but for many millions of others.

Toupee was aware that Putin controlled the news. But he didn't know just how extensively the president had robbed the nation of its assets and built up pharaonic personal funds in Switzerland. I asked him, and he denied it.

*

'If you want to see Byzantium, go to Pskov.' I wanted, Byzantium or not, to look around a city where Pushkin had spent time, and besides, it was on my way north, where I was headed to seek out Dostoyevsky. Mist hung low in the forest when Irina and our driver Sergei, a saturnine figure with a high-fringed basin haircut, picked me up. The day was overcast, the sun a stain, but the occasional showers, even hard ones, were over in minutes, and the fields emerged greener than ever. Conical haystacks alternated with wildflower meadows and wood stacked high and tight in outbuildings of cottages with corrugated-iron roofs. Many houses, all small, had no electricity. Forty per cent of homes in the countryside and small towns are without not just electricity, but running water and sewers as well. Yet just before Ostrov, I could see the glittering roofs of a nuclear facility.

Onion domes flashed in sunlight as Sergei accelerated into town. Ecclesiastical chronicles mention Pskov as early as the tenth century. The town grew so wealthy that its burghers invited Greek icon and fresco painters up to decorate their churches, and within a couple of centuries a distinctive Pskov school of architecture matured, using limestone slabs simply plastered and whitewashed. In 1510, Moscow took Pskov; my guide said people cried until their eyes almost fell out. But the distinctive architecture continued to flourish. At one point every street had a church. 'When you live close to a border', according to Anna, the guide who had joined us on her patch, 'you learn to depend on God and yourselves.' This tied in with apolitical atomisation. Perhaps that explains the cosy human dimension that characterises churches like the black-domed Transfiguration Cathedral in the Mirozhsky Monastery – the opposite of the European gothic that makes man small. Emigrés wishing to preserve something uniquely Russian in a foreign land have built places of Orthodox worship with Pskov-style cupolas and drums from Helsinki to Canberra via London and the banks of the Jordan. Le Corbusier stopped in Pskov en route from Moscow to Paris, and a fifteenth-century church inspired the Ronchamp chapel.

The town played a part in the drama of Russian history beyond the artistic sphere. Before the snow melted in spring 1917, Nicholas II signed his abdication documents in Pskov railway station. While we took coffee in a hotel, Anna told me that recently, almost a century after Nicholas had written himself into oblivion, an old man appeared from the Pskov shadows and handed a copy of the Old Testament from that era to a priest. It had annotations. Could it have belonged to the last tsar? Anna's husband, a criminologist, arbitrated on the veracity of the claim. He took the train to St Petersburg and photocopied documents bearing Nicholas' handwriting, to make a comparison. Not finding what he needed, he proceeded to the Moscow archives, where he located notes the tsar had written about debts from a card game. This confirmed the authenticity of the Bible – or so they say – and the volume is now locked in a glass case in the priest's church. We finished our coffee, paid, left and climbed into the tiny car to drive what turned out to be 100 metres to the kremlin, at which juncture we clambered out again.*

In exile Pushkin was allowed to travel within the Pskov district. He went to town often, and sat in a gazebo in a nook in the kremlin under what is now called Pushkin's Tower. When he was a free man, he travelled on the Kiev road from Pskov. It took four days to reach Petersburg and almost a week to get to Moscow – longer in spring, when the tracks turned to mud. The world still melts into slush and mud in western Russia in April. I was in Moscow once during that month, and roads disappeared under small lakes of brown water and towering piles of exhaust-blackened snow. It snows in Moscow almost every April. Lack of drainage contributes to the chaos. According to a much-quoted Russian saying, 'the country has two eternal problems, roads and idiots'. Looking at the indices of corruption in road maintenance in Russia, these two 'eternal problems' form a Venn diagram.†️ Russia spends $237 million to build a kilometre of road. The US spends $6 million.

*

Ten days earlier, before visiting Pushkin's estate, it had taken me eighteen hours to reach Pskov from the capital. At the Leningradsky station I had settled into a second-class compartment on the night train north-west. The journey led to my first sustained attempts at conversation in Russian. I had started learning two months previously using three methods: a Linguaphone course which I installed on my

* Many Russian cities have a kremlin (fortress), not just Moscow.

† In the latest Transparency International Corruption Perception Index, Russia stands at 134 out of 176, well below, for example, Paraguay and Liberia. But Russia does better than South Sudan.

phone; an evening class at King's College London; and the services of a private tutor who proved rather more interesting than my studies. I equipped myself with a two-volume Russian–English/English–Russian dictionary which I found at my local library's annual book sale, not on the sale tables, but propping the door open. I was hoping a degree in Greek would help me, but it hindered. Here's an extract from my diary the day I began.

2 April. One of the first nouns in my Linguaphone course is *plastinka* – vinyl record. Useful. As instructed, I have an exercise book ready to write the simple words over and over, to get used to Cyrillic. Persistently, many letters come out in Greek – the left tail of the m down beneath the line, the a like a Greek alpha, the left tail of the B down, the d all over the place. Immediately begin to worry that if ever I do gain a modicum of Russian, I will lose Greek, which would be counterproductive, given my goal of going to embassy parties to talk in Russian and Greek. Demoralising news that letters are handwritten (cursive) in a different form to the printed versions – in some cases, unrecognisably different.

I found pronunciation hard, but a couple of websites helped: Russian speakers spoke the words. I found this useful, though I grew tired of sidebars offering me Ukrainian women.

At the Leningradsky station, Oleg Gazmanov's Soviet anthem 'Moskva!' belted out of the speakers. Inside our compartment, my two female companions exchanged vertiginous heels for railway-issue slippers, and began preparing for the night. One, Svetlana (though we had not yet got on to introductions), removed an apricot nylon blouse with a tie at the neck, and jeans, and changed into cotton pyjamas, after which she buffed manicured nails and applied cotton pads to her eyes. I was touched at the way in which the train people put women passengers together; soldiers stocked the next-door compartment. The other woman, Masha, who had black hair to her waist and wore no makeup, stripped to change into a Columbia University T-shirt. Once settled, the pair laid out picnics on a lower bunk of our second-class, four-berth compartment. As the train chugged west, I learned that Svetlana, from Belarus, was working at something unintelligible in Moscow, and that Masha, from Kazakhstan, was pursuing the equally mysterious 'Expansion Management'. They were typical fellow passengers (as I was to learn): frosty at first, they quickly thawed. I offered picnic contributions, and the three of us talked while eating *pirozhki* (small meat turnovers), *kolbasa* sausage and of course cucumber, as the butterscotch light of a late midsummer evening settled over Zelenograd, a Russian silicon valley, and after that on swathes of forest, the odd factory, and sharp-roofed chalets set in fields of purple flowers. The train continued to move slowly, often stopping for long periods. I didn't care. What could be more agreeable than watching Russia roll by?

*

Pushkin arrived in exile a romantic poet. When time weighed heavily, he read multi-volume histories, and their themes seeped into his work. Mikhailovskoye turned him into a historical poet, so the north-west forged the transitional hinge of his life. The verse-play *Boris Godunov* was his major achievement in exile. The protagonist – Russians pronounce his first name 'ba-REECE' – ruled medieval Muscovy, and the play opens when Ivan the Terrible dies, leaving a weak-minded son, Fyodor, and humble Boris is anointed regent. When Fyodor in turn expires in 1598, Boris ascends the throne. Pushkin wrote the play in the political turmoil of the twenties – the Decembrists' era – and it was actually, of course, about Nicholas I, and could just as well be about contemporary Russia and its miasma of rumour, intrigue and killing. Boris Godunov was a member of the *oprichniki* – Ivan's thuggish secret police, ancestors of today's FSB (formerly KGB). When

Ivan's illegitimate son Dmitry died mysteriously aged ten, many accused Boris of murder. He cuts an ambiguous figure.

In the play Pushkin began to alternate comic scenes with the main action, trying to craft dialogue that would pass the censor. But neither Nicholas I nor the censors were used to the coarse language which Pushkin put into the mouths of his comic characters. The censors banned the play. The Communists banned it too, 150 years later, and exiled the director. 'Though written in a good spirit,' Pushkin wrote, 'I could not quite hide all my ears under my holy fool's cap. They stick out.' Six years after composition, in 1831, he revised the play.

I once saw it on a foggy November evening. It was the première of Adrian Mitchell's adaptation at the Swan Theatre in Stratford-upon-Avon. While I was watching, the authorities were arresting journalists hundreds of kilometres away in Moscow, so it remained as relevant as it had been when Pushkin conjured it out of the thin air of the north-west. The protesting mob resembled a shoot from a Toast catalogue – earthy-coloured draped felts and jerseys. Lloyd Hutchinson played Boris with a sharp suit and a tic, screwing his nose up like a rabbit. He opened the play marching silently down the stage wiping blood off his hands before holding forth in an Ulster accent, presumably pointing up the tsar's outsider status. The two princes played the next scene like Morecambe and Wise. Mitchell's adaptation followed Pushkin's original 1825 text and deployed lots of Shakespearean references – mossy beds, uneasy heads wearing crowns and the rest. The audience saw Boris disintegrate. By the end, a string vest had replaced the suit. Here was man riddled with self-doubt, and with a bad conscience to boot.

*

On returning from Pushkingrad to London I remembered the *pirozhki* I had eaten on the train. I decided to learn to cook them.

It was an attempt to keep Russia close as I made my way through many tens of metres of books in the Topography: R. stacks of the London Library and, I hoped, a way to stay on the scent of my writers. So I began to trawl *The Best of Russian Cooking*, by Alexandra Kropotkin, published in 1947. The author was a princess of White blood, though she had grown up in England and, when she wrote the book, lived in America and had been married to an American for thirty-six years. She speaks for her class and era: 'Russians are nice people, though in certain parts of Russia the admixture of Oriental blood may lend a definite touch of deviousness to their thought and behavior.' Princess Alexandra enjoyed adapting recipes for her adopted homeland, contributing the results to the ladies' page of *Liberty* magazine, though a sentence in upper case in the preface to *The Best of Russian Cooking* expresses an acute source of anguish concerning the produce available in Massachusetts: 'NOT ENOUGH DIFFERENT KINDS OF MUSHROOMS.'

Kropotkin exemplified the kind of Russian – one of the kinds – who fled during the Revolution. You can see her on YouTube, in a 1951 television interview in which she sports a hat set at forty-five degrees to her head and sticking twenty centimetres into the air. The two interviewers quiz her as if they had never seen a Russian before. 'The whole of Russia is a prison camp,' Kropotkin declares briskly, proceeding to explain the nature of state-sponsored terrorism. One of her interlocutors asks her advice on increasing the effectiveness of US propaganda in Russia. 'What can we do', he pleads, 'to drive a wedge between the Kremlin and the Russian people?'

In the many pages of recipes for both *pirozhki* pastry and filling, Kropotkin stipulates that the cook must make more than she needs, because the little turnovers go quickly. And in my house, they did. My children's spirits rose at the prospect of a year of Russian cooking (they were soon to fall again). I began with sour-cream pastry and a traditional meat and dill filling. 'I must warn you,' Kropotkin writes when issuing instructions, 'your true Russian entertains a violent passion for dill – and dill is a herb that can permeate your life if you don't watch it.' Before my next trip, I tackled my first *borshch* (let's not worry about the fact that the soup is of Ukrainian ancestry). I liked the Lady Macbeth look, though I didn't realise I had actually cut my hand until I did the washing up.

II

A Heart's Journey

Sergei at the wheel, we set off north-east from Pskov along empty roads. We entered the *oblast* or region of Novgorod. Light the colour of an unripe lemon slanted through the birch forest. Yuliana, my guide, had brought a picnic, and we dined leaning against a wall, the field opposite flaunting sunflowers. She had slices of homemade pizza, a pail of blackcurrants, jellied fruit sweets called *marmelad*, and mint tea in a flask. Sergei was on a diet, and ate all the black-currants. Yuliana pointed out a village across the field occupied by Seto people, an ethnic group dwelling on either side of the border between Russia and Estonia. Sergei said something disparaging about 'primitive' Seto culture. Like almost all indigenous peoples across Russia, the Seto are embattled. During the Soviet era the authorities banned their language and communities buried their traditional costumes in an attempt to preserve them. The Seto have a king, and a few shamans linger on, despite the fact that nominally the Seto are Orthodox. It was a familiar story, and not only in Russia: young people leaving and folk memory fading. Dostoyevsky worshipped the idea of 'folk culture'; he would have been horrified, at least in theory. What he thought and how he acted were often at variance.

I was looking for Dostoyevsky in a declining spa town on the river Polist 160 kilometres east of Pushkin's estate. Enterprises had died post-perestroika. Nonetheless, as the town sits on Ilmen, a natural lake sixty-six times the size of Windermere and a nineteenth the size of Lake Ontario, Staraya Russa enjoys the patronage of rich Muscovites who keep handsome shoreside houses. It is an eight-hour slow drive from the capital.

The Dostoyevskys arrived in 1872. They had set off by train from Petersburg, transferred for Novgorod, then taken a boat across Ilmen. Anna Dostoyevskaya wrote, 'The sun shone bright on the river's far shore from which the crenelated walls of its Kremlin rose up, the gilded cupolas of the Cathedral of St Sophia were ablaze, and in the chilly air the bells were loudly calling to matins.'

In a coffee shop on a quiet main street, we met our local guide, Valentina, an Amazonian figure in an orange patterned dress and a white lace hat. We walked in the chequered shadow of the elms. A statue of Dostoyevsky glowered over the former market square. The main resort within Staraya Russa occupied a twelve-hectare site in the centre of town, and had three man-made mineral lakes. 'The spa is something God has given us,' said Valentina. A group of hardy swimmers took the plunge year round; she called them *morzhi* (walruses). Thousands of stuffed toys welcomed us to an old-fashioned entertainment centre. Linden, fine-fingered birch, oak, ash, chestnut and willow shaded the lakes' banks. Kurort had been receiving guests for 185 years. Gorky visited for mud treatment, and wrote to his son saying that he had become salty as a herring.

Of all big-beast Russian writers of the nineteenth century – Pushkin, Gogol, Herzen, Goncharov, Lermontov, Turgenev, Tolstoy, Leskov – Fyodor Mikhailovich Dostoyevsky was the only one not born into landed gentry. His father had risen from the priestly class to become a doctor: when Fyodor was a child, seven Dostoyevskys slept in a windowless flat in the grounds of Moscow's Mariinsky Hospital for the Poor, where the future author's father worked. They shared beds, yet they had servants.

Dostoyevsky moved to Petersburg when he was sixteen, and his novels are closely associated with that city. But Muscovites have not lost the opportunity to claim him, and they have restored that apartment – his birthplace, after all – and opened it to the public. It was not as gloomy as biographies indicate. It would have been crowded when Dostoyevsky was growing up, but the rooms were not poky, and the vaulted interior entrance hall was rather beautiful. One of Fyodor's brothers had left a detailed account of the furnishings. The visitor sees childhood toys of the period on a rug, but it is difficult to imagine that Dostoyevsky was ever a child. His mother died from TB before he turned sixteen, and two years after he left for Petersburg, his father died, probably murdered.

Dostoyevsky was precocious, becoming famous in educated circles in his mid-twenties with his debut novel, *Poor Folk (Bednyye lyudi)*. He believed in a world of living love, a sphere in which God existed for the poor, the dispossessed and the lonely. He is the poet of the slums. In 1848 revolutionary turmoil in western Europe caused panic in the Russian establishment; overexcited Petersburgers climbed on tables to read newspapers aloud. The young Dostoyevsky was all for revolution, especially if it meant the liberation of serfs. He became involved in a freethinking secret group, like the Decembrists, the aim of which was to spread discontent with the existing order everywhere.

Nicholas I did anything necessary to suppress independent thought. Dostoyevsky was imprisoned in the Peter and Paul Fortress for printing and distributing anti-establishment literature. Early one morning, jailers yanked him and his colleagues from their cells and carted them (literally) to Semyonovskaya Square, where fresh snow had fallen. The sun had just risen, but a crowd had gathered. Soldiers led the men to a scaffold, lined them up and read out their sentence: death by firing squad. A priest walked along the condemned, giving each man a cross to kiss. The first three prisoners were tied to stakes, and hoods pulled over their heads. Dostoyevsky was waiting in the next batch of three. The firing squad stood ready. The people fell silent.

Suddenly, hooves pounded through the square. A rider carried a message from the tsar commuting the sentences. Soldiers released the three from their stakes. Punishment had been changed to four years' hard labour in Siberia. It turned out that the tsar had specifically ordered that the prisoners should not be told that their sentence was commuted until the last minute; so it had been a mock execution from the beginning.

A million convicts marched east in the nineteenth century, the journey a *via dolorosa* which killed thousands even before they reached their destination. Dostoyevsky was held in a military prison in Omsk. The jail was a literally rotten wooden construction where convicts slept on bare boards. In winter temperatures fell to minus forty. In a letter to his brother Mikhail, Dostoyevsky wrote of 'filth on the floors an inch thick … We were packed like *herrings* in a barrel … fleas, lice, and black beetles by the bushel.' He was often in the prison hospital. In *House of the Dead (Zapiski iz myortvogo doma)*, the fictionalised account of his incarceration, Dostoyevsky conjures the bath-house. 'Two hundred men in a room twelve paces square, the floor inches thick in slime, the convicts, their leg chains clanking, piled on benches pouring dirty water onto the shaven heads of the men crouched below – a phantasmagoria of crimson steaming bodies ridged with the scars of the lash. It was not heat: it was hell.'

After prison he served, as a term of his sentence, as a common soldier in Siberia. He married Mariya Isayeva, a widow with a son, Pavel (Pasha), and the family returned to Petersburg at the end of 1859, a year and two months before the liberation of the serfs. Five years after their arrival, Mariya died of TB.*

*

Besides providing a cast of villains to populate the novels to come, the prison experience affected Dostoyevsky's ideas; how could it not? 'I learned [there] that I had always been a Russian at heart,' he wrote. He rediscovered God, and in his imagination the deity became inextricably bound up with the Russian people, who thereby achieved a kind of sanctity. 'For real Russians', Alyosha says in *The Brothers Karamazov*, 'the questions of the existence of God and immortality ... are of course first and foremost.' Dostoyevsky felt united with his countrymen, and with God, in an indissoluble three-way bond. This was the foundation of his worship of folk culture. In the words of Joseph Frank, the formidable Dostoyevsky biographer, 'Time and again he will show in his major characters the persistence of something he considers "Russian", even in those who are most powerfully and corrosively affected by western European ideas ... [he believed] that the instinctive sentiments and loyalties of Russians would always break through.' After Siberia Dostoyevsky distrusted the progressive ideology which had influenced him as a young man. He came to consider such things harmful – it was all very well to have a revolution, but anarchy

---

* In about 1862 he took a lover, 23-year-old Apollinaria 'Polina' Suslova. Her younger sister Nadezhda was the first woman to obtain a medical degree in Russia. The sisters were of serf stock.

might be worse than tyranny, or, as actually was to happen in Russia after 1917, a fresh tyranny might be worse still.

*

The wooden two-storey house with yellow-and-blue glass windows wrapped round a closed veranda was the only home Dostoyevsky ever owned: he was even more restless than Pushkin. He did, though, spend most of the last eight years of his life watching the costive river from his study window in Staraya Russa. The town provided the setting of *The Brothers Karamazov* – the character Grushenka lived in a house modelled on one still standing on the opposite bank to Dostoyevsky's. The family home is open to the public. Dostoyevsky wrote about humility, but didn't have much of it; even the sympathetic Frank writes of his subject's 'boundless vanity and overweening sense of self-importance'. But as I walked through the empty rooms, light gilling on the floor through shutter slats, I empathised with this agonised and deeply moving figure.

He suffered ill health throughout his adult life: epilepsy, emphysema, rheumatism, constipation, haemorrhoids. He had nervous tics. When he edited a literary journal in Petersburg, his second wife described him leaving the house in freezing temperatures and sitting for hours in an overheated proofreading room. He often worked fifteen hours a day and had six fits a week. He frequented spas in Germany for his emphysema, but remained a committed smoker. A student remembered spotting him on a bench in a church park, 'hunched, emaciated, with a yellowish face, hollow cheeks, sunken eyes'.

A copy of the famous Vasily Perov portrait hung in the house. Painted in 1872, when the author was fifty-one, it depicts a stooped figure mired in thought and beset by passionate doubt; a man obsessed with his message for the Russian people – a message begging them not to abandon the Christian faith of their ancestors. Dostoyevsky was finishing *Demons* at the time, and was about to start *The Brothers Karamazov*. The greatcoat worn indoors indicates a man too distracted to engage with the world beyond his own imagination; the long, locked fingers suppose a profound, tense concentration.

In his study, a cool, shaded room overlooking the river and the green leaves of the oaks, a pair of candles stood on the desk. Dostoyevsky disliked lamps. He wrote through the night, went to bed at dawn and slept until two in the afternoon, when he drank tea from the samovar and rolled cigarettes made with thick yellow paper. At three he had a wine glass of vodka with a meal, went for a walk along the cobbled embankment, returned to dine with the family, then started work again. Pages from his notebooks are a thing to behold – a dense, tiny hand, paragraphs circled and inserted elsewhere with arrows, sketches of faces in the middle of it all, Himalayan doodles and thickets of crossings out.

His second wife, Anna Grigoryevna, took shorthand for him in the study. They had met when she came to him as a stenographer in Petersburg. They married in 1867 in the Izmailovsky Cathedral – she was not yet twenty-one, he turned forty-six later that year. A first infant died when they were living in Switzerland. Years after his baby girl's death, Dostoyevsky visited her grave in Geneva. The couple had two more children before they moved to Staraya Russa. In the house there, the one with the yellow-and-blue glassed veranda, Anna Grigoryevna gave birth to a third child, the boy Alexei, in an upstairs bedroom. Alexei died of epilepsy when he was three. Fyodor Mikhailovich spent the whole night on his knees by his bed after his son passed away. He was a tender man, and when separated from the family he could not bear to see other people's children playing in the street. The worst part of travel is the sight of ordinary people doing ordinary things, like paying bills or watching their children kick a football.

*

God notwithstanding, Dostoyevsky was a rabid xenophobe and anti-Semite (he hated Jews first and Germans second). On his final visit to the Bad Ems spa he was writing about Zosima's message of love and universal reconciliation in *The Brothers Karamazov*. At the same time, in his private letters he poured out bile on Jews.

He was a compulsive gambler. When he pawned Anna's clothes and jewellery, she said she began to envy all the other people in the world. What Anna endured beggars belief. She is one of the great wives of history. When I read about her, I marvelled at how good a person can be, though one could argue that she was a victim of female oppression. His letters – he often sent her two a day – brimmed with hysterical apologies and self-castigation. Dostoyevsky spawned good intentions like a herring. Yet theirs was a happy union. Passion lasted. He wrote to his 'Anechka' from Bad Ems in 1876 to say he had fallen in love with her four or five times since their marriage. 'I love you to the point of torment,' he wrote, saying he could not imagine anyone other than her 'in this regard'.

If you know his story, it makes the Perov portrait authentic – a man tormented with guilt, doubt and longing, addicted to the roulette table. And gambling was only one of his financial problems. His stepson Pasha was a living drain. When Dostoyevsky's much-loved brother Mikhail died, the author supported his sponging family. He even gave money to Mikhail's mistress and her son. A Dostoyevsky biography reads like a Greek tragedy.

*

As we left the house, Valentina said, 'The Nazis knew this had been Dostoyevsky's house, so they didn't destroy it.' This seemed unlikely: but who knew? German troops occupied Staraya Russa for two and a half years during the Great Patriotic War, and when they left they burned it down.

As we stood at the side of the road, Valentina's son drew up to convey our party to a fish restaurant. There we sat in an ersatz temple in the garden and dined on mediocre freshwater fish baked in an outdoor oven. Birds sang and dogs barked. The dieting Sergei sat apart, eating an apple. A full-sized billiard table abutted a wall painted with a fleet of boats. A man sat slumped over the bar. The two guides discussed their housing. The main point seemed to be the thick- or thinness of the walls: I'd heard many people complain that they could hear knives and forks clattering on neighbours' plates. Yuliana, billeted in a Khrushchev-era block in Pskov, felt she was lucky. 'I can only hear my neighbours when they shout,' she said.

The proprietor had fired up the *banya*, so after coffee we three put on felt cloche hats and went in. Yuliana beat me with a *venik*, a bouquet of birch twigs, then I beat her.

*

Like Dickens', Dostoyevsky's work came out first in serial form, in periodicals and journals. In his mature years he wrote obsessively about the competing tensions between the West and Russia. Like almost all his compatriot authors of the period, Dostoyevsky wrote about European moral stultification. He left no stone unturned to 'prove' his belief that Russian life was intrinsically superior to the European civilisation in vogue in educated circles. In *The Brothers Karamazov*, Father Paissy insists to Alyosha that ideas from Europe in the form of rational inquiry damage Russia since they blind people to Christian truth. 'The science of this world,' trumpets Paissy, 'having united itself into a great force, has, especially in the past century, examined everything heavenly that has been bequeathed to us in sacred books, and, after hard analysis, the learned ones of this world have absolutely nothing left of what was once holy.' The monk Zosima writes, 'In the enlightened world of today ... the spiritual world, the higher half of man's being, is altogether rejected, banished with a sort of triumph, even with hatred.' As for Russians of 1880, the author's contemporaries, they 'live only for mutual envy, for pleasure-seeking and self display. To have dinners, horses, carriages, rank, and slaves to serve them ...' If only he'd known how things were to turn out.

On an eight-day visit to England in 1862, Dostoyevsky decided that the Crystal Palace offered up an image of the unholy spirit of modernity that brooded over London. He enjoyed predicting the downfall of European civilisation and once told a French author, 'We possess the genius of all the peoples and also have our own; thus we can understand you and you cannot understand us.' By 1876 he was not only ranting that the Russian nation, inseparable from the Russian people, had a God-given destiny to create a new Christian world order. He also had a vision of peoples of other nations living peacefully under Russian tutelage, believing so firmly that Constantinople would soon be Russian that he called it Tsargrad.

The European turn away from spirituality towards materialism evidently had a moral component. In the *Karamazov* trial scene, the women think Dmitry Fyodorovich will be wrongly acquitted of murder because of 'the new ideas, because of the new feelings that are going around nowadays'. 'Enlightenment' and progress are flagged as pernicious. The drunken, self-pitying Fyodor Pavlovich – the Karamazov father – screams at the monks, to justify his behaviour, 'This is the age of liberalism, the age of steamships and railways.'

Pushkin's verse, Dostoyevsky determined in the context of his good-Russia-versus-bad-West agenda, marked the moment when educated Russians divided into 'Slavophiles' and Europeans. He perceived his country to be experiencing a convulsion, uncertain in which direction to turn – inward or outward. He became increasingly Slavophile himself, and came to understand that Russia could never be truly European. Time has proved him right.

Allied with this preoccupation with spiritual decline, there was much agonised probing of religious issues. After Siberia, Dostoyevsky began to think of human life as an eternal struggle between the material and the spiritual: Europe embodied the material, while Russia was spirituality incarnate. This spirituality, however, necessarily involved pain and agony. He once wrote – and this quotation is often cited:

The most basic spiritual need of the Russian people is the need for suffering, incessant and unslakeable suffering, everywhere and in everything. I think the Russian people have been infused with this need from time immemorial ... There is always an element of suffering even in the happiness of the Russian people, and without it their happiness is incomplete.

What is one to make of this? Redemption through suffering. It is a nice idea. But is it true? When I wrote this chapter I was still in deep shock from my own experiences in the suffering department, and was dealing with its practical consequences. I did not feel redeemed. And by the way, don't read Dostoyevsky's account of wife beating.

But I swam in a Russian lake at sunrise, and stillness came upon me like a benediction.

*

After Siberia, the golden years. Three of the four great novels appeared before the move to Staraya Russa: *Crime and Punishment* (*Prestupleniye i nakazaniye*), *The Idiot* (*Idiot*) and *Demons* (*Besy*). *The Brothers Karamazov* (*Bratya Karamazovy*) was published in one volume in 1880. All four books revolve around murders.

On 4 April 1866 a poor student who had been expelled from the university for not paying his fees fired a pistol at Alexander II as the tsar walked his Irish setter in the Winter Garden. The event shocked the nation, even though the bullet whizzed past the imperial barnet. Up until then, the decade had shown signs of political thaw, but repression followed the attempted murder. *Crime and Punishment* appeared in one volume the year after the assassination attempt. The story focuses on the psychology of its provincial protagonist, Rodion Raskolnikov, also an impoverished former student expelled from university for not paying his fees. (Dostoyevsky played with names. A *raskolnik* is a dissenter.) Raskolnikov wields an axe to murder a decrepit money lender, and by accident slaughters her feeble-minded sister as well. His ensuing inner turmoil is half real and half theoretical. The reader inevitably wonders why he committed his foul crimes. Dostoyevsky hints at reasons – social pressure, mental illness, spiritual death – but none convince. Part of the greatness of *Crime and Punishment* lies in its depiction of the unknowability of motives.

A competition in a British magazine once asked readers to summarise a book in four lines of verse. One of the runners-up chose *Crime and Punishment*. Her entry read:

> *Raskolnikov, student of nonsense,*
> *Engages in brutal attacks,*
> *But finds that his own bloody conscience*
> *Is sharper by far than an axe.*

Dostoyevsky does not go in for neat conclusions. His narratives are often open-ended. It's one of the things I like most about his books. There are rarely neat conclusions in life. The reader follows Raskolnikov's tortured search for meaning, and it turns out to be a failed project, as he finds no meaning in his crime. He arrives at a spiritual rebirth of sorts through the agency of the dignified prostitute Sonya. What is the conclusion to these hundreds of pages spent wandering through the former student's mind as he lies in his tiny, low-ceilinged garret (Dostoyevsky uses the word 'coffin')? There isn't one. What is to become of Raskolnikov? The reader doesn't know. In *The Brothers Karamazov*, who murdered the brothers' despicable father? Apparently Smerdyakov, though Dmitry takes responsibility, responsibility being a major Dostoyevskian theme. (The author was working on a second volume of *The Brothers Karamazov* when he died.)

The uncertainty mirrors Dostoyevsky's insistence on doubt. What could be more human? After his youthful radical philosophy, he became increasingly sceptical of theories or solutions, often finding himself muddled about which way to turn. And like all the truest Christians, Dostoyevsky was uncertain about his faith. This is unfashionable today, when the only flourishing branch of the Anglican and Episcopalian churches is the evangelical variety, which is absolutely certain about absolutely everything. Dostoyevsky made Ivan Karamazov such a convincing atheist that readers believed in him, as the author had feared they might. The great novels all deal with the unresolvable tension between reason and faith, and the unendurable challenge of believing in a God who lets the world immolate itself.

What of Dostoyevsky as a writer of prose? He is no stylist. As Richard Pevear, one of his translators, says, 'He will get stuck on a particular word, repeat it five times in half a page, and then never use it again.' The pained translator continues, 'His sentences tend to flounder most when he is most serious.' Book Five, chapter five of *The Brothers Karamazov* includes a seven-page paragraph. What Vladimir Nabokov called 'wastelands of literary platitudes' slow the narrative drive. There is little character development; most of the cast are one-dimensional, and his veneration for the simple heroes of Russian folklore is naïve. After all, there is no such thing as 'Russian culture' – the place is too big, and too ethnically fragmented and socially divided. In addition, there is in Dostoyevsky's writing little of what Dr Johnson called the significance of the trivial – food, clothes, weather – and these are the things that make a book human. Dostoyevsky never gave the ordinary its beautiful due.

But. At his best, images spill onto the page like mercury from a broken thermometer. Again, in *The Brothers Karamazov*, the reader meets a judge 'with a haemorrhoidal face', while as Alyosha prays, 'fragments of thought flashed in his soul, catching fire like little stars and dying out at once to give way to others'. In the same novel the author perfectly describes that curious experience of waking from a dream: 'Ivan wanted to rush to the window; but something seemed suddenly to bind his legs and arms. He was straining as hard as he could to break his bonds, but in vain.' Dostoyevsky can conjure a sense of place, most notably the shadowy side of Petersburg, the dank alleys, gloomy staircases and low-ceilinged bars with their unendurable stench in the area between the Yekaterina (later the Griboyedova) and the

Moika canals, Sennaya Square – Hay Square, or the Haymarket – and Kolomna, a seedy, slummy area where the adult Dostoyevsky lived. 'They reached Liteyny Avenue at last,' he writes in *The Idiot*.

> It was still thawing. A warm, damp, oppressive wind went whistling up and down the streets, carriages splashed through the mud, the horses' hooves struck the cobbles in the road with a ringing sound. The people on the pavement slouched along in wet and dejected crowds with here and there a drunken man among them.

The critical success of *Crime and Punishment*, set in those grim alleys, catapulted Dostoyevsky into the front line of Russian writers: he was level with Tolstoy (seven years his junior) and Turgenev (three years his senior). But for many years his books didn't sell. In 1874 he called into the distribution offices of his publishing firm and learned that *The Idiot*, which had just appeared in a one-volume edition, had shifted precisely two copies. Like most writers, the agonies of literary rivalry plagued him. He found out that a publisher had bought *Anna Karenina* (which came out in serial form between 1873 and 1877) for 500 roubles a sheet, which was twice what Dostoyevsky got. He read the novel while receiving compressed air treatment for emphysema, which required him to sit under an apparatus called a bell. He found the book 'boring'.

*

Demons, sometimes translated as *Devils*, sometimes as *The Possessed*, was published between 1871 and 1872. It satirised the Nihilists, a group that had been enjoying favour among Russian intellectuals for a decade. (They were atheists, of course, but, ironically, some critics have argued that Russian Nihilism actually grew from the Orthodox rejection of the world.) By the time *Demons* appeared, the loose group had ratcheted up its revolutionary intent. Nihilists rejected all forms of authority, as their name, from the Latin *nihil*, meaning 'nothing', suggests, but in fact they did not believe in nothing. They championed science, for example, as an engine of progress. In Dostoyevsky's mind they represented danger – they were the *possessed*. (The novel paints a prescient portrait of the moral quagmires that suck down the socialist ideal in our own age.) Nikolai Stavrogin represents Russian Man, fruitlessly trying to regain the Orthodox faith, while at the same time fighting the ideological *devils* Dostoyevsky believed were plaguing Russian culture. It is a book about misguided idealism.

Stavrogin's torments echo the existential anguish of Onegin. Dostoyevsky was sixteen when Pushkin died, and the poet's work influenced him deeply. In a speech at the unveiling of the Pushkin memorial in Moscow in 1880, an event attended by tens of ʼthousands, Dostoyevsky praised Pushkin as the embodiment of the spirit of the motherland, hailing him as a poetic herald of the glorious mission Russia had been called to accomplish on behalf of humanity. He liked to think he was linking hands with Pushkin over the decades, as others, in time, were to think they touched Dostoyevsky. Sometimes this involved retro-fitting. Dostoyevsky interpreted Tatiana's faithfulness to the crusty general in *Onegin* as a manifestation of her deep-rootedness in the values of the Russian folk soul. Perhaps, in part, it was. But Stavrogin connects with a prototype popularised in Turgenev's *Diary of a Superfluous Man*, published in 1850, seventeen years after *Onegin*. Still, the Onegin–Stavrogin type, superfluous or not, became a staple of Russian literature.

Instalments of *The Brothers Karamazov* appeared between January 1879 and November 1880. In the middle of the run, in February 1880, a bomb exploded under the Winter Palace dining room. It was the fourth assassination attempt against Alexander II. The explosion killed eleven, but the perpetrator failed to murder any member of the royal family. Thirteen months later, another bomb finally blew Alexander to bits.

Dostoyevsky died at fifty-nine in St Petersburg. Since those early days of poor sales, he had burst onto literary Russia and won (almost) all hearts. The funeral procession stretched for kilometres. He ended his life as a spiritual leader, a man who had transcended ideology. His was a heart's journey. As the philosopher Vladimir Solovyov said in a lecture to female students shortly after Dostoyevsky died,

> Just as the highest worldly power somehow or other becomes concentrated in one person, who represents a state, similarly the highest spiritual power in each epoch usually belongs in every people to one man, who more clearly than all grasps the spiritual ideals of mankind, more consciously than all strives to attain them, more strongly than all affects others by his preachments. Such a spiritual leader of the Russian people in recent times was Dostoevsky.

Anna Grigoryevna turned thirty-five that year. She never remarried.

*

The night train to Tver arced south-east, skirting lakes and forests until the line passed out of Novgorod and crossed the Vyshny Volochyok waterway. An engineering feat when it was constructed in the 1700s, the Vyshny Volochyok was the first waterway to connect the Baltic and Caspian basins, and is now one of three canal systems joining the Neva to the Volga. At about three in the morning, the sky a pearly ultramarine and the carriage silent bar the rhythmic creak of the suspension, a railway bridge conveyed us over the Tvertsa, which flows into the Volga at Tver.

Famed now for its railway manufacturing plant, in the fourteenth century Tver was the Russian capital. I was told numerous times during my brief stay, by proud burghers, 'Moscow paid taxes to us then.' I walked aimlessly in the rookeries of the medieval city. Dostoyevsky had to transit in Tver when he returned from Siberia in 1859, and languished there for six weeks under state surveillance awaiting permission to depart for Petersburg. He wrote about a vision of the promised land – the Russia west of the Urals. When he arrived home at last, it was to a heady sense of freedom and reform. Since his departure, radical and liberal compatriots had started scores of newspapers and periodicals. Here was promise indeed. But he was no longer sure.

*

Not long after this trip, a newspaper commissioned me to write about a river cruise from Petersburg to Moscow. I'm not fond of cruising, but I took the job to see a little more of Russia, and to catch another glimpse of Dostoyevsky.

Before boarding, I took the Petersburg metro to see the courtyard where Raskolnikov killed the old moneylender with an axe in *Crime and Punishment*, and the murky canal where he disposed of his weapon.

It was a long way, then and now, from the divine baroque created by Catherine the Great's architect Francesco Rastrelli, where a hot Italian palette replaces the greys and blacks of Dostoyevsky country. The police building on Sadovaya Street where Raskolnikov confessed is now an Apple Store.

The 129-metre *Truvor* began its twelve-day voyage at a pier next to Sverdlov Bridge. It was a hot summer, and Spam-coloured Russian bodies lay on grassy banks outside the Peter and Paul Fortress where Dostoyevsky had been in jail, only occasionally cooled by a salty Baltic headwind. Light floated from the Gulf of Finland and infused the sky and the mint-green baroque façade of the Winter Palace with a pearly sheen. It was the period of white nights – *belyye nochi* – so late evening shimmered as brightly as noon. The *Truvor* pulled out of Petersburg accompanied by the low elephant grief of its horn. It was hard to leave the deck. That night we proceeded south-east at a dignified pace across lakes and along rivers before meeting the Volga–Baltic waterway. The difference in water level between the two cities of 150 metres required seventeen locks, triumphs of Soviet gigantism.

The 150 other passengers were mostly American, with a sprinkle of British, Dutch and German. I got to know some over dinner as Russia swam by in buttery evening light. We went on excursions every day. In Uglich, some of us visited a *kommunalka*, a Soviet-era communal living space (a dozen passengers went in each group), and took tea with our hostess, Irina. Twelve people lived in a ten-roomed flat with shared kitchen and bathroom. (Putin grew up in a *kommunalka*. His family had lived in one through the Nazi siege of Leningrad – except for Putin's elder brother. He had died of diphtheria.) Electronic devices were in evidence, but the twenty-first century could not prevail over a stench of boiled cabbage that had predated and outlived the Soviets. Irina had occupied her room for forty years, and had been permitted to purchase it post-communism for a token sum. We ate pickled gherkins and drank home-distilled vodka at eight-thirty in the morning.

Later only five of us opted for the *banya* experience. After baking ourselves, we leapt naked into the Volga.

We cruised past islands, the blanketing forest dotted with wooden cabins and churches. Timber travelled down centre stream, as it has for centuries, though on barges now, rather than just floating. On Lake Onega, an expanse of water so big that the *Truvor*'s captain considered it to be a sea, we disembarked to inspect an open-air museum on Kizhi Island, which preserves wooden chapels, houses, windmills and granaries that reflect Karelian culture. At the 1714 Church of the Transfiguration with its twenty-two domes, aspen shingles silvered by wind and humidity stood proud against an enamel sky striated with cirrus cloud, like bacon.

Ospreys patrolled the riverbanks of Vologda, and wild orchids bloomed in sedge. It's hard to conjure the scale of Russia. Denmark, Holland, Belgium and Switzerland could fit into this one province.

On board, lectures on national history enhanced proceedings, especially as the tour leaders who delivered them (all Russian) were not afraid to introduce their own comments. Raisa Gorbacheva, we heard, was the first Russian First Lady who weighed less than her husband.

The *Truvor* entered the capital on the Moscow Canal, a waterway sometimes called the Intellectuals' Canal, because gulag prisoners culled from the intelligentsia, loathed by Stalin, built it. It was a Saturday, sunlight sparkling, and on the banks families sat on folding chairs with picnics and splashing children. Yachts began to appear as we approached the metropolis, and one had the sense of returning to the world.

*

Dostoyevsky writes little about what his characters ate. According to his wife's memoir he himself enjoyed washing down boiled chicken with warm milk. At breakfast – a repast which came late for him – he drank grain vodka with a lump of brown bread. He had fastidious tea-making rituals. He often asked his cook to prepare *shchi*, cabbage soup, staple of Russian staples. I turned to my old friend the Princess to have a go at making *shchi* in London.

13 April
My first *shchi*.

Mouldy swede in veg basket so I used it instead of Alexandra's three potatoes. Dilemma over which type of cabbage – she stipulates white, but can this be what Russians use, or is she being American (as she often is)? As usual, Princess enthusiastic about pints of consommé. As with *borshch*, dithers about meat or not. Took her advice and put meat in bottom of pan, but was a mistake. Fortunately, my *shchi* was delicious, as the boys have been complaining about too many hard-boiled eggs in their new Russian diet. Meat at bottom of pan rancid, so decided in future to serve meat separately, if at all.

Russian pancakes, *bliny*, go down well, though the boys wouldn't eat them with anything savoury (Russians have them with melted butter and smoked, pickled or salted fish). So we became a proper Russian–British–Canadian household and tucked into *bliny* with maple syrup. (The boys' father is Canadian, and they have dual citizenship.) Princess dilated on advantages of yeast-raised batter, but admitted that she could not toss high, *à l'américaine*. 'Clark Gable tried to teach me how,' she wrote, 'and he was an accomplished pancake chef, but I just couldn't seem to learn the trick.'

*

After *Poor Folk*, and still in his twenties, in 1846 Dostoyevsky published the novella *The Double* (*Dvoinik*). Golyadkin, a low-level civil servant, encounters a man who is his double in looks and the opposite in personality: the doppelgänger is confident and extrovert, whereas Golyadkin is a weed. The book charts their evolving relationship, until the real Golyadkin goes mad. Petrine St Petersburg, its bureaucracy, and the effects of the latter, are omnipresent. Scholars have long wallowed in muddy waters regarding the interpretation of *The Double*. It seems to me the story explores the psychological search for identity. And it's funny (the subtitle, 'A Petersburg Poem', mocks Golyadkin's unlyrical environment). If you do see this book as a reflection on a universal characteristic of the human condition – the quest for identity – the story is easily adaptable.* A week after returning from the cruise I saw the 2013 film version, starring Jesse Eisenberg as both protagonists and rather brilliantly directed by Richard Ayoade.

---

* Despite expanses of theory in Dostoyevsky's novels, they are surprisingly filmic. Think of all the falling candlesticks clanging in the darkness in *Demons*, and the endless shots ringing out.

Part of it is set in a tube train, the identical men swaying along with the carriage as they talk, evoking dips in and out of reality. The film doppelgänger is more sensitive than Dostoyevsky's original: he coaches Simon, his shy counterpart, in how to court the love interest (Mia Wasikowska). The office environment is deliberately Soviet; it works so well that one understands how much Sovietness existed proleptically in tsarist Russia (institutionalisation of every corner of life, hierarchies) and endures in dystopian aspects of contemporary society (identical and faceless pod offices). Ayoade said in an interview that Dostoyevsky never wrote an ending with which he was satisfied. His interlocutor asked if that would not make the director's job easier, as it removed any issue of authorial infallibility. 'Yes,' Ayoade replied, 'we'll help Fyodor get it right for once.'

Eighteen years after *The Double*, Dostoyevsky produced *Notes from Underground* (*Zapiski iz podpolya*), a soliloquy by a miserable, nameless former civil servant and self-imposed outsider whose liver problems represent the generalised suffering Dostoyevsky was so keen to publicise. 'I am a sick man,' goes the first line, 'I am a wicked man.' (The adjective *zloi* can also be translated as 'spiteful'.) In the second part of the novel, the narrator records events that happened decades earlier, in a kind of memoir. The reader enters the half-crazed vortex of a man's mind. I found this book almost unreadable – there is a kind of shattering dullness about it – and had little idea what it was about, beyond ideological issues and a general sense that the West was gaining ground in Russian thought, which was a bad thing.

The only occasion I glimpsed the meaning of *Notes* was at a one-man production performed and co-adapted by Harry Lloyd at London's Print Room. The set consisted of teetering piles of books. As the audience entered, the smouldering Lloyd sat in a threadbare armchair, barefoot, directing us where to sit. The performance, set in contemporary London, bridged the gap to modern life. A programme note said:

Dostoevsky was tormented by the infinite amount of perspectives one can have of any single thing. As we today are bombarded with a seemingly endless supply of unclassified information, we flit from source to source, unable to focus, prioritise or even make decisions. So we find ourselves longing for stability, but caught in an unending, internal vortex.

Questions the play raised hung in the air, like motes of dust, long after the curtain fell.

*

I had been making slow progress learning Russian, and was apt to get demoralised. Following my euphoric discovery that there was only one past tense, my tutor hit me with the concept of aspect (whether an action, event or state denoted by a verb is specific and finite or not, and whether or not it brings about a change of state. Yikes). 'To go' had four versions: going by foot and by transport were different, as were going repeatedly and going in a way that was already over and done with after one journey. A *cauchemar*, as they say in French and Russian. A Greek plumber came to our house and when I tried to explain the problem with the U-bend I realised I could now speak neither Greek nor Russian. The words came out like a metronome in a mixture of the two that would have been unintelligible to anyone at embassy parties. As the *Penguin Russian Course* confirmed, 'the stressing of nouns in the plural often gives the student some difficulty' – *oknó* (window, pronounced 'ak-NAW'), for example, mutates in the plural to *ókna* ('AWK-na'). I had bought this book second hand and became more interested in the marginalia of its previous owner than in irregular verbs. Who was J. P. Roberts, learning Russian in 1980? He was obviously fed up with his studies. In the chapter on interrogatives, after the word for 'who' – *kto* – he had written, 'Kto cares?'

There were happy moments. Another book I was using, the *Ruslan* course, centred chapters on situations one might encounter as a tourist. An early one taught the student how to book into a hotel in Russia. The picture depicted a cockroach (*tarakan*).

In the light of my ineptitude I determined to take an immersive course: I hoped it might deliver a short, sharp shock. In spring, through a Swedish company found on the internet, I booked myself onto a ten-day course of one-to-one Russian lessons in Petrozavodsk in the north-west (though it was not as far west as Pskov). Besides lessons, the firm organised homestay accommodation. It was a package.

*

A gang surrounded me as I was boarding the metro at St Petersburg's Moskovskaya station. The would-be robbers deployed a familiar tactic, pressing and jostling while one tried to put his hand in my bag. I saw in time, and kneed the perpetrator in the balls, but it was an unnerving start to my trip.

At the Ladozhsky station, departure point in Petersburg for trains heading north, displaced Uzbeks proffered leaflets advertising mobile phone companies. We set off on time. Even in April the sky did not die until 10.30. Skirting the southern shore of Lake Ladoga, about half way through the overnight journey to Petrozavodsk the train crossed into Karelia, an autonomous republic within the Russian Federation, veined with rivers and spotted with lakes. There were no roads until the middle of the twentieth century. Karelians were fine riverine navigators.

The railway ticket included breakfast, and at six in the morning an attendant ferried in a compartmentalised plastic tray containing an omelette the size, shape and consistency of half a tennis ball, two smooth-skinned *kolbasa* sausages, a pack of brown biscuits, a pot of yogurt and a carton of water. Four of these trays made a mess of the small, fold-out table, especially when augmented by extra food donated by my three companions, all bound for Murmansk, poor buggers (I was there once).

Lake Onega appeared through the smeared window, stretching north like a hand. (Indeed it is the shape of a Quentin Blake hand, splintering into bony fingers.) It was the lake that the *Truvor* captain considered a sea. The winter had been heavy, and the lake was still mostly frozen. Snow cobwebbed stubbled fields.

We pulled into Petrozavodsk station in the rain.

My hosts, Vera and Sergei, met me, accompanied by Galina, the university administrator who looked after language students. I could see immediately that they were a jolly crew, and much chatter and kindly laughter accompanied my attempts at conversation as a taxi sashayed to a four-storey sixties block. The air outside was vaporous, but Vera and Sergei's third-floor flat was light and airy. Over tea, I learned that Sergei built traditional wooden houses, and Vera, a former national cross-country ski champion, worked as a part-time receptionist at a health centre. She was strong and wiry and completely flat on both sides, like an ironing board. One of their daughters, a librarian, had married, and lived nearby. The other, seventeen-year-old schoolgirl Masha, was a competitive dancer of waltz, samba and rumba. Her troupe had recently toured Nepal.

My room was spacious and almost empty; I suspect it was a living room normally, and that they cleared it out it for paying guests. Outside, birch trees grew higher than the window. At a trolleybus garage in the foreground I watched a mechanic manipulate a pair of batons attached to parallel wires – like an oversized kite mechanism – to get a trolleybus hooked up.

On the road into town, a few wooden houses remained, dwarfed by the ubiquitous apartment blocks, which were shrouded in misty rain. It took about twenty minutes to walk in. The overall effect of Petrozavodsk was not as leprous as I had seen elsewhere, though roads were pitted and muddy from melted snow. Trolleybuses plied up and down, and young women teetered on high heels.

I walked back home along the shoreline, which ran parallel with the road. At an open-air gym overlooking rills of sand at the edge of the lake, ingeniously engineered without springs, an elderly woman pedalled on a bike and a man in a bomber jacket worked a cross-trainer. Close to town, the edge of the lake was attractive, tarted up with statues, decent hotels and public buildings, but around Moskovskaya, the street where I lived, it was strewn with litter and rutted with tyre tracks and dirty ice.

The next morning, my teacher arrived. Owing to my visa status, I was required to have one-to-one lessons at home, rather than at the university. Marina was slender, with long blond hair; she was perhaps thirty-six or thirty-seven. She lived alone, and over the course of ten days, when we talked to each other about our lives, she gave the impression that she had not been happy in love. She had a vegetarian dog called Nadar, of which she spoke often. Marina had once been to a conference in Greece, and spoke of the country like the Promised Land. The weather! The fish restaurants! (I saw numerous photographs of these piscatorial paradises.) She was artistic, and enjoyed painting boxes and mirrors with flowers. She usually wore jeans and a thin acrylic sweater. The internet, she said, was ruining her life, because she wasted so much time on it.

The first full afternoon, after my lesson, it took Vera and me ninety minutes to fill in my mandatory registration form at the post office. We did the first one in blue ink, which turned out to be unacceptable. The second we filled in with black ink, but in Roman characters. This too was unacceptable (even though it said at the top of the form that both Roman and Cyrillic were all right). They took the third.

My lesson each day was from nine until one. We tackled grammar, pronunciation and vocabulary, and at the end Marina set me homework for the next day. Nuances inevitably emerged. After we had learned the word for 'room', *komnata*, I asked how to say 'bedroom'. Marina looked at me with a wilting mien. 'Most Russians', she said, 'only have one room in which to live and sleep, so it's the same word.'*

---

* I later discovered that there is a word for 'bedroom': *spal'nya*, and many Russians do have a second room, but I assume Marina didn't know any two-roomers.

*

Vera and her family had few possessions. There was little unnecessary consumption. On the subject of consumption, my stay was on a bed-and-breakfast basis, and Vera, who started work early each morning, always left something in the pan for me. I ate on a stool in the small kitchen, pondering the words of a fridge magnet quoting Spinoza in English: 'If you want the present to be different from the past, study the past.' The first morning brought forth a cold fried egg and tinned diced vegetables. The next day, small slabs of processed chicken served with yesterday's boiled rice had steamed under the lid of the frying pan for several hours. A gelatinous boxed tiramisu marked the nadir of the breaking of the fast; the zenith came in the form of *kasha* – buckwheat porridge. It was easy to scrape off the congealed veneer. Vera and her family were fastidious about food. One rarely saw them eating, and a medium bar of chocolate lasted them three days.

We often took tea together. I viewed photographs of Masha dancing. Vera hid Sergei's cigarettes, rationing them out one by one, and he smoked in the stairwell, where etiolated plants stood on a windowsill next to a jam jar filled with butts in cowslip-yellow water.

As part of her job, Marina had to teach and examine foreigners who had applied to work in Russia. To qualify for an employment permit, they were required to prove they could speak Russian. Most of her students were Uzbeks, Azerbaijanis and Tatars. She gave a speech on 'taking our jobs' and so on. How wearyingly familiar it all sounded.

*

Every day the lake ice thawed a little more at the edges, but it was still thick in the middle: I saw a man standing on it. The whiteness cast an iridescent band over browned-out banks and tatty blocks of flats. Vera, Sergei, Marina and Galina – everyone I knew – referred to Onega as 'our lake', proud of its status as the second largest in Europe with an astonishing 1,650 islands to boot. I wondered how this could be, given that I could see the other side. But it turned out that bit was just a bay.

To pass the time in the afternoons, after a session at the open-air gym I went swimming at Akvatika, a grand indoor pool. I got told off for not wearing a swimming cap, but a lifeguard went to find one I could borrow. Afterwards I sat in the sauna with liver-spotted pensioners wearing shower caps, having been careful to observe knicker etiquette. (I was once told off in a women's hammam in Tripoli for taking my pants off.) Here nudity was optional. In the changing room, the hair drier was the kind you sit under, head in a dome.

On Thursday afternoon rain fell hard and brown lakes gathered in potholes. Later that evening, my brolly (*zont*) vanished from the stairwell. Vera was horrified, exclaiming loudly with her arms folded tightly across the place where her bosom would have been if she had had one.

On Saturday, women were selling sheaves of *verby* – willow – on the streets because the next day was Willow Sunday, *verbnoye voskresenye*, what we call Palm Sunday. The day had begun auspiciously with much victorious shouting after a neighbour returned the *zont*, having taken it in error. As I had no lesson, I had arranged to look round the university with Galina. Her British students, she said, 'have a glass in each hand and a pack of cigarettes in each pocket. They think I'm a freak because I don't drink or smoke – why don't you, they say, when it's so cheap?' She had her first child aged forty, an eventuality also considered freakish by her compatriots.

Galina introduced me to her colleague Nastya (short for Anastasia), a young teaching assistant with eyes the colour of freshly sliced cucumber, and we cooked up a plan to take a bus to Salomineya, a fishing village on the other side of the bay. She brought her new-that-day friend Raban, who was staying with her via a couch-surfing website. Both were free spirits. They talked non-stop. Couch-surfing was popular.

Only a few small clouds clippered across the sky, though in the shade a chill descended – it was one of those days when it was summer in the light and winter in the dark. The bus was a filthy boneshaker. We discussed national characteristics. 'Compared to the US,' said Nastya, 'Russia seems closed.' 'We wear a *maska* – a mask,' chipped in Raban. 'But it's only a street face. In reality, Russians are friendly.' This I believed to be true, though it took time to get acquainted with the *maska*. I remember my friend Colin Thubron, an accomplished Russia watcher and fluent speaker, saying that in decades of visiting, he had never met a smiling Russian. It was during a lecture he was giving, and Russians in the audience applauded.

Logs had been stacked outside wooden houses on the outskirts of Salomineya. Towards the centre, solid new-builds displaced older structures. The village smelled of fire, as people were burning foliage in their gardens. 'The smell of spring,' Raban said. A well was still in use, protected in a cupboard, and a shadouf-like lever arrangement hoisted water out. We crossed a rickety bridge to get to the main part of the village, one-way traffic controlled by lights. The ice had melted out, and men were fishing. Bundles of willow lay in the porch of a yellow and grey church.

Raban worked for a railway company and couch-surfed when he could; he also hosted surfers. He had just had a Thai woman to stay for a month. Couch-surfing had taken him to Germany and all over Russia – once he hitchhiked 6,000 kilometres to Sakhalin, a Russian island in the Pacific. He was only nineteen, but was, apparently, deeply engaged in his country's twentieth-century history. 'I came to Petrozavodsk', he told me, 'as a kind of pilgrimage.' He went on to explain that the pioneering Yury Dmitriev, a son of Petrozavodsk and a man committed to exposing the truth of the communist past in the north-west, had found sites near the city where Stalin's prisoners had been executed and buried. 'I have been to Krasny Bor near here, where many corpses lie, to pay homage,' Raban said. Many of the condemned had been transported from the Solovki islands in the White Sea. In 2014 Dmitriev used the Day of Remembrance to condemn the annexation of Crimea and the conflict in eastern Ukraine. A decade before he had unsuccessfully protested against the erection of a statue of the corrupt Yury Andropov in Petrozavodsk, briefly Soviet leader in the 1980s and once chief of the city's Komsomol (Communist Party youth wing).

*

Galina arrived at the flat with two tickets to a concert at the nearby *konservatoriya*. Vera came with me. Once we were seated, she pointed out, a few rows in front of us, the regional minister of culture, of whom she had a low opinion. The orchestra were playing traditional instruments, including balalaikas and dombras (round-bellied, long-necked lutes). The evening began with speeches. I thought the first might have been a simple speech of welcome. After three addresses, each introduced at length by a woman in a black dress, I feared we were in for a reprise of the seventeenth party congress.

A white-haired tenor arrived, to a fanfare, wearing a dinner jacket that reached to his knees. The programme was varied. On the one hand we heard a scene from Prokofiev's opera *The Gambler* (*Igrok*), based on Dostoyevsky's novel of the same name. On the other, the audience clapped in time to 'Those Were the Days, My Friend', a favourite from my childhood: I can see Mary Hopkin now. Turns out it was originally a Russian song, '*Dorogoi dlinnoyu*'. The row of female dombra players bowed forward on the chords like wheat in a field. They wore white tops, long black skirts or trousers, and little black ties.

At home, we talked over tea. Sergei said there were never serfs in Karelia on account of the lack of agriculture. White Sea fishers and hunters produced for themselves, which affected the mentality. But he lamented that nobody works any more. There is no heavy industry. Peter the Great built large-scale ironworks in Petrozavodsk for forging cannons (the town's very name means 'Peter's works'). These were no

longer operational. Vera said it was good that there was no industry, as it meant the air was clean.

*

The next evening, Galina had arranged to come over – it was her responsibility to check on my welfare. Vera had her hair done for the event, and bought supplies. But Galina rang to postpone, so we had a party without her – wine, slices of cheese and ice cream (from locally made cones, Vera was quick to point out). Sergei said I was good at languages, and I said yes, but at fifty-two it's not like the old days. He agreed. Vera said, 'But we are wise now.' 'I'd rather be young than wise,' Sergei replied. Then we watched television. I struggled through the weather forecast every night. A national version came on before the local one. As far as I could make out, the weatherman seemed to say, every day, 'Tomorrow it will be cold in the north and hot in the south, with loads of other stuff going on in the middle.'

*

When we said goodbye, Marina gave me a notebook with columns listing Russian words next to English ones. She had told me that she decorated a friend's coffee shop in Anokhin Street, and in the early evening, when dusk had not yet fallen on Petrozavodsk, I went there. It was called Cherchez la Femme, and Marina's paintings looked fine.

III

The Heart within the Tomb

Blue-eyed Ivan Sergeyevich Turgenev (pronounced 'Toor-GAY-nyeff')was six foot three and handsome, spoke fifteen languages, played chess to an international standard and was a fabled raconteur as well as a popular landlord whose 5,000 serfs literally sang his praises. And of course he wrote like the Angel Gabriel. You've known his characters all your life: Rakitin, agonisingly alert to his own superfluity, and Natalya, torn between passion and self-criticism.

He was three years older than Dostoyevsky, and more or less his opposite. The pair appeared together at readings of their work, representing the twin poles of Russian culture: despotic tsarism (Fyodor Mikhailovich) versus a liberal Western-style constitution (Ivan Sergeyevich). Turgenev thought Dostoyevsky's ravings about mystical Russianness a load of rubbish. Equally, Dostoyevsky had a low opinion of the author of *Fathers and Sons*: 'I went to see him in the morning at noon,' he wrote to a friend in 1867, 'and found him at lunch. I tell you frankly: even before this I don't like the man personally.' An uncharacteristically humorous and self-deprecatory comment followed. 'Most unpleasant of all, I owe him money from 1857 from Wiesbaden … Also, I don't like his aristocratic pharisaic embraces when he advances to kiss you, but presents his cheek. Terrible, as though he were a general.'

The E105 south from Tula, an arrow of a highway, flies through the pinstriped darkness of birch forest. On the verges, men in tracksuits and plastic sandals touted pails of the mushrooms Russians call 'horn of plenty', perching the goods on top of rusty Ladas. The mushrooms were 300 roubles a pail, compared with 3,000 roubles in Moscow. The wide-open spaces of the Oryol *oblast* lead to Turgenev's ancestral estate, Spasskoye-Lutovinovo, buried in the forest a couple of kilometres off the E105. Turgenev said the air at Spasskoye was full of ideas. He had over 7,000 trees, mainly ash, a thousand of them between 150 and 300 years old. 'Do you not think', Arkady says in *Fathers and Sons*, 'that our Russian term *yasen* is particularly suited to the ash tree? For no other tree cleaves the air with such airy brightness.' *Yasen* comes from the adjective *yasny*, meaning clear or bright.

In 1834 he planted an oak tree, and asked everyone who ever came to bow before it. So I did. It was knobbly now, and ringed by iron railings. I felt the air dense with ideas, just as he had.

At the main house, an unpainted wooden staircase led to a veranda and the front door, flanked by greenery which had been trained with twine like guy ropes to grow straight to the roof, giving the appearance of a Big Top. The balcony posts were carved into flanges at the summits, and similar carving appeared over the lintel. Red flowers sprouted among the foliage all around. The house was painted lilac, and had a green roof. A smaller balcony led off the first floor. To the right as you looked at the house, a cream-coloured wing had a portico, and its own larch tree. The veranda of the main house appears in *Fathers and Sons*.

> Nikolai Petrovich, however, continued sitting with head bent, and his eyes contemplating the ancient steps of the veranda, up which a stout speckled hen was tap-tapping its way on a pair of splayed yellow legs, and thereby causing an untidy, but fastidious-looking cat to regard it from the balustrade with marked disapproval. Meanwhile the sun beat fiercely down, and from the darkened interior of a neighbouring granary came a smell of hot rye straw.

Inside, dark furniture was oppressively empire-style. Elaborate curtains were swagged low over the windows. The master's desk was baize-topped, and in his study he had a winged leather sofa, a 400-year-old icon of Veronica's Veil and chandeliers. A polished hall floor reflected pale blue watered silk wallpaper and a blue self-striped silk sofa on one side of an oval walnut table. A plainer dining room had apricot soft furnishings, double doors and an English grandfather clock, which still works – a man comes from Moscow every year to service it. There was, of course, a six-foot white porcelain stove in a corner. Turgenev had a piano, and played it often. In his dressing room he had an English washstand. 'English washstands', says Bazarov in *Fathers and Sons*, 'represent progress.' And then there was Zakhar's room. He was Turgenev's personal servant. When Ivan Sergeyevich died, Zakhar wrote a note to go on his tomb in St Petersburg, extolling the humanity and greatness of the man he had served. And he said how proud he was to have known him.

Nursery nurses, valets and a procession of French and German governesses and tutors populated Turgenev's childhood. When the family carriage crunched up the drive after a shopping trip to Tula, the serf orchestra started up, drowning out the hissing of geese. The estate was an almost self-sufficient village. Besides the serf quarters, Spasskoye had an icehouse, a *banya*, a smokehouse, a tannery, workshops which made the serfs' clothes and shoes, a well, and a mill for making wallpaper and stationery. For an especially grand dinner, however, Turgenev's mother ordered viands from Moscow, more than 300 kilometres away. And comestibles went in the other direction too. For part of the winter the Turgenevs shifted to their house in Moscow, sending ahead wagons of pork (the pigs were dead) and geese (they were alive), followed by other carriages conveying laundrymaids and clerks. It would not be right to call Turgenev's Spasskoye feudal, as the serfs were property.

Sergei Nikolayevich, the author's father, was a military man who fought Napoleon's troops. He was at Borodino. The estate was not his – his wife inherited it from an uncle at the age of sixteen. She was Varvara Petrovna. Her clothes were not made on the estate; she sent to Moscow, Berlin or Paris for them. Spasskoye included twenty villages which Varvara ruled as an absolute sovereign. Her retinue was divided by rank and title. There was a chamberlain; her personal maids were ladies-in-waiting; and her private office had a dais on which she sat with her portrait behind her, ringing bells – she had a mania for bells – issuing orders and receiving deputations. Supposed miscreants paraded before her window so she might select who was going to Siberia. Serfs could not marry without her permission; many she ordered to marry. They were allowed to have children, but once a child was born it was sent away. The police were not permitted to come to Spasskoye, although the local chief of police amused Varvara so she let him come in through a back door.

Like others of her class, or caste, Varvara regarded Orthodoxy as the religion of serfs and poor people. She had a French translation of Thomas à Kempis read at table. Cholera was an unwanted visitor to the district, often, and many poor people died. Some said Varvara feared the disease so much that when it was on the prowl she had herself carried round in a glass-enclosed chair.

When Turgenev started his career, the tsar's censor was the most influential figure in literary life. After *A Sportsman's Sketches* (*Zapiski okhotnika*) appeared in 1852 Ivan Sergeyevich spent a month incarcerated at the local police station, in a stifling cell bizarrely located in the archive building, so he read files to while away the hours. Later, after his release, he wrote of the frustrating agony of being a writer in Russia during this period. 'Times in those days were difficult,' he wrote. 'In the morning, perhaps, you have had your proofs returned to you, all scored and disfigured by red ink, as if covered with blood. You may even have to pay a visit to the censor, offer him vain and degrading explanations, or justifications, and listen to his verdict, often derisory, from which there is no appeal.'

Still, he achieved fame in Russia with *A Sportsman's Sketches*, published first in serial form in the *Contemporary Review* and sometimes translated in English as *Sketches from a Hunter's Album*. The volume was a collection of sensitive and often lyrical stories about the social and natural life of the Russian countryside around Spasskoye. The pieces depict peasants, for the first time, as rational human beings, not victims. A nobleman hunts with a hound and a serf companion. The two men sleep side by side in huts and barns, eat the same food, and talk intimately. Turgenev's father's serf valet had taught the boy to read and write Russian, and, unlike his mother, the author perceived serfs as people like him. He had experienced them as such. Varvara's cruelty affected him. In his early short story *Mumu* he records a landlady ordering a serf's dog to be destroyed because it bares its teeth when she approaches. Decades later, he said that the proudest moment of his life came after the liberation of the serfs when, on a train from Oryol to Moscow, two former serfs approached him and bowed to the ground 'to thank him in the name of the whole people'.

Behind the main house at Spasskoye there was a simple, one-floor green building with cross-hatched wooden window shutters. This was Turgenev's home for two years in the early 1850s, after the tsar exiled him from Moscow and Petersburg for writing an article in praise of Gogol in which he expressed un-tsarist political views. Under house arrest, Turgenev wrote *Ottsy i deti* (*Fathers and Sons* traditionally in English, but the accurate title is 'Fathers and Children'). Talk about turning adversity to advantage.

Varvara Petrovna died in 1850. After she perished Turgenev freed his house serfs and put the others on quit rent, encouraging them to take advantage of freedom, with the redemption payments reduced by one-fifth. 'There is nothing in it to boast of,' he wrote to a friend, 'but also, I believe, it cannot bring me shame.' Turgenev said of his mother, 'She never regarded me as a writer and never read a single story or article of mine, not even my *Sportsman's Sketches*.'

*

After the isolation of Spasskoye Turgenev lived mostly in self-imposed European exile, first for eight years in Baden-Baden. A few kilometres across the Rhine from Strasbourg, Baden-Baden had grown into a thriving summer resort, especially for Parisians. Europeans of a certain class gathered there for health and amusement. They strolled in the mountains and in the Black Forest, attended the theatre and haunted the two *Schlösser* and the Rhineland orchards. They caught trout from the river Oos, lay in baths of ionised minerals, drank the water at a *Kurhaus* and played at the gambling tables. Later Turgenev moved to Berlin, where he wore a green swallow-tail coat, a blue-eyed Slavonic giant. He also spent time on the Isle of Wight.

Although Turgenev lived most of his adult life in Europe, he returned home to Spasskoye often, and wrote five of his six novels there. He must have felt he was out of the world. The journey from Petersburg alone took a week, though in 1863 a train service started between Moscow and Oryol.

Some say that the West discovered Russia through Turgenev. European literati loved him and his work. Gustave Flaubert was in thrall to him. The pair met in Paris in a Left Bank restaurant at the end of winter in 1863, when the Frenchman was forty-one and the Russian forty-four. They corresponded for seventeen years. Flaubert wrote:

> I have considered you a master for a long time. But the more I study you, the more your skill leaves me gaping. I admire the vehement yet restrained quality of your writing, the fellow feeling that extends to the lowest of human creatures and brings landscapes to life ... Your work has a bittersweet flavor, a sadness that is delightful and penetrates to the very depths of my soul.

Flaubert sent Turgenev cheese from France. In 1872 he wrote, 'There's only one man left in the world now with whom I can talk, and that's you.'

*

The Heart within the Tomb

In *Fathers and Sons*, two young men visit their family homes in the country during a summer break from Petersburg, where they have just graduated from university. The first line might not quite be universally acknowledged as the best, but it's close.

> 'Well, Peter? Cannot you see them yet?' asked a squire of about forty who, hatless, and clad in a dusty jacket over a pair of tweed breeches, stepped on to the veranda of a posting-house on the twentieth day of May, 1859.

The translator Constance Garnett, who turned most of the Golden Age writers into English, said Turgenev was the most difficult of the Russians to translate 'because his style is the most beautiful'. The squire in the first line of *Fathers and Sons* is Nikolai Petrovich Kirsanov. His father served as a general in 1812, like Turgenev senior. The book is about the collision between old and young, liberals and radicals, traditional civilisation and sceptical rationalism.

Turgenev wrote the novel in response to his own time, but it might just as well be about now. The young Nihilist Bazarov, a restless hero and the one who likes English washstands, is what today we would call a disrupter, and he'd live in Shoreditch or Williamsburg. His friends sit around discussing topics like 'Is marriage a prejudice or a crime?' Arkady is his acolyte. On a visit to a relative in a neighbouring province they meet Anna Sergeyevna, the widowed Madame Odintsova, a figure who, 'like all women who have never known what it is to fall in love, was sensible of a persistent yearning for something wholly undefined'. How did Turgenev know that? From her marriage of convenience 'she had derived a certain aversion to the male sex in general, which she conceived to be composed exclusively of creatures slovenly idle, wearisome and weakly exacting in their habits'. Odintsova is one of Turgenev's greatest creations. Bazarov likes her sister more at one juncture, and judges Anna 'yesterday's loaf'. I fancied this as the title of my autobiography.

When Bazarov tells his adoring father Vasily Ivanovich that he has pricked his finger when dissecting a dead typhoid patient for his medical experiments, the line crashes onto the page like a Beethoven chord. No one is right and no one is wrong in this book: Turgenev said he didn't know whether to love or hate Bazarov. In these pages you see life in all its cruelty, randomness, indifference and brevity. Turgenev was a lyrical prose poet, a Schumann to Pushkin's Mozart. Read the book again and you'll see what I mean. The Russian critic D. S. Mirsky said Turgenev's characters, like those of other Russian realists, 'are not good or bad, they are only more or less unhappy and deserving of sympathy'. Isn't that more or less how it is off the page too?

When *Fathers and Sons* came out in 1862 it annoyed almost everyone. It was considered incendiary. Both sides of the intellectual polarisation hated it for different reasons. The revolutionaries thought Bazarov a libellous caricature of themselves. The old guard considered him the glorification of evil. The novel's critical reception in Russia naturally wounded Turgenev. In his next novel, *Smoke (Dym)*, set in Baden-Baden, those wounds took on a life of their own in Turgenev's caricature of Russian society (the smoke of the title is railway smoke). He complains in letters that he missed many things from his homeland; but he was bitter that Russia had turned her back on him. He clung to his homeland's images, though. At the end of his violent story 'An Unhappy Girl' he uses the image of a bit of herring in a man's hair to express the chaos in a restaurant when plates are thrown and tables overturned.

As I prepared to leave Spasskoye, the sun dropped behind an aspen copse which was trailing long shadows over the motionless fields. The light faded with intemperate haste. 'Bazarov rose,' Turgenev wrote in the room I was standing in. 'The lamp was casting dim light, while into the fragrant, darkened, isolated room there came wafted at intervals, under a swinging blind, the sensuous freshness of the night, and the sounds of its mysterious whisperings.'

*

The Heart within the Tomb

In the grounds near the main house, they had buried Soviet soldiers who died in Oryol in the Great Patriotic War. 'In a remote corner of Russia', Turgenev wrote at the end of *Fathers and Sons*, many years ahead of the war, 'there lies a little country cemetery. Like most cemeteries of the kind, it is depressing of aspect. Over its fences dense masses of weed have grown, its drab wooden crosses are rickety and turning mouldy under their blistered, painted canopies, its stone paths have lost their alignment, and look as though someone has displaced them from below, its two or three ragged trees diffuse only the scantiest of shade, and sheep wander over its tombs.'

Bazarov's grieving parents visit this fictional cemetery. Are their tears fruitless, Turgenev asks in the final paragraph:

> No, no and a thousand times no! For, though the heart that lives within that tomb may have been passionate and wild and erring, the flowers which bloom in that spot contemplate us with eyes of naught but peace and innocence, and speak to us of naught but the eternal, mighty calm of 'unheeding' nature, as an image of the Eternal Reconciliation, and of the Life which shall have no End.

*

Who was Turgenev? His forebears were Turkic-speaking nomads who galloped across the steppe with Genghis Khan – the name Turgenev derives from the Mongol word for 'swift', *türgen*. As an adult, Ivan Sergeyevich told a friend that the only things he liked were music, poetry, nature and dogs. His themes as a writer were twofold: the changing world of Russia, and the finely calibrated shifts of feeling that make a person human. 'His large nature', his admirer Henry James wrote, 'overflowed with the love of justice but he was also the stuff of which glories are made.' His work is set in the magnanimous and brutal world of the gentry – the world he grew up in. The stories and plays reflect his ambivalence about that world. He was a man and a writer of restraint, and could not stop himself from seeing both sides of an argument. People are difficult to pin down in Turgenev. His vision was not of a beautiful world, but his gift was to see beyond the boredom and the horror, and glimpse beauty.

Unlike his near-contemporaries Tolstoy and Dostoyevsky, who were better known in both life and death, Turgenev was not susceptible to nationalistic romanticism. He wanted neither to lead nor to follow. 'I agree with no man's opinions,' says Bazarov; 'I have some of my own.' This surely was Turgenev.

Having said that Turgenev's imagination was rooted in ambiguity, there was one point on which he was as sure as he ever was about anything – perhaps that would be eighty per cent sure. This was the tension between the semi-Asiatic world of Muscovy and the Russia that looked to Europe. To the poet Afanasy Fet Turgenev wrote, 'I feel a strong physical revulsion from anything Slavophil … it's flabby, unpleasant, rotten and sticks to one's gullet. And it smells of the icon lamp in church. No, I am an incorrigible westerner.' He did not go in for guff about the 'Russian soul'. He stood far from the visions of Pushkin, of that genius Alexander Herzen, of Dostoyevsky and the other Slavophiles who believed it was Russia's destiny to save the fallen West.

*

One of his stories, *First Love* (*Pervaya lyubov*), tells how a man and his son fall in love with the same young woman. Turgenev said the story came directly from his youth and he draws a moving portrait of his own father in it. And at the end, when the fictional father is dying (Sergei died at forty-two), he says something to his son that Turgenev repeated in many stories: 'My son, fear the love of woman; fear that bliss, that poison.'

Turgenev never married. He was in love his whole adult life with Pauline Viardot, a famed mezzo-soprano and composer. Of Spanish descent and French nationality, she lived mostly in Paris and was married with four children. Turgenev fell for her when he was twenty-five. Two minutes before he died forty years later, he said she was the tsarina among all tsarinas. The last time he was at Spasskoye he said he had lived all his life at the edge of another family – the Viardots. He learned to love without possessing.

He wrote best away from Pauline. Some book-loving Russians thought she damaged his talent, as obsessions can. Turgenev had an illegitimate daughter with a Spasskoye serf. The child went to live with the Viardots, adopting the first name Paulinette and the family surname. Turgenev had not taken any interest in his daughter in her early years, but after the move to Paris he played a fatherly role of sorts, though the relationship was troubled. Poor Paulinette.

*

After a Moscow production of his play *A Month in the Country* (*Mesyats v derevne*), Turgenev told an actress, 'Rakitin is myself. I always portray myself as the unsuccessful lover in my novels.' That play is performed in English more than any other work of Turgenev's, but many think a fortnight in the country would have been enough. Perhaps in recognition of that, Patrick Marber's version, first produced at the National Theatre in 2015, is called *Three Days in the Country*.

In 2002 Turgenev's play *Fortune's Fool* (*Nakhlebnik*, roughly translatable as 'sponger'; the play sometimes appears in English as *The Parasite*) ran for 127 performances on Broadway. It's funny, and in a Russian way turns tragic. The second act in particular is alternately farcical and tragic. The scene depicting a panic before a party might be the best thing Turgenev ever wrote. In a recent production at London's Arcola Theatre, wealthy landowner Tropatchov strutted in an emerald frock-coat, a small-brained peacock delighting in torturing the impoverished hanger-on Kuzovkin for the sake of it. Even Tropatchov's stature was perfect: thin legs and barrel body and curled black hair with a side parting.

*

Turgenev wrote to Flaubert from Moscow on 26 June 1872:

Old age, my dear friend, is a great dull cloud that envelops the future, the present and even the past, which it makes more melancholy, covering our memories with fine cracks, like old porcelain ... In fact I think a journey to Russia, the two of us together, would do you good. I've just spent four whole days, not on the top of a haystack, but wandering along the paths of an old country garden, full of rustic perfumes, strawberries, birds, sunshine and sleepy shadows, with two hundred acres of gently waving rye all around! It was superb!

When he knew he was dying, he wrote to Tolstoy, ten years his junior, 'to say how glad I was to have been a contemporary of yours'.

*

I was missing Russia and struggling with my work, so in the dreary evenings of a London winter I turned again to cooking *à la russe*. Abandoning the Princess briefly, I looked at *Mastering the Art of Soviet Cooking* by Anya von Bremzen. I chose her *kulebyaka* (fish, rice and mushrooms in pastry), largely because it appears in Turgenev and he loved to eat it. I grew suspicious when von Bremzen instructed me to mix yeast with sugar and warm milk and leave until it bubbles: I knew it wouldn't. Worse, once I had the required elastic dough, it failed to rise a millimetre, let alone double in size. But as the cook said, 'The sour cream in the yeast dough ... adds a lovely tang to the buttery casing.' It did. And the filling was sublime – a bosky base of wild mushrooms cut with the tang of lemon juice and the sweetness of sherry served with mountains of dill and flat-leaf parsley and the solidity of boiled rice and little chunks of hard-boiled egg. I glazed the top with egg yolk and decorated it with a cut-out pastry fish and a ring of olive for the eye.

Mastering the Art of Soviet Cooking tells the story of post-Revolutionary Russia through the prism of one family and what they ate. The author and her mother arrived in Philadelphia in 1974, stateless refugees with no winter coats. They were also, von Bremzen asserts, 'thoroughly gentrified Moscow Jews', abandoned some years previously by the infant Anya's father. The book is structured chronologically, beginning with an account of maternal grandparents in the 1920s and proceeding to the present. Historical material is interspersed with flash-forwards and commentary – when the author returns to Moscow in 1987, for example, she presents the reader with a disquisition on Russia's 'steeped and saturated history with vodka' or, in its absence, with *politura*, which is wood varnish.

An award-winning food writer, to confect this volume Bremzen and her mother raked through the past, using their overheated kitchen in Queens 'as a time machine and an incubator of memories'. Deploying the hallowed 1939 *Book of Tasty and Healthy Food*, known to Soviet citizens as simply *The Book* (*Kniga*), they have fun recreating old dissident get-togethers, preparing Stalin's Deathday Dinner, and brewing their own kvass, a drink made out of fermented bread. In reality, *The Book* promoted a communist fantasy, as most of the ingredients were not available. It was cookbook as propaganda. But its influence lives on. In 2017 the beatific Mary Berry adapted a herring-and-egg *Kniga* recipe on British television.

There is much that is harrowing in *Mastering the Art of Soviet Cooking*, the pages on the Great Patriotic War especially. The author moves artfully between longshots ('He cleared minefields by sending troops attacking across them') to her schoolgirl mother's ritual lunch ration of *podushechka*, a sweet the size of a fingernail. Her grandfather was a military spy who contracted pneumonia after leading General Zhukov's catastrophic amphibious reconnaissance mission across Lake Ladoga during the siege of Leningrad. Dying in hospital a few days later, he wrote to his wife, 'Liza, teach the children to throw grenades. Make sure they remember their papa. He loved them so.'

The chapter on the 1950s includes a short essay on the culture of queuing: 'Your average *Homo sovieticus* spent a third to half of his non-working time queuing for something.' The author reaches her own birth in 1963, a year remembered for one of the worst crop failures in post-Stalinist history.

The descriptions of meals are delightful, despite the anomaly at the heart of this book, namely that during the entire Soviet period there was nothing decent to eat unless you were a Party official. After the Revolution, von Bremzen writes, 'in just a bony fistful of years, classical Russian food culture vanished'. Inevitably, therefore, 'a story about Soviet food is a chronicle of longing'. But von Bremzen conjures the whiff of fermenting sauerkraut in an enamelled bucket, the glisten of sinew and fat in a cheap goulash 'with an ivory palette', and the sharp and creamy taste of the ubiquitous *salat Olivier* in the 'kitschy, mayonnaise-happy seventies'. The gunky Olivier, she writes, 'could be a metaphor for a Soviet émigré's memory: urban legends and totalitarian myths, collective narratives and biographical facts, journeys home both real and imaginary – all loosely cemented with mayo'.

When the USSR imploded, the author was tucking into wild duck with a fiery sauce in the rebellious Georgian sub-republic of Abkhazia.*

Through austerity, the elite, as always, lived off the fat of the land. Take the 1930s, a period of unimaginable hardship for most Muscovites. In the House of Government (*Dom pravitelstva*), a titanic structure of 507 flats on an island facing the Kremlin, those on the right side of the government gorged on duck and goose pâté, oranges, cheese and dishes of rich food from *kisel* to *knysh* ordered from a kitchen on the ground floor. The building, known to some Russians as the House on the Embankment (*Dom na naberezhnoi*), was built on swampland in 1931. For decades resident politicians and prominent supporters of

---

* A growing foodie movement has emerged in metropolitan Russia over the past decade, partly in response to economic sanctions. Celebrity chefs such as Vladimir Mukhin at Moscow's White Rabbit restaurant have reimagined Russian cuisine by drawing on the vibrant culinary traditions that the Soviet regime erased. (If you want to see new Russian money's vulgarity at its finest, head to the sixteenth floor of Smolensky Passazh and have a bite at White Rabbit.)

the regime had use of a bank, a theatre, a library, a shooting gallery and a cinema. The thugs of the NKVD – the People's Commissariat for Internal Affairs, *Narodny komissariat vnutrennikh del* – could get into the flats through the rubbish disposal room. The NKVD also kept an apartment in the building from which they could monitor tenants' telephone calls.

Yet even this place was a House of Terror. However important a tenant might be, a knock on the door hung in the air before it came. And it often came. Stalin's stooges tortured many tenants previously of impeccable record into making false confessions for which they were duly executed; others were executed anyway. Between 1937 and 1940, some of the flats in the House had five sets of tenants, so swiftly did Stalin kill them off. Those moving in knew they were walking in dead men's shoes.*

Tolstoy famously wrote that all unhappy families are unhappy in a different way, but this is not true. The families in the House were all unhappy in the same way. The knock on the door, the telephone call, the black car purring into the courtyard. Thugs forced children to denounce their parents. A son of one Bolshevik grew up in the House. As an adult, he interrogated, in the Lubyanka, a woman with whom he had played throughout their childhoods. She went to the gulag for twenty years and there learned, through taps on the cell walls from a fellow prisoner, that they had murdered her husband. The men and women in the revolving doors of the House of Government knew what was coming: they kept bags packed. Many had already denounced their own colleagues and collaborated in their execution. One tenant refused to open the door to NKVD henchmen. So those 'policemen' bricked him in. He died of starvation.

---

* The House of Government, near Borovitskaya metro station, is in private hands now. A lifelong tenant opened a small museum in one of the apartments. I went there. You could see the ghosts.

This building came to my attention through a book almost as monumental as the House itself. Published in 2017 in English, its author, Yuri Slezkine, is a professor of history at Berkeley. His name rang a bell. In *The Magnetic North*, my 2009 volume about travelling in the Arctic, I had quoted from a book by Yuri Slezkine called *Arctic Mirrors: Russia and the Small Peoples of the North*. That author turned out to be this Yuri Slezkine's grandfather. The grandson too has written on Russia's treatment of its Arctic minorities (there are more than thirty discrete groups). And so the horror passed down the generations, more misery inflicted by barbarian rulers. It used to be dog eat dog. Now it's the other way round.

Here's what I wrote at the time, involving Slezkine senior. The Tobias in the text was a young German anthropologist with woolly ash-blond hair. I met him in Anadyr, the capital of Chukotka. He was studying the practice of *ukrupneniye*, by which the state, from 1957 to the mid-1980s, 'centralised' semi-nomadic Chukchi reindeer herders and walrus hunters in the Russian Far East, rounding them up into purpose-built factory towns. The goal – to boost production – was never achieved; the consequence was social and cultural disaster.

The 'disaster' Tobias had witnessed in the villages was not the result of Soviet collectivisation, but of the years following 1991. He returned to the subject again and again, using the phrase 'post-apocalypse' to mean 'after the collapse of the Soviet Union' – for example he spoke of the abandoned villages he had visited as 'post-apocalyptic ghost towns'. He told me he was interested in how people relate to their empty villages when they return. 'Why do they go back?' I asked. 'To hunt,' he said, 'and to escape the shattered utopia of Soviet modernisation.' In the words of Yuri Slezkine, author of the best book on what Russian academics call 'the small peoples of the north' (*malye narody severa*), 'No matter how fast the circumpolar peoples adapted to their changing economic circumstances, for most of them it was not fast enough.'

Like every regime that had preceded it, the new Russia that emerged after the collapse failed to embrace its indigenous peoples, particularly when Putin's 'vertical power' strategy removed the little autonomy enjoyed by the regions. This was particularly evident in Chukotka. The Russian nationalism that seeped into the space left vacant by Communism further alienated peoples not considered quite Russian enough. When powerful voices of the right express a longing for a traditional Russia, they do not mean reindeer and walrus.

After many years working with indigenous peoples in the Arctic, Tobias had an informed idea about the reality of their lives. But he was able to find redemption in the spirit he encountered among the hunters who had not succumbed to despair and booze. More than once, as we were talking over a coffee, he cited Hemingway to express what he discovered in Chukotkan villages: the world breaks everyone and afterward many are strong at the broken places. 'They have a certain resilience,' Tobias continued. 'They have carved out a place in a hostile world.'

*

Turgenev was the first love of my gnome-like Russian teacher, Edward Gurvich. We met through the agency of our mutual friend Colin Thubron, who had himself learned Russian from Gurvich. The gnome came to my house for ninety minutes every week and we sat at a desk in the library overlooking a plane tree that reached to the third floor. The first time he came, I went to meet him at the station close to my house. I carried a book for purposes of recognition, he wore an *ushanka*, the hat with earflaps – *ushi* means ears. He looked like a Soviet aviator from the sixties. He was the best kind of teacher, in that he disliked talking in English.

As I was making tea for us before proceeding to the library I told Edward I was shortly going to Russia again. He launched into anxious advice about taking off all jewellery prior to departure, regarding everyone with suspicion, and telling people I was Sarah, not Sara, the latter having Jewish connotations which Russians don't like. This set the tone. He made it clear that Russians are a rum lot and would be waiting to trip me up or otherwise murder or annoy me at all times. He declared himself a Jewish anti-Semite, said several times that he was ninety-five, and professed to be sexist to boot, the evidence for the latter being that he treated his son and daughter differently. He was a vocal royalist ('The Queen gave me passport') and *hated Russia*.

Edward's father had emigrated from Argentina to the Soviet Union in 1931, and never went home again. (When I complained that the Russian 'ui' sound, represented in Cyrillic with the letter ы and normally transliterated *y*, was extraordinarily hard to master, Edward said his father didn't manage it in thirty years.)

From the first meeting, we laughed. In the second lesson he started telling me about a succession of wives – it seemed that there were three or four, the story varied: either that or I misunderstood. His first wife was a psychoanalyst. She was the mother of Edward's beloved 26-year-old son, a doctor who spoke six languages and lived in Germany. Our common profound suspicion of analysis often came up during lessons: we both enjoyed venting our spleen on the topic.

In the third lesson, for the purposes of conversation, we showed one another photographs of our families, and the wife count seemed to have risen. Asking me about my family, I tried to tell him my then partner and father of my children was Canadian, but ended up saying, in my hopeless Russian, that he was a comedian, and for the rest of our acquaintance, that was how the man remained. 'Is this the comedian?' Edward said as he inspected a family photograph. During this session Edward announced that he had Munchhausen syndrome.

'How does that manifest itself?' I asked.

'I am a compulsive liar.'

'Have you lied to me?'

'Oh yes.'

His most frequent word, when discussing contemporary Russia, was 'bandit' (it's the same in Russian and English). Putin was bandit number one. He (Edward, not Putin) emailed me the moment I got back from a trip to the Caucasus as he feared I might have been kidnapped. He was pleased to hear how much I hated Sochi, and after an anti-Putin rant we discussed the unfortunate national physiognomy. Edward believed it was to do with Stalin's purges, which wiped out the intelligentsia. He said that Russian men's faces are like bottoms.

He gave me a copy of his autobiography. It was in the form of an alphabet – *Stories of a Soviet Childhood from A to Yazyk*. For my homework, I had to read the chapter on 'Love'. At our sixth lesson, he gave me a bilingual photocopy of Chekhov's 'The Lady with the Little Dog', one of the greatest short stories ever written.* He had photocopied on both sides of the pages, but each side was the opposite way up, so I had to rotate the sheets. I was thrilled at the prospect of picking my way through Chekhov in Russian for the first time, no matter how painstaking it might be.

At our next meeting Edward kicked off as soon as we got upstairs and sat at our small desk overlooking the plane tree, now in June in full abundance and swaying in the light summer breeze. He made a start with a speech about moral relativism. This was a challenge. I wondered where it was leading, and of course it was to 'The Lady with the Little Dog'. We struggled on. He refused to accept my

---

* This glorious story is often translated as 'The Lady with the Dog'. But is also appears in English as 'The Lady with the Little Dog'. The reason for this is that there are two different words in Russian – one for dog, and one, with an extra letter, meaning little dog or doggy. Chekhov chose to use the latter, and to my mind it conjures a wholly different picture and a more appropriate one – the reader sees a creature more accessory than hound, an image in keeping with the story's tone of delicacy and restraint. The tale is sometimes also translated as 'The Lady with the Lapdog'. It is a fixture on the literary landscape. The London-born short-story writer Clive Sinclair (1948–2018) brought it up to date as 'The Lady with the Laptop' (1996).

fumbling suggestion that there was indeed something resembling moral absolutism. He had his arsenal ready, and drew from his briefcase a newspaper cutting about Mr and Mrs Prokofiev. When Sergei left her, Lina went to the gulag for twenty years. I wasn't sure what that was meant to reveal. Anyway, then we looked at the story. If Edward's first love was Turgenev, his second was Chekhov's short stories.

Part of my homework one week involved watching the 2011 Russian film *Elena*, directed by Andrei Zvyagintsev, on the grounds that it would be good for my Russian. I was surprised, therefore, when nobody spoke for the first eight minutes, but I did enjoy the film. The two settings, both in Moscow, were a rich man's apartment and his servant's son's slummy flat. I had seen so many of the latter, there being proportionately more of them by a factor of about a hundred thousand. The plot involved the servant, Elena, paying to get her grandson into university so that he would not be conscripted. That was true to life – I had met many people who had done this. You can buy anything in Russia. Even Edward liked the film.

Much later, when I was heading for an intensive language course in Moscow, he asked me in which district I was staying. When I said Vykhino, he put his head in his hands. At about this point we read a newspaper article together about Mikhail Khodorkovsky, the oligarch businessman who had just been released from a jail sentence for fraud, money laundering and embezzlement. He was once crowned the richest man in Russia, and when the government turned against him he won political asylum in London. 'At the root of the conflict between Putin and Khodorkovsky', stated writer and activist Masha Gessen,

lies a basic difference in character. Putin rarely says what he means and even less frequently trusts that others are saying what they mean. Khodorkovsky, in contrast, seems to have always taken himself and others at face value. He has constructed his identity in accordance with his convictions and his life in accordance with his identity. That is what landed him in prison.

Much feather spitting ensued from Edward, who perceived the affair, plausibly enough, as a paradigm of the state of Moscow politics.

In February, when the plane tree was bare, we discussed the speech recently made in the Bundestag by Daniil Granin, an author then in his nineties (he died in 2017), to mark Holocaust Memorial Day. Edward had directed me to a YouTube video of this speech. It was hard to make out. Angela Merkel and other grandees sat solemnly in the front row wearing headphones. Granin fought at the siege of Leningrad. Edward called him an 'old Soviet fool camouflaged as a dissident'. I made the point that a speech about the reality of war might be a good thing, and after all, the Nazi movement was on the rise in Germany. (Edward loved Germany, in a good way.) In response he extrapolated on the siege of Leningrad, asking why the authorities had not shipped supplies over the not-then-frozen Lake Ladoga. It was either, he concluded, because Stalin was an idiot, or because he didn't want to relieve Leningrad. His point was not that the latter was true, but that it was impossible to address the situation to find out: an independent television channel had recently made a documentary on the subject, and Putin promptly shut the channel down. In the YouTube clip, Granin droned on about horrible Germans, but what, Edward fulminated, was Stalin's role? He had already sent ill-equipped Russian soldiers to their deaths in the Winter War in Finland.

Stalin had deployed the Red Army over the whole frontier, a 900-kilometre line from the Baltic to the Arctic Ocean. The campaign was a disaster for the freshly purged Soviet army. The newly installed high command was incompetent, junior officers revealed a fatal lack of spirit, and Russia, the country with the longest Arctic coast in the world, dispatched men to wage winter war in their usual brown uniforms and without skis or adequate tents. Soldiers regularly froze to death in the frosted silence of the forest. The highly adapted Finns, on the other hand, wore white ski apparel and lived in specialised bell tents which they pitched round a portable wood stove, using the flue as the central pole. Their flying columns that worked through the maze of lakes and waterways were so effective that Russians called them *belaya smert*, the white death. Finnish troops even enjoyed shallow sauna dugouts near the front. In the negotiated peace that ended the Winter War the Russo-Finnish border moved west as Stalin had wanted, but the debacle was a pyrrhic victory after 250,000 Red Army men perished.

Occasionally, Edward revealed himself, despite his protestations, to be a true Russian, and that was when I liked him best. I found it satisfying, on the grounds that there is no escaping birth and destiny. When Crimea exploded, Edward, beginning by making it clear that he was not a patriot and hated most aspects of Russian life, concluded, with some vehemence, 'Crimea is Russian. That fool Khrushchev gave it away.'

IV

I Am Yours in Heart

Turgenev met Mikhail Lermontov, four years his senior, at a Petersburg party. Wearing the uniform of a Hussar regiment of the Imperial Guards, Lermontov did not take off his gloves or discard his sabre the whole evening. 'Hunching his shoulders and frowning,' wrote Turgenev, 'he glanced morosely at Countess MP [a noted beauty] from time to time ... Lermontov's appearance: a certain gloomy and unkind force, pensive disdain and passion emanated from his swarthy countenance, from his large and steady eyes. Their heavy gaze strangely disagreed with the expression of his almost childishly tender and protruding lips. His whole figure, squat, bow-legged, with a large head and wide stooping shoulders, roused an unpleasant feeling. But all who met him were immediately conscious of his inherent strength.'

Turgenev noted that this man was like the fictional Pechorin, the protagonist of Lermontov's 1840 novel *A Hero of Our Time* (*Geroi nashego vremeni*): 'When he laughed, his eyes were not laughing.' Lermontov wore a droopy cavalry moustache, and suffered chronic arthritis. One of his legs was shorter than the other.

He dropped out of Moscow University and enrolled in the military. Fame came quickly, when it came – many saw him straightaway as Pushkin's heir. He had never met the master, but revered him, as they all did. Within months of Pushkin's death, Lermontov, then a junior cavalry officer, wrote the elegy 'The Death of a Poet' ('*Smert poeta*'), in which he excoriated everyone responsible for Pushkin's end. (I like

Sasha Dugdale's recent translation: 'Haven't you heard of God's court, you scum? | He's waiting up there, scale and sword.') Lermontov's poem rocketed him to fame, and into exile.

The tsar sent him to the Caucasus, where Circassians with flashing daggers fought Chechens in camelhair jackets and danced with Dagestani girls whose arms jangled with silver bracelets. Actually, Lermontov was exiled twice. The second time he joined the Tenginsky Regiment on the wooded coast of the Black Sea. Orders came from Petersburg folded in the leather panniers of couriers, and gun-running English merchants supported four Tenginsky battalions fighting the tribal chiefs who attacked the 'forts' – in reality disorderly piles of mud built with earth and brushwood. Muslim warriors inserted horse-hair under the skin of prisoners' feet, so the soles swelled, thereby preventing escape. Circassians carried javelins as they galloped. Kazakhs sowed and ploughed while armed. Malaria and typhus lurked in the shadows.

Lermontov never washed during this period, and he let his hair grow long. He fought bravely in the forests of Chechnya (which is part of the Caucasus), riding a white horse; his unit, wrote a fellow officer, 'was like an errant comet, ever seeking the most dangerous places'. He showed selflessness beyond praise, said Prince Golitsyn, a cavalry commander. He was writing poetry all this time.

> *Far off, with wild and jagged peaks,*
> *But ever proud and still, on high*
> *The mountains in their snowy clothes*
> *Stretched, and above in loftiest sky*
> *Kazbek's sharp-pointed turret rose.*
> *With secret, bitter sadness then*
> *I thought: 'O miserable men!'*

Rereading it now, I don't think it's much good. He was a prose writer. That said, Russians know him best for his lyrical and narrative verse.

Lermontov was passionately involved with the Caucasus, or at least with a romanticised version of it, as writers have been from Pushkin to Tolstoy (both of whom fought there alongside Cossacks against the Muslim tribes) and beyond. It was his spiritual home: 'I am yours in heart, | Forever and always.' *A Hero of Our Time* conjures the region's aromatic air.

Lermontov painted watercolours of the mountains, and in one self-portrait he stares out wearing a Caucasian cloak and Circassian sword, with tribal cartridge cases pinned onto his tunic. The fictional Pechorin of *Hero* fell in love with the Caucasus too, as well as with the Circassian Bela.

He had a family connection with the region which fostered his love for it. A rich and sad grandmother, who brought up little Mikhail – his mother died when he was four and his father was a wastrel – had a sister with a summer house in Pyatigorsk, a spa town in the Caucasian foothills. When Grandma and Mikhail made the 2,000-kilometre journey from Petersburg they took a French tutor, a German governess, a doctor (also French) and a squadron of cooks, servants and grooms. Beyond the steppes of the Kuban the landscape began to change – the song of the cicada replaced the northern cuckoo; fraxinella, bellflower and wormwood flourished; and pelicans flew overhead from the Sea of Azov.* The Lermontovs had to cross the fabled Line, sometimes called the Cordon. It was the frontier between Russians and tribesmen, mostly following the river Terek. Sheepskin-clad horsemen manned the Line brandishing red lances, Cossack lookouts scrambled up ladders along the river, and brigands crossed the Terek on *bourdouchs*, inflated animal skins, to steal women. The Russian army fought to subdue the Islamic mountain peoples for two generations. Cossacks were Russian, but of particular descent – the word comes from the Turkic *quzzaq*, meaning horseman.

Many of the Decembrists who had not been exiled, or who had returned from exile, were serving in the Caucasus when Lermontov was there, and some, in their writings, popularised the region – there was even a school of Romantic Caucasus writers (Alexander Bestuzhev wrote, 'Wildly beautiful is the resounding Terek in the mountains of Darial', and so forth). It was a potent region, in all senses. Its glorious savagery provided an ideal canvas for a man compelled to write about freedom. In literary terms, it belongs to Lermontov.

*

One summer, to find Lermontov, I took my sons, Wilf, almost sixteen, and eleven-year-old Reg, to the Caucasus. Their father, Peter, joined us a few days after the off. We flew from Gatwick to Kiev, then on to Sochi, the hub of the Black Sea Riviera, its infrastructure transformed by the upcoming Winter Olympics and Paralympics. We stayed

---

* In the wheat-growing land between the Don and the Caucasus, during Stalin's engineered famine government troops burned Cossacks alive in locked buildings.

first in the resort of Adler at the mouth of the river Mzymta a short way south of Sochi. My old friend Mark Collins joined us from Cape Cod; we all thought of him as family, and he had travelled with us through China the previous year.

The Adler sea front was like Coney Island, without the charm. The beach constituted a spectator sport: a monkey in a nappy posed for photos, and two men of colour dressed up as African 'natives' also posed for photos. Loudhailers hailed, loudly. We stayed at the moderately horrible Hotel Palma close to the beach. The open-sided canteen, where we ate *kasha* at self-service breakfast, had a tiled faux-Byzantine floor, and sparrows swooped onto the tables. My luggage did not arrive for two days.

The children jetskied every day, and Reg careered down a monster inflatable slide. Early in the morning impossibly small cars parked up in leafy back lanes selling watermelons and grape juice under magnolia canopies, and holidaymakers strolled on boardwalks or set up camp in wooden beach huts on the edge of Naberezhnaya Parade – think of that Chekhov short story from the previous chapter, 'The Lady with the Little Dog', except now girls wear bikinis rather than berets. A legless man sat on a folding chair drinking beer and reading on an electronic device. Perhaps Sochi presents an image of modern Russia – a stark division between rich and poor – but Adler is the real thing: tatty lino, strings of dried fish, people battling on. At night, the city faded upwards into weak violet heights. But overall Adler was revolting, Sochi disgusting, and the hotel horrid.

Cocooned on the front, one might not realise that Adler was equally if not more affected by the Olympics than Sochi itself. The smaller resort sparkled with new bridges, a light railway system and a gleaming regional airport owned by London-based aluminium tsar Oleg Deripaska, a corporate raider who also owned Sochi airport and had a major stake in the Olympics. Pedestrians navigated seas of mud and floodlights glared all night, as workers were on the job twenty-four hours a day. The disruption and waste revealed an ugly irony.

The Soviet Union did not participate in the Olympics until 1952, on the grounds that the event reeked of competitive bourgeois individualism.

Most sporting events were to take place in the Imeretinskaya valley, much closer to Adler than Sochi, in a 'coastal cluster' that included the Central Stadium, the Bolshoi Ice Palace Figure Skating Rink, and much else. The Olympic Park, like Petersburg, rose up on swampy land.

An apocalyptic night thunderstorm threatened to split our hotel in two, and lightning flashed red on the mountains, illuminating oxides leaking from iron-bearing rocks (the famous blood snows of the Caucasus). This climate had already contributed to the exorbitant cost of a Winter Olympics remorselessly touted before and after as the most expensive Games ever. Summer temperatures regularly hit the high twenties in subtropical Sochi and winters are mild, obliging organisers to orchestrate the biggest snow-storing operation the world has ever seen. Specially designed reflective thermal blankets covered thousands of tonnes of snow pyramids. The road and rail link ferrying tourists from the airport to the slopes alone cost $43 billion. One Moscow radio host commented that it would have been cheaper to construct the road with gold. Putin financed forty-nine new hotels, twenty-two tunnels, fifty-four bridges, a cathedral and a hospital. The kickbacks alone cost billions. But it was worth it. Putin had seen the West expand NATO to the frontiers of the motherland, court Ukraine and bomb the shit out of Serbia and Kosovo. It was time to fight back, and show who was boss.

The G8 convened in Sochi shortly after the Games, when Russia held the rotating chairmanship, followed by a Formula One Grand Prix, and the region hosted the men's football World Cup in 2018. Perhaps the infrastructural investment will keep on giving, though one wonders what local people will ever get out of it – they haven't got much yet.

*

The Russian segment of the Black Sea (500 kilometres, counting the
Sea of Azov) curls north from Adler then up to the marshy delta of
the River Don, the cleaver peaks of the western Caucasus rising behind.
The tallest mountain in Europe presides – the one Russians call
Dedushka (grandfather) Elbrus. The dove from Noah's ark landed on
the pinnacle of Elbrus.

Larger than California, the Sea is only a little smaller than Spain.
Six basin nations own a slice of coast: Bulgaria, Romania, Ukraine,
Russia, Georgia and Turkey. Each has its own aspect, but the Russian
Riviera is sui generis, because the mountainous skirt has such a narrow
coastal hem. Russia's heavy loss of maritime access when the USSR
collapsed drew attention to the role of that stretch of shore in the
national imagination (Novorossiisk on the Black Sea is now among
the nation's largest commercial ports). People cherish their slender
strip of sunshine. I have heard Siberians talk fondly of the Black Sea
while crunching across permafrost.

Putin had showcased his country for the Games, smoothing
appalling roads and hoping to clear them of the hellish *probki* (traffic
jams) that clog the coast. Private money dutifully followed: Louis
Vuitton has five stores in Russia, and one of them is in Sochi. Still,
vestiges of tsardom persist on certain wide avenues and in a spec-
tacular late nineteenth-century arboretum. Elsewhere in the region,
enterprising Russkies are busy challenging the Old World at its own
game: a subtropical climate has enabled Château Le Grand Vostock,
a winery on the hills close to the coast, to produce wines that they at
least call premium.

With few planning laws, much of Sochi (population about a third
of a million) is a horror story. On the other hand, the communist
regime ensured that generally developers didn't get their hands on
waterfront land, and, miraculously, the current regime has flogged off
little of it. Given the narrow, crowded littoral – Sochi is the longest
city in Europe – the best way to enjoy the Riviera is from far out.
Partly to amuse the boys, we went sailing for two days in the

eight-metre *Shambala* owned by brothers Yegor and Ivan, competitive sailors and Olympic-standard snowboarders, all plaited ponytails and walnut-brown ropey legs. They were, of course, of the Russian elite. Out on the blue the water was warm, clear and a curious blend of saline and fresh. In late afternoon, the light was bright. When a pair of dolphins fluked around the boat, my boys swam alongside them.

We stayed the night not on board but at the Sochi Yacht Club, a major shithole in what locals call the arse end of town. Soviet service prevailed: 100 rooms and all washing machines broken, regular power cuts, sheets that did not fit the beds, unconcealed electric wires, jobsworth staff, wardrobes that fell apart when you shut the door. There was no wifi unless you crouched in a corner on the second floor, and then it was tortoise slow. The boys were not allowed to swim in the adjacent hotel or play football in the adjacent stadium. A kind of bad taste amounted to squalor. In and around the club, people were ill favoured, badly dressed and overweight.

Looking south from the water, it was hard to reconcile the stillness of the scene with the nationalist upheaval indigenous to the region. That eternal landscape has sustained a constantly shifting human population: Black Sea people have been in movement for at least 5,000 years. (You wouldn't think this, though, after reading Soviet archaeological texts. In these books and articles both Russia and Russians appeared ready made since life began on the steppe, with nobody else ever having a look-in.) It could be romantic, if the current regime weren't increasingly authoritarian here as elsewhere. The economic squeeze Russia has applied to Georgia and the rest of the Caucasus reflects intense competition for regional influence. Russia panicked when the US tried to gain control of oil and gas in and around the Caspian. Though I've come to the conclusion that Russia foams with aggressive paranoia towards the whole of the outside world. And anyway this war too was never won, as present-day Chechnya reveals.

In town, the place to be seen was BSBC (Black Sea Beach Club), an ultra-chic bar and restaurant in the Grand Hotel Rodina, a well of tranquillity with gardens rolling to the water, the whole festooned with pillars and golf buggies. I was writing a piece for *Vanity Fair* to pay for the trip, and BSBC was right up that magazine's street. Deripaska owns it. A charming pair of young PR women entertained me. When the sun set, well-heeled locals drank with visiting oligarchs who had moored yachts at a private pier. We listened to the tinkle of a grand piano. Indoor and outdoor pools, an immense spa, a cinema, private parties – what more could one want? At the Black Magnolia restaurant, a partnership with chef Anton Mosimann, we ate prawn and scallop salad served by staff in white gloves. I have eaten a lot of bad meals in Russia, but at its best, the cuisine is fine indeed, and at the Beach Club I had the tastiest *okroshka* of my long life (it's a cold soup made of uncooked vegetables, eggs, meat and kvass, served with horseradish and sour cream).

The Olympic committee, naturally, had booked out the whole hotel. Nothing is too good for them. 'Otherwise', said one of my companions, 'ninety per cent of our clientele is Russian, and of the rest, most are Kazakhs and Ukrainians. People feel private and protected here.' It was quiet as a mausoleum. You can get an average room for 1,000 euros a night.

*

A branch of the broad-gauge North Caucasus Railway runs along the coast from Sochi, the monumental Stalinist station a work of art in itself, and we watched the Riviera unfurl from a slow-moving carriage with a restorative samovar at the end (plugged into the mains now, but still). An hour out of Sochi the land remained undeveloped. Russian Black Sea beaches are shingle – there is no sand – but at least north of Sochi they are empty. As the train doesn't go through the mountains, to reach Caucasian spa territory, where Lermontov lived and died, the line travels two sides of a triangle. A twelve-hour journey from Sochi conveyed us inland to Pyatigorsk. A second-class sleeper carriage has nine compartments, each called a *kupe* and each with four berths, two upper (*nad*) and two lower (*pod*). Wherever you board, you find on your bunk a polythene-wrapped package containing linen, towels, a toothbrush and a pair of slippers. The smartly uniformed *provodnitsa* plays a vital role in the megalithic monopoly that is Russian Railways and rules over her fiefdom like a benign dictator with a weird hairdo. After an hour ours yelled that 'facilities' were temporarily closing, and set about her regular cleaning task. She unhooked the net curtain rail from a window in the corridor and used it to plunge the lavatory — though she did slip the net off first. Later she ferried in a meal of chicken and pasta served on polystyrene trays, with a pat of coleslaw and two slices of stale white bread. Mark's chicken portion consisted of a foot.

*

Lermontov describes the spa in *A Hero of Our Time*:

Yesterday I arrived in Pyatigorsk and rented rooms on the outskirts of town, at its highest part, at the foot of Mount Mashuk. When there is a storm, the clouds will come right down to my roof. Just now, at five o'clock in the morning, when I opened my window my room was filled with the scent of flowers which grew in the modest little front garden. Boughs of flowering cherry look in at me through the window and from time to time the wind scatters their white petals over my writing table. I have a marvellous view in three directions. To the west, five-peaked Beshtu rises up like a shaggy Persian cap and covers the entire northern part of the horizon. In the east, the outlook is more cheerful: down below me is the trim, spotless, colourful little town and the noise from the medicinal springs, the chatter of the polyglot crowd. Farther away the mountains become darker and mistier, rising in a semi-circle ... But it is time for me to get on. I am going to the Elizavyetinski spring: they say that all the spa's society meets there in the morning.

We disgorged from our train early in the morning and walked for thirty minutes to reach the Hotel Bristol. Pyatigorsk was cool and provincial, its wide streets planted with limes and acacias. The name means five mountains, and the town lies on the river Podkumok. It is one of the oldest spa resorts in Russia, and its streets have changed little since the Petersburg elite strolled up and down to take the waters and Cossack braves galloped into town with dead men's heads swinging from their saddles. In those days the air was so sulphurous that officers' buttons turned yellow. Patients were advised to walk between the springs, hence the shady trees on Kirov (formerly Tsar) Avenue. They lay on Persian carpets in front of the Grotto of Diana, a scene depicted in *A Hero of Our Time*.

Pyatigorsk is pre-Revolutionary Russia in aspic. A pair of inward-leaning stone gateposts kept guard at the top of what is now Karl Marx Street; grand fin-de-siècle hotels, empire-style, neo-renaissance, pseudo-gothic – every architectural fashion that came and went, from the neoclassical Narodnyye Baths to the iron and glass Lermontovskaya Gallery in Tsvetnik, the flowerbedded park laid out in 1828. On Sundays Russian families strolled in Tsvetnik, a touch seedy now, perusing honey stalls. A salesman was keen to show that his milk-chocolate-coloured honey was good for maintaining an erection (he acted this out). Trams trundled up and down Kirov past faded restaurants staffed by bow-tied waiters, and on Saturday night the street throbbed with electronic music and bands of bored youth. The Nostalgia restaurant on Kirov was a study in benign decay. The food as always came in dribs and drabs, but then, we had nothing else to do.

*

Outside Proval, the main spring, visitors rubbed the nose of a bronze statue of a ticket seller. It ensured good fortune, and explained why the poor fellow's nose was gold and the rest of him black. His name was Ostap Bender, a fictional trickster whose name has become synonymous with conmen throughout Russia. Bender first appeared in the 1928 satirical novel by Ilf and Petrov (the authors used pen names) called *The Twelve Chairs*. The always sockless hero tries to beat the system, and in doing so he entered the national psyche, not least because, increasingly, entrepreneurialism and con-artistry were synonymous. Successive generations have continually reinterpreted the Bender figure according to the zeitgeist. Ilf and Petrov were writing among the smoking ruins of the Civil War and the subsequent famine, but Bender was a man for all seasons. Film makers have produced three Russian versions of *The Twelve Chairs*, Mel Brooks made an American one, and another appeared in Cuba. It was significant that there was no sign at the statue – Bender is too familiar to require explanation. Many of his catchphrases have entered the vernacular, for example, the ironical 'The West will help us. Don't give up'.

The spring water inside the cave was pale blue and bubbling far below, but a scum on the surface made it look solid. Afterwards we sat with our feet in another spring next to one of the ubiquitous Soviet-era sanatoria where workers, if they were lucky, took holidays (most of these institutions were linked to trades, so metalworkers went to their own special sanatorium, and so on). People still take the waters at a modern public drinking gallery in town. The beverage was free, but a plastic cup cost two roubles. If you didn't sniff it first it wasn't too bad. People stood at rows of basins filling babies' bottles. Next door, the Spa Research Institute occupied the site of the Restoratsiya, the town's first hotel, where Pechorin waltzed at a ball with the velvet-eyed Princess Mary.

Next day we hired bikes and cycled round the forested foot of Mount Mashuk, the only place in the world I've seen blue spruce look blue. There was nobody there. I had been reading Vasily Grossman's

Life and Fate, and although he was describing the north, his description of the Russian woods rang true:

> From the forest and lakes came the breath of an old Russia ... Ancient tracks ran among these lakes and forests; houses and churches had been built from the tall, upright trees; the masts of sailing-boats had been hewn from them. The Grey Wolf had run through these forests ... This vanished past seemed somehow simple-minded, youthful, naïve ... [the river], quick and slim, flowing between steep, many-coloured banks, through the green of the forest, through patterns of light blue and red – was a symbol of this vanished past.

Grossman was born in 1905 in that part of the Pale of Settlement which is now in Ukraine. He worked as a correspondent for the Red Army newspaper during the Great Patriotic War, spending three years on front lines. He finished *Life and Fate* in 1960, whereupon the KGB confiscated it (they even took the typewriter ribbons) and announced that it could be published – perhaps – in 200 years. *Mirabile dictu*, dissidents microfilmed a copy of the typescript and smuggled it to the West. It was published posthumously: Grossman died in 1964.

The author's prose reinforced my opinion, forged both through direct experience and through reading, that for most people, being Russian has always been miserable – before, during and after communism. Grossman brings out this national fate, as his multitudinous cast of characters lie speared like butterflies between ghastly rulers and filthy fascist invaders.

At close to 900 pages, *Life and Fate* is a long read, and the prose is both dense and intricate at the same time, which makes it impossible to dispatch quickly. To talk of pleasure from pages on German camps, or the horrors of the Battle of Stalingrad, seems perverse. But that is what literature is for – to illuminate both beauty and horror. The ultimate success of *Life and Fate* – now almost universally proclaimed a triumph – proves V. S. Naipaul's dictum that a good book always makes its way in the end.

In the summer of 1841, Lermontov spent his last months in Pyatigorsk in the rooms mentioned earlier, on a small estate belonging to a company commander. The complex takes up a whole block now and is no longer on the outskirts of town. The writer kept two race-horses and four servants, took the waters, and danced in his grey uniform ('Gambling, wine and fighting make us feverish,' he wrote). I went alone to visit. The garden was vaporous, fountains gurgled listlessly and clouds raked the Caucasian mountain tops. The modest estate consisted of three small houses and some outbuildings. Lermontov occupied a thatched, one-storey guest cottage, now open to the public. As he sat at his desk he could reach out of the window and pick cherries.

In *A Hero of Our Time* Pechorin says, 'I have a congenital desire to contradict; my whole life is merely a chain of sad and unsuccessful contradictions to heart and mind.' This was surely Lermontov (not that it matters whether it was or wasn't). One day he picked a fight with an acquaintance over a trivial matter and goaded the fellow to challenge him to a duel.

At the Upper Market, Peter, Mark and I took a *marshrutka* (a deregulated and knackered minibus that travels along a fixed route – *marshrut* – dropping off and picking up passengers at any point along the way) to find the spot on the west flank of the mountain where Lermontov expired. A white obelisk erected among the pines in 1915 marked it. Lermontov had arrived for the duel wearing a raspberry taffeta shirt. (In *A Hero of Our Time*, freakily, Pechorin perishes in a duel.) A row of fresh bouquets around the obelisk bore witness to the sacerdotal role of the writer in Russia. But even with the faint rattle of *marshrutki* in the distance, it seemed a lonely place to die. He was twenty-seven.

I Am Yours in Heart

Did Lermontov, approaching that site, feel the tenderness that dying people often report when they know life is closing in? Pechorin describes walking to his own duel: 'I remember, at this point, I felt a love for nature greater than at any time before. How interesting to watch a single dewdrop, quivering on a wide vine-leaf and reflecting millions of rainbow rays!' In real life, Lermontov's friend Glebov remembered spending hours alone in the forest with the corpse after the bullet hit, sitting on the grass in the rain. An acquaintance of Glebov's wrote down the man's account.

> The head of the dead poet was resting on his knees – it was dark, the tethered horses neighed, reared, pawed the ground with their hooves, the thunder and lightning was incessant, it was frightening beyond words. Glebov wanted to lower the head carefully onto his greatcoat, but this movement caused Lermontov to yawn convulsively.

*

A ride on the cable car to the top of Mashuk revealed the volcanic nature of the steppe: extinct cones of lava and ash shot out of the fertile plains. Though apparently Mashuk was active in the nineteenth century: in *A Hero of Our Time* the top 'smoked like an extinguished torch'. You could see Granddaddy Elbrus. Amusing ourselves with *pirozhki* (turnovers) and our books at an outdoor cafe at the top of the mountain, we witnessed a wedding. Under an arch wreathed in white lace, a bride in full meringue sang a rap love song to her groom, a fidgety giant wearing a shiny suit and no tie. A woman gave a running commentary through a faulty mike, and they inflated a red heart with a lantern in it and set it free, whereupon it dropped two metres to the ground and frazzled out.

*

With the snap of the censor at his heels, Lermontov venerated Byron's verses in praise of freedom.* He often cited the older poet in his work ('It is Byron I wish to emulate') and his borrowings have provided academic fodder for decades. But Lermontov is a better writer than Byron. Like so many Russians he drew on folk tales, a deeply embedded genre (more deeply than in Europe, and even more than in the US). He used the speech of the ordinary man, sometimes, and viewed the world from that man's angle, for example in the poem 'Borodino', written to commemorate the twenty-fifth anniversary of victory over Napoleon. The narrator is a peasant soldier.

> *For three whole days without a change*
> *We only shot at distant range;*
> *No use at all!*
> *You heard men saying left and right,*
> *It's time to buckle up and fight.*

*

The same stewardess appeared outside our carriage on train 644 from Pyatigorsk back to the coast, and, standing on the platform and spotting us, she flung her arms wide and greeted us like family. It was a cloudy day, the ridged arable land quilted with solid greens and yellows and spiked with baled hay. Trees sprouted through the roof of an abandoned cement factory and sprawling farms lay in ruins. The villages were poor; you could see the decay on the faces. The Black Sea Riviera exemplifies the baleful collision between two Russias. We ate the same dire food as on the inbound journey – well, not the same (it was rice and fish), but it achieved the same overall effect. The five of us grew incensed when we saw our *provodnitsa* carrying a whole steaming chicken on a tray. To whom was she taking it, and why couldn't we have one?

* Russia has a Byron cult, on the basis (presumably) that he is the nearest equivalent to Pushkin. In fact, Lermontov in many ways is more Byronic.

When the train reached the coast, a sickle moon rose, and the sea turned black indeed.

My only bad experience on Russian railways occurred on this journey. Four of us were in one *kupe*, and Mark was sleeping on one of the lower bunks in the adjacent carriage. At some nameless station in the night two young women tottered into his compartment with a bottle of vodka, chattered volubly, and started prodding Mark. When he turned over, they began laughing at him and sticking their bottoms in his face. Then he heard the word 'gay'. They were insulting him, as they perceived it, for not responding to their advances. One of them lay down next to him on his bunk.

As it happens Mark is gay – and this was the time when Putin had introduced anti-homosexual legislation that fostered gay baiting. The Games were to become a focal point for this legislation. Artists such as Cher had already turned down a Sochi gig in protest. The Russian Orthodox Church, characteristically, had weighed in with a call for homosexuality to be criminalised. Mark's behaviour had nothing to do with his sexuality. But he felt vulnerable and frightened, and I sensed the dark side of Putin's Russia entering the carriage with the girls that night.*

The Orthodox Church had been synonymous with the state for a thousand years, but the degree to which the contemporary leadership did the government's bidding was obscene. Everyone knew it. I lost track of how many people told me the story of the patriarch's watch. Kirill's office had put out a photograph of him sitting at his desk in full ecclesiastical fig. Eagle-eyed readers soon spotted a Breguet watch on his wrist, a timepiece worth $30,000. Once the comments appeared, Kirill's people withdrew the picture. The image duly reappeared without the watch – but the reflection of its face remained on the patriarch's desk. Bloggers responded with vim – one produced the original photo

* Gay rights groups did what they could to protest. A brilliant video circulated in which famous non-Russians learned to say '*Gde ya mogu kupit raduzhny flag?*' Which means, 'Where can I buy a rainbow flag?' It included clips of all the usual suspects, including Stephen Fry, Peter Tatchell and Rupert Everett.

depicting the Breguet alone, the patriarch himself having been 'vanished'. Patriarch Kirill enjoys presidential status, which means a cavalcade escorts him to public appearances. On his name day, the great and the good pay homage. One year, at the celebration, the Japanese ambassador presented Kirill with a full-length mink coat. Meanwhile 55,000 children sleep rough in Moscow on any one night. Many have trench foot, a condition not seen since the First World War.

Moral authority? I don't think so.

*

Pechorin is a 'superfluous man', that creature indigenous to nineteenth-century Russian literature. Lermontov was writing in the 1830s, a period in which Nicholas I suppressed literature with gusto. Who among writers might not be disillusioned? That said, Pechorin is not merely a 'type'. Nabokov made a distinction between him and Onegin:

> Pushkin's Onegin stretches himself throughout the book and yawns. Lermontov's Pechorin does nothing of the sort – he laughs and bites. With his immense store of tenderness, kindness and heroism behind his cynical and arrogant appearance, he is a deeper personality than the cold lean fop delightfully depicted by Pushkin.

Pechorin was beset with disillusion:

> I run through the memory of my past in its entirety and can't help asking myself: why have I lived? For what purpose was I born? … There probably was one once, and I probably did have a lofty calling, because I felt a boundless strength in my soul … But I didn't divine this calling. I was carried away with the bait of passions, empty and unrewarding. I came out of their crucible as hard and cold as iron.

*

Snowcock wheeled across the dawning sky, southbound to Abkhazia. From the peaks, saffron light slipped down the Achishkho Ridge, at length reaching the bowl in which we had pitched our tiny camp. The western Caucasus is 1,600 kilometres from Moscow and its oligarchs (or, as my youngest son referred to them throughout our holiday, 'ogilarchs'), but at that moment, looking out over the Russian wilderness, one might have been on another planet.

When I made enquiries about family holidays in the region, nobody knew what I was talking about. But I found a couple of guides via *Lonely Planet* and the internet, and after our coastal and Pyatigorsk experiences, we went wild camping in the mountains. Canadian Peter is indigenous to the great outdoors and a handy asset when wrestling a tent to the ground. As for the younger boys, their perfect holiday is one in which washing is not required.

I had had constructive Skype conversations with the guides, Tatyana (Tanya) and her husband Ivan, prior to departure using my patchy Russian and Tanya's rather better English. The pair agreed to provide all camping equipment including sleeping bags and mats; we had only to bring packs, trekking clothing, including full waterproofs, and boots. The point of departure was to be their hometown, Krasnaya Polyana, an hour from the Black Sea coast.

We travelled there from Adler standing up for an hour in a *marshrutka* with stony-faced construction workers including a pair of Turks. We were to stay the night with our guides before heading to the hills in the morning. I will not say the holiday was easy to organise. Like anything off the beaten track in Russia, it was not for the faint-hearted.

'City of contrasts' is judged the most baleful travel writing cliché, with good reason: what place does not have contrasts? So I believed, until I arrived in Krasnaya Polyana, a town of unremittingly horrible concrete homogeneity. Construction for the Winter Olympics had erased all trace of the vernacular architecture that previously characterised these hills. At any rate, with some difficulty we found Tanya and Ivan's ramshackle house at the end of a gravel dead end.

A monk opened the door and took us through to the garden. The wheat there was as high as an elephant's eye, and alongside it five adults were standing at prayer. This was not the Russia we had been expecting.

The house, it emerged, operated as a hippie Orthodox hostel run commune-style by Tanya and the ponytailed and bearded Ivan. Tanya was effortlessly stylish – she couldn't help herself – all headbands, long skirts and droopy tops. Ivan was fond of barking orders.

Seventeen Russians were in residence in Skithostel, all in flight from the nine-to-five. Most people avoided us except to say good evening. Two further monks arrived from Abkhazia, and a whey-faced youth straight out of a Dostoyevsky novel – he even wore a kind of frock-coat – was cooking up wild mushrooms in the kitchen when we sat down there, and when the fruiting fungi were done, he wordlessly gave us a plate. Possibly uniquely in the whole of Russia, there was no television. Later we went to a shop to buy pasta and other ingredients for supper from a member of the sizeable Greek community who settled in Krasnaya Polyana a couple of centuries ago when the authorities booted the indigenous Circassians off their fertile land. The town was in many ways typical of the symbiosis of the many nationalities, religions and languages embedded in the Caucasus. The pasta turned into paste on contact with water.

Next morning, prior to departure, Tanya set off to the post office with our passports to undertake the business of 'registration', a procedure required of independent travellers to Russia, as I had discovered in Petrozavodsk (though only under certain circumstances, details of which are mired in obfuscation). While she was gone, Ivan got out a chess board and a clock with a timer, proceeding to thrash us all in turn at speed chess.

The road to the trailhead was atrocious, and we were obliged to hire a four-by-four taxi in which we were so tightly packed that Mark could see nothing but the back of his rucksack in his lap. That part of the Krasnodar *krai* (a *krai* is a federal subject region) is a controlled area, a portion of it administered by the National Park Service and the rest by a federal biosphere organisation, a set-up guaranteed to deliver a poor outcome for all. Ivan had secured the complicated permissions required to get us past a remote security barrier. And so we arrived at the trailhead, where the authorities had prepared the way by erecting a sign indicating that high heels should not be worn. With no footwear concerns we headed straight off into alpine meadows threaded with lakes and shimmering with the violet blooms Russians call *kolokolchiki* (little bells). The five of us looked around in exhilaration, after so many uncertain months of preamble. We listened to branches cracking underfoot and smelled the crushed juniper. The 3,000-metre peaks of Tchugush and Pseashkho stood on one side, and on the other rose the greater Caucasian ridge, chopped up by its numerous river valleys.

The ridge ran from the blocky uplift of Fisht to the Aibga glacier in the Roza Khutor plateau. After a couple of hours, approaching Zerkalnoye (Mirror) Lake, on the shores of which we planned to set up our first camp, we passed three young people who invited us for herb tea, dried wild apricots and hazelnuts – one of them cracked the latter with his hand, which impressed Reg. This nutcracker was talkative, lively and peculiarly happy, for a Russian. Tanya later told us he had been sampling the local variety of psilocybin mushrooms. Yet over the course of the week, everyone we met on the trail – maybe two groups of three or four hikers a day – offered us something to eat or drink. Russians can seem unfriendly, and rarely ask any questions (a Greek will have details of your divorce out of you in five minutes). But they are often generous.

We bathed in a waterfall in dappled sunshine. A mist hung low as we picked our spot to settle for the night, each of us bearing an armful of kindling. The boys were dispatched to the lake with containers: one of the joys of camping in this part of the Caucasus is that some of the lakes have drinkable water, so one doesn't have to cart gallons.

The guides made a good job of catering. Of course we had to eat a lot of dried food, but there was also cheese, salami, apricots and biscuits as well as herbs and blueberries picked along the way, and Tanya had packed chocolate to keep us going. The boys sucked pouches of condensed milk. Instant potatoes in a plastic pot were surprisingly good, we all agreed, though perhaps anything is good after five days on the trail. For lunch we ate raw garlic with salt and bread. Like all Russians, Tanya and Ivan were tremendously interested in mushrooms (though not the psilocybin kind, alas) and we ate their pickings fried in butter, straight from a pan set in the fire. Tea brewed from mountain herbs was always on the go when I emerged from my tent, and we drank it accompanied by the sound of Caucasian parsley frogs croaking at the edge of the lake.

Particular air patterns and a wet mass that blows in from the Black Sea and crashes into the 2,000-metre Achishkho Ridge makes the zone we were hiking through the most humid place in European Russia. We were fortunate with the weather: hot days, cold nights, and no rain. But you could see there *had* been a lot of rain. The mushy landscape alternated between meadows and Oriental birch forest interspersed with cherry laurel, ferny underbrush and Caucasian blackberry bushes. Many lakes were covered with sedge grass and moss that formed strange patterns, like amphibious crop circles. Often, on narrower, higher paths, we enjoyed views over hundreds of kilometres of virgin hardwood forest and the shaved ribbon of the Olympic ski run. At night Ivan picked out the constellations, recounting folk tales behind the names.

A fifteen-year-old is hard to amuse when disconnected from Facebook, but by some minor act of God Wilf is interested in wildlife. I had promised creatures, and fortunately (for me), the western Caucasus did not let us down. Wilf spotted a rather beautifully patterned, persimmon-coloured Dinnik's viper (less glamorously the common newt, and obligingly asleep), plenty of griffon vultures and a West Caucasian tur, resembling a cross between a goat and an antelope. And we saw the rare, snow-coloured, high-altitude butterfly *Parnassius nordmanni*. I was not sorry that we failed to meet a brown bear. Ivan had seen one the previous month, though he did not carry a gun. It would have been against his principles.

We warmed to Tanya and Ivan, despite the fact that the latter told us off for not rolling up the sleeping bags correctly. I noted that they crossed themselves each morning as we set out. When a pair of fellow trekkers joined us round the fire one night, they loosened up. 'We reject politics and politicians; this is a corrupt country, and we opt out,' Ivan said. As the days unfurled we realised that everyone in the hills belonged to an alternative community, one that refused to participate in the horrors of Putin's administration, identifying instead with the unchanging wilderness of Mother Russia. This explained the spirit of Tanya and Ivan's unconventional home. It was an ironic development, given the region's historical reputation as a crucible for independence movements and nationalism. (And it goes on. We could see the mountains of the breakaway Georgian republic of Abkhazia from the top of our ridge.) Earlier that day we had a bird's eye view of the famous new ski run. 'Nobody here wanted the Olympics,' Tanya said. 'All that environmental desecration, and for what? To show how modern Putin's Russia is?' Everyone in the Caucasus complained about labour conditions imposed on the (mostly central Asian) migrant construction workers, pointing out that nothing had changed since 2010, when riots among them filmed on phones went viral. 'Did you see all the new hotels in Krasnaya?' fumed Tanya. Indeed I had seen many, with glaziers' stickers still on the windows.

The second night we camped at a shelter with a corrugated iron roof. Sunrise was a magical time, a drawn-out transition from cold to hot. First rays illuminated the tips of the mountains, then gold poured down Achishkho Ridge.

The peaks of the western Caucasus are snowbound for seven months a year; the stuff weighs branches down, releasing them sharply during the spring melt – you walk at that time at your peril, as a bouncing branch can kill. We were there during the short, crazily verdant summer. Like polar ice, summer rolls in and out over the mountains in a tide. On our last afternoon we camped near a waterfall and bathed in its sunny pools before celebrating my firstborn's sixteenth birthday with a jar of herring. A three-hour evening hike took us to a saddleback, past hundreds of tonnes of grey moraine slashing the hillsides, debris left behind after glaciers moved through thousands of years ago. A delicate green lichen covered the boulders, highlighted that evening by the westering sun. From the top, we looked down at our camp, where smoke rose vertically from the fire. The air was transparent; even the saucepans were distinct. Much further below we saw Krasnaya Polyana, where lines of tiny trucks were churning dust for Olympic venues. A new infrastructure for the Caucasus indeed. But the hotels and roads will vanish in time, just as Putin will be a footnote to history. The Caucasus will still be there; still the same.

*

Back at Skithostel, in transit to Sochi, we watched as residents eddied in and out. This time we were sleeping in an eight-bed dorm. Construction workers occupied the other beds; one, with a teddy on his pillow, was plugged into his computer all evening, wearing headphones.

We had hired one of our sailors, Yegor, to pick us up from Krasnaya Polyana and convey us back to the unlovely Palma in Adler, where we were to ready ourselves for international departure. He was 105 minutes late, so we got up at six o'clock for nothing. The gravel street at that hour was still, the whole scene washed.

Yegor brought his girlfriend Margarette, even though there was not enough space in the jeep for a party of seven. It poured with rain the whole way, and the traffic jams were murderous. Yegor and Margarette talked with disgust about the spiralling cost of the Olympics. 'The government controls the weather', said Margarette, 'by spraying the air to keep it dry for construction.'

'But it's raining,' I said as we sat like sardines in the back of the jeep.

'That is the result of spraying,' she said. So an effort to keep the land dry made it wet. Maybe I had misunderstood. I was losing the will to live. Yegor worried about the environmental effects of weather control.

'And locals can't get tickets to the Olympics.'

They complained, but one sensed an air of resignation. What, after all, would be the point of protesting?

*

Back at home in London, media attention on the Games reached a climax. One heard relentlessly, all over again, that these Olympics were the most expensive ever. This, of course, was partly because the Games were being held in the wrong place. John Sweeney's *Panorama* programme, 'The Truth about Putin's Games', aired ten days before the opening ceremony. Sweeney interviewed construction workers who had been cheated and abused. Human-rights campaigners spoke about non-payment of wages – one labourer got paid only after sewing his lips together in front of a television camera. The whole extravaganza, said Sweeney, was a 'pet project of Putin's'. The president likes Sochi – he holidays there. Many of the major contractors in the Caucasus at that time had known him since childhood. He wanted 'his' Games to 'project Russia's image'. And it did: a Dagestani leader called the Sochi Olympics 'Satanic dances on the bones of our ances-tors'. *Panorama* showed footage of Sweeney in altercations with police who stopped him from driving to sports sites. Villagers talked to camera of having no pavements or working wells because of construc-tion and landslips – I'd seen this for myself in Krasnaya Polyana. Houses literally rocked on their foundations. An environmentalist said the damage would be felt for years to come. In addition, Sochi was the most corrupt Games in history, according to Sweeney, with fifty per cent of the budget 'trousered'. Vladimir Morozov, a former contractor now living in Surrey, testified in court to the scale of corruption. He said the authorities threatened that he would be 'drowned in blood' if he spoke out. 'The Sochi ski jump', announced the portentous Sweeney, 'is possibly the most mismanaged project in the world.' Now, this would be a hotly contested field. But I believed the claim. Fingers in the pie, irons in the fire, snouts in the trough – every metaphor ever invented applied to Sochi. The ski jump and surrounding infrastructure was owned by a company called Krasnaya Polyana, the main investor in which was a business tycoon called Akhmed Bilalov. When costs spiralled Putin sacked him live on prime-time television. Bilalov fled the country and later claimed his enemies had tried to poison him.

Elsewhere, the flow of corruptly acquired money continued to reach London, as it had done for some years. The investment firm Heritage Capital has estimated that between 1998 and 2004, £54 billion in capital left Russia. Much of it was spent in London and Surrey in a frenzy of real-estate purchasing. (Deripaska, mentioned above, had a portfolio including an eleven-bedroom Grade I-listed Regency pied-à-terre in London's Belgrave Square, and, through a company registered in Cyprus, a titanic mansion in St George's Hill, a private estate in Surrey.) There were investments elsewhere of course, notably France, but Britain was the oligarchs' favoured choice. Why? According to Olga Fedina, who wrote an entertaining book called *What Every Russian Knows (and You Don't)*,

Britain is so fascinating for Russians because it represents, more than other cultures, what is most absent in Russia: calm self-respect and conservatism coupled with independence of spirit and self-assurance. More importantly still, it has habeas corpus, the rights of an individual versus the authorities, an unshakable respect for property and private life and the sanctity of the law.

Russia's own Economic Development and Trade Ministry says that between $210 billion and $239 billion drained out of Russia during post-collapse 'reforms', about half of which was dirty money linked to laundering or organised crime. The statistics go on. The IMF estimates that $170 billion left in the seven years before 2001. Think what that could have done for the crumbling infrastructure. Mobutu himself couldn't have done a better job. There were voices at home speaking the truth, even at the time. A satirist called Viktor Shenderovich, writing on the site of an independent radio station, compared the Sochi Games to those held in Berlin in 1936. It was brave, as Shenderovich must have known what was coming. Within days, the authorities posted a video of him masturbating.

V

We All Come out from under Gogol's Overcoat

Lermontov spent a month in Moscow in the spring of 1840, on his way to Stavropol. He met Gogol, five years his senior, at a dinner in a friend's garden to celebrate Gogol's name day, and recited a new poem, 'The Novice' (*'Mtsyri'*), the story of a Georgian boy in flight from kidnap and imprisonment. The censor had now banned the word 'freedom', so Lermontov smuggled in his theme through an imaginary escape.

> *Far off I saw, through vapoury strands,*
> *Where, glittering diamond of the snows,*
> *Grey, bastion Caucasus arose;*
> *And then, for some strange reason I*
> *Felt light of heart.*

Biographers say Lermontov recited the whole poem, but can he really have done so? At almost 800 lines they would have been there half the night.

*

Gogol's mother was proud of her son and in old age told neighbours that Nikolai Vasilyevich had invented the railway engine. He grew up in a Cossack Ukrainian village and went to school in Nezhin. Far back the family belonged to the Turkic Gogels – their name comes from the Chuvash word *gögül*, a bird of the steppes. Gogol's mother was Ukrainian, and at home the family spoke both her language and Russian. On leaving high school, Gogol (pronounced 'GAW-guhl') moved to Petersburg and became a civil servant, then a teacher, both for short periods: in 1829 he went abroad, and travelled restlessly for many years. He spent summers wandering from spa to spa. He had a long sharp nose which he could touch with his lower lip. Perhaps that is why he wrote so much about odours. Gogol's early stories smell of black Russian earth and the pungency of sheaves of corn on a blazing afternoon. He had short legs and an awkward gait, and wore his straight hair in a low parting; it flopped around his neck. A tuft of beard complemented a wispy moustache. His face was out of proportion, as if reflected in a teaspoon. In Rome Gogol entered into a relationship with a 23-year-old Russian count, but the man died of TB.

Besides smells, noses feature in Gogolian prose. One of his stories is actually called 'The Nose' ('*Nos*'). In the opening scene a Petersburg barber finds a nose in his breakfast bread. The appendage, which previously belonged to a medium-level civil servant, takes on a life of its own, rising further up the hierarchy than its previous owner. This was a typical theme for Gogol – the absurdity of government apparatus. A minor elevation from one particular level to another required, for example, a change from black to white trousers. Lonely and impoverished functionaries hurrying home in the cold haunt Gogol's Petersburg writings.

In 1831 Gogol met Pushkin. They became friends, and the elder man encouraged Gogol to write on demotic subjects. Pushkin said of Gogol that 'behind his laughter you feel the unseen tears'. Pushkin sketched his friend.

Pushkin's unexpected death shocked and moved Gogol, as it had Lermontov. Gogol understood the freakish poetry of life in a way that Pushkin never did.

According to Nabokov, Gogol's *Government Inspector* (*Revizor*) is 'the greatest play ever written in Russian (and never surpassed since)'. It is 'poetry in action, and by poetry I mean the mysteries of the irrational as perceived through rational words'. It was Pushkin who had suggested the plot. It is a play about corruption, and again a satire on Russian civic bureaucracy. Some critics said it was an insidious attack on officialdom, and the negative coverage bit deep. It may have marked the start of Nikolai Vasilyevich's persecution mania. But the play brought fame and praise in equal measure to the attacks.

*

In the opening pages of *Dead Souls* (*Myortvyye dushi*), in my opinion Gogol's chef d'oeuvre, the protagonist, Chichikov, rolls into a provincial town in a troika accompanied by Selifan the coachman (who had 'his own peculiar smell') and a valet. He is on a journey visiting landowners with dead serfs on their property registers (serfs were known as 'souls'). Chichikov's mission is to buy these deceased assets, persuading landowners that as the government taxed landlords on all serfs held, they would be better off without the dead ones. He himself wanted the names, as with legal ownership he could take out a loan against them and retire to a pleasant estate and a life of indolence. He is a scoundrel and magnificent liar, the Tartuffe of the east.

Pushkin had a hand in this plot too. When Gogol read him the completed manuscript, Pushkin said, 'God, what a sad country Russia is.' Tolstoy listed the book as one of the works that had most influenced him between the ages of fourteen and twenty.

Gogol is a master of detail. Think of the flies patrolling a landowner's kitchen in *Dead Souls* as the housekeeper cuts a sugar loaf into cubes. The insects were there for the purpose

> of showing themselves in public, of parading up and down the sugar loaf, of rubbing both their hindquarters and their fore against one another, of cleaning their bodies under the wings, of extending their forelegs over their heads and grooming themselves, and of flying out of the window again to return with other predatory squadrons.

Or the two-pronged fork at the inn after the carriage overturns: 'The landlady … returned with a plate, a napkin (the latter starched to the consistency of dried bark), a knife with a bone handle beginning to turn yellow, a two-pronged fork as thin as a wafer, and a salt-cellar incapable of being made to stand upright.'

Note the elegiac description of the miser Plyushkin's rank garden:

> The united tops of trees that had grown wide in liberty spread above the skyline in masses of green clouds and irregular domes of tremulous leafage. The colossal white trunk of a birchtree

deprived of its top, which had been broken off by s
or thunderbolt, rose out of these dense green masses
disclosed its rotund smoothness in midair, like a well-propoi
tioned column of sparkling marble ... Strands of hop, after
strangling the bushes of elder, mountain ash and hazel below,
had meandered all over the ridge of the fence whence they ran
up at last to twist around that truncated birch tree halfway up
its length ...

*

Educated Russians parrot Gogol. Grotesquely, at the 1988 Moscow
summit between Reagan and Gorbachev, the US president co-opted
the writer. 'I am reminded', he lied in a speech at Moscow University,
'of the famous passage near the end of Gogol's *Dead Souls*.
Comparing his nation to a speeding troika, Gogol asks what will
be his destination. But he writes, "There was no answer save the
bell pouring forth marvelous sound."' A White House official later
told the *Los Angeles Times* that 'the president was not overly familiar
with the works he quoted'. The spokesman said that Reagan's speech-
writers had clocked up a fortune in overtime poring over Russian
books.

Gogol excavated vocabulary from folk tales and was a collector of
new and arcane words: he was an anti-intellectual, in a way. The
educated classes still regarded Russian as inferior to French. At the
top girls' school in Moscow, a pupil heard talking Russian had to wear
a red bell and stand in the corner all day. Gogol was a great popu-
lariser of the Russian language – and a pioneer when it came to the
deployment of street terms. As a result, some regarded his prose with
contempt. One princess told her daughter that his books were for
coachmen. But just as Pushkin set Russian poetry free, in the long
run Gogol did the same for prose. He created Russian realism. He

was poetic and lyrical – the original subtitle of *Dead Souls* was 'A Poem'.*

In 'The Overcoat' ('*Shinel*', sometimes translated as 'The Cloak'), Akaky Akakiyevich, a poor government clerk, commissions a one-eyed tailor to make him a coat, the cost of which involves much privation. The garment is the pride of Akaky's life, and on the first night he wears it, bearded assailants steal it. The story reminds one of Maupassant's 'The Necklace', as one knows disaster is looming from the first page. Akaky Akakiyevich expires of grief, and his ghost haunts Petersburg. This is Gogol's account of the theft:

Soon there spread before him those deserted streets, which are not cheerful in the daytime, to say nothing of the evening. Now they were even more dim and lonely: the lanterns began to grow rarer, oil, evidently, had been less liberally supplied. Then came wooden houses and fences: not a soul anywhere; only the snow sparkled in the streets, and mournfully veiled the low-roofed cabins with their closed shutters ... Afar, a tiny spark glimmered from some watchman's box, which seemed to stand on the edge of the world. Akaky Akakiyevich's cheerfulness diminished at this point in a marked degree ... He glanced back and on both sides, it was like a sea about him ... He suddenly beheld, standing just before his very nose, some bearded individuals of precisely what sort he could not make out. All grew dark before his eyes, and his heart throbbed. 'But, of course, the cloak is mine!' said one of them in a loud voice, seizing hold of his collar.

Here's a stamp the Russian post office issued in 2009, depicting a scene from 'The Overcoat'. Nabokov considered that with this story, Gogol 'became the greatest artist that Russia has yet produced'.

---

* *Poema* in Russian means a long narrative poem as opposed to lyric poetry (*stikhi*).

РОССИЯ
RUSSIA·2009
8.00

Н.В. Гоголь
«Шинель» 1842г.

*

Gogol spent the last four years of his life in Moscow, and the state has turned his house into a museum. One September I took a week-long language course at Moscow's Grint Institute, and visited on a free afternoon. Originally a seventeenth-century merchant's mansion, the house was on Nikitsky Boulevard, close to Arbatskaya metro station. A statue of Nikolai Vasilyevich kept guard. The entrance ticket depicted a silhouette of a man with a huge nose. The house, originally in the countryside, was primrose yellow, with stone arcades and bal-conies. Gogol lived there as a guest of Count Alexander Tolstoy – a relative, as well as a friend – and his wife Anna. Turgenev was also in residence for a brief period, and Gogol wrote in praise of the younger writer's work. Gogol had been going properly bonkers for years, as well as becoming obsessed with God. When a friend's wife died and the man was frantic with grief, Gogol wrote to him to say, 'Jesus Christ

will help you to become a gentleman, which you are neither by education nor inclination – she [the dead wife] is speaking through me.' He
was, he thought, an instrument of God. His mind was unfathomable.
He was incontinently human, which is why I love him.

He had begun to write more about religion, and had made a
pilgrimage to the Holy Land. Like many artists he sought guidance at
the Optina Pustyn monastery close to the river Zhizdra south of
Moscow. His quest was bound up with a lifelong search for the Russian
soul. Gogol believed in the spiritual community of the Russian Church
– the only true Church – and in the destiny of Russia to save the
West. Think of the passage referred to by Reagan when Chichikov is
on the road: 'Russia, are you not also like the bold troika which no
one can overtake? The road is a cloud of smoke under your wheels,
the bridges thunder, everything lags behind and is stranded in the rear.'
But at the end Gogol broke off relations with Optina, and felt he had
failed before God.

He was a Slavophile who believed in the corruption of the West.
Paris, he declared, had only a surface glitter that concealed an abyss
of fraud and greed. The reader might wonder why, in that case, Gogol
spent so many years in that sink of iniquity. It reveals an ambivalence:
like many educated Russians in the nineteenth century he was in thrall
to the educative properties of European travel at the same time as
obsessing over the decayed moral values of the West. And of course,
even in exile he could not escape the mental map of his native land.

What a house guest the anorexic and barking genius must have
been. He prepared almost-raw macaroni and cheese with a fervour
bordering on mania. Gogol was working, at the time he lived on
Nikitsky Boulevard, on the second volume of *Dead Souls*, and wrote
standing up in a cornflower-blue study. But he burned the manuscript
in the ground-floor fireplace. Gogol died in the house aged forty-
two, weakened by malaria and malnutrition and so thin that the
doctors could feel his spine by pressing his stomach. They had put
leeches on his nose (his nose!), tied his hands to the bed so he

couldn't tear the leeches off, and plunged him alternately into cold and boiling baths.

In the room where he died, the attendant dimmed the lights, and the death mask glowed. Gogol is in Moscow's Novodevichy cemetery now (they moved the body from a monastery in 1931 – the Soviets liked shifting graves around, controlling death as they did life). His epitaph mangles an Old Testament quotation: 'I shall laugh my bitter laugh'.

The house had a large library on the second floor where people were sitting in front of computers, newspapers lay folded in racks, and heavy wooden drawers held handwritten card catalogues. Three students were playing music from scores propped on silent keyboards, wearing headphones. There was a white sofa. People rushed out to take mobile calls, just like I do in the libraries where I work. It was the only time I felt at home in Moscow.

*

The Grint Institute, where I took my lessons, was situated in Vykhino, a south-eastern district on the Tagansko-Krasnopresnenskaya metro line. I mentioned earlier that my teacher Edward had put his head in his hands when I told him I was going there. A comment on the internet said it was 'the most unpleasant and dysfunctional district of Moscow'. At this news, my spirits rose. But it wasn't that bad. I was billeted as usual in a homestay. Tamara, my host, was a widow who lived in a second-floor, one-bedroom flat in a standard block. I had the sofa in the living room. The institute was a five-minute walk away. Grint was part of the private Moscow Humanities University. In the 1940s, during the Great Patriotic War the international Komsomol High School occupied the buildings, and subsequently the place became a female sniper college. Some of the surrounding streets were named after snipers.

'I have been to Gogol's house,' I told Tamara when I got back from my visit. We were sitting in the kitchen drinking tea and watching a quiz show. A row of soft toys sat atop the humpbacked TV.

'No you haven't. Museums are closed on a Monday.'

'I was lucky that this particular museum is open on a Monday.'

'It must have been Gorky's house.'

'No it wasn't.' I got out my ticket, date-stamped, and several post-cards I had purchased. The soft toys looked at me sceptically.

Later, after we had eaten *shchi*, I asked her if she would like to watch Grigory Kozintsev's 1926 adaptation of *The Overcoat*, which I had downloaded from YouTube. She narrowed her eyes, and I could tell she was puzzling over whether the film was in Russian or English.

'It's a silent film,' I said. So we watched it, sitting side by side at the kitchen table. The movie, which incorporates another Gogol story, perfectly portrays the crowded offices where clerks sat hunched over quills and teetering piles of government folders rose towards the ceiling like uneven pillars. Out on the streets the flickering black-and-white footage contributed to a general atmosphere of menace, as did a dramatic score which hinted at danger around every corner. Akaky looks terrified throughout. Tamara's only comment was that she did not like the male characters' sideburns.

When the film was over, she produced a spiral-bound street map of Moscow, with an index at which she was pointing.

'Look, there is no Gogol house. Here is a Gorky house.'

I lay down on the kitchen lino, and closed my eyes.

*

Cherry trees outside the classroom window, foaming with blossom, glowed in late afternoon sun. I had two different teachers, both friendly women. One lived with her mother and daughter in a small flat, and the daughter was expecting a baby, 'so we will be four generations of women together!' Sounded like hell. The other was younger and un-Russian-looking, with a sculpted head that looked like it had been washed up from the Aegean. Vykhino, they told me as we admired the cherry blossom, used to be one huge orchard. Over time people had chopped down the trees and a produce market took their place. According to my teachers, the government had recently destroyed this market, which by then had sprawled across the district, because markets elsewhere had trouble with central Asian immigrants. So Putin razed the whole Vykhino market to dispel racial tensions and show what a strongman he was. It used to be the last station on the metro, a position normally considered dangerous; then, in 2013, the line was extended. On the island platform of the station I noted, from the advertisements, that the word 'selfie' had entered the Russian vocabulary. In many ways the district was characteristic of the suburbs. Half-finished developments, cranes, pools of standing water, sand pits, scrubby wasteland, litter, lots of litter, beige-coloured Russians bathing in dirty rivers.

A group of American undergraduates was in residence at the university, all taking a six-month Russian course. Several expeditions were organised for them, and they invited me on one of them – a boat trip. The Moskva afforded a good view of historical treasures of the capital. The toothy red walls of the Kremlin must be one of the most famous vistas in Russia. Moscow was first settled as a provincial trading post far from the magnificent medieval cities of Kievan Rus. Wooden churches came and went on the site (most accidentally burned down), until in the sixteenth century Italian stonecutters, German cannon founders and Persian smiths created the foundations of the walls known to the whole world today. The Kremlin appears to have been designed to foster centralised, secretive regimes. It was not always grand. According to Catherine Merridale, a Kremlin historian, in the days of Ivan the Terrible,

> gowned, whey-faced officials ... laboured in the barely furnished, poorly lit rooms. If there were windows, they were small, and any light that entered would have had to pass through a film of mica or fish-bladders rather than glass. Meanwhile, the stoves and tallow candles that burned almost all the time would have

made the atmosphere permanently sooty … only the chief clerks had the luxury of desks or chairs; the rest spent long days squatting on the floor.

No wonder Peter the Great bailed out.

Every regime has remade the Kremlin in its own image. The Bolsheviks turned its medieval palaces into canteens. Stalin dynamited at least two of its churches. A leading conservationist who led a campaign to save early frescoes in those churches perished in the gulag.

We disembarked from the trippers' boat and walked to the Moskva Hotel, just outside the Kremlin walls. It had recently been demolished and rebuilt as a crude replica. Rows of traditional painted wooden dwellings had also been destroyed, and at least 200 listed buildings. Many churches have gone, including the Church of the Saviour in the Pine Forest, outside the Kremlin, once among the oldest in the city. There is little incentive to conserve historic buildings, despite the lure of tourist cash. Mayor Yury Luzkhov (in office 1992–2010) sanctioned demolitions on his watch. Moscow property laws differ from the federal variety, the disparity creating tension, with buildings often the victims. At any rate before returning to barracks we went to view Voyentorg, an Art Nouveau military department store built in the second decade of the twentieth century on the corner of Vozdvizhenka Street and Bolshoi Kislovsky Lane. The shop closed in 1994. It initially became the property of the Moscow city government, and, owing to eighteenth- and early nineteenth-century finds on the site, was part of the Kremlin conservation area. But Voyentorg went under the wrecker's ball anyway. They built a vulgar replica of the façade, and in 2017 a Chinese billionaire bought the site.

*

Ten minutes on foot from Grint, the Kuskovo palace sprawled elegantly in heavily landscaped grounds. Kuskovo was the summer home of the Sheremetev family. The first of that name to live at the site distinguished himself as a field marshal under Peter the Great. His son built the extravagant palace. I visited on a Friday, which turned out to be a popular day for weddings. Couples posed in the eighteenth-century parterres and in front of the lake, ogled by the statuary, while awkward young relatives in ill-fitting clothes sidled behind the grotto to smoke. The main house was peachy pink, and lowish, with a green roof, high windows and a grand staircase sweeping up to the porticoed entrance, and a carriage drive where bejewelled visitors stepped out to dance at one of the famous Sheremetev balls.

I had caught a cold, and was congested, sneezing and in discomfort, as well as embarrassed about introducing germs to Tamara's small flat. When I got back she had taken her dentures out. She made me *kasha*, which she said was good for colds. I had asked permission to wash my smalls in the basin and peg them on the line strung uncertainly over the bath. Tamara had inspected the garments overnight. At breakfast the next day, she said that my knickers were too brief.

To access the internet, I walked to a large McDonald's near the metro station. There I could buy a coffee and do my emails. It was always busy. In the Ladies, Uzbek women washed their hair. *Babushki* squatted on pails on the street outside selling produce, often a pitifully small amount of it. I bought Tamara a pineapple. She said, 'Mayakovsky thought pineapples were bourgeois.' She often surprised me.

I got my diploma at the end of the week. I was even more proud when Tamara said I had the smallest bag of any paying guest she had ever had (she had a regular relationship with the Grint Institute, and had hosted students for years). The last morning, we watched the Welsh Open on television. I said I hated golf and had never liked anyone I met who played it. She agreed, so after an hour and a half we turned the television off. We ate *bliny* and a kind of stiff cottage cheese called *tvorog* with bilberry jam spooned onto the plate.

The language-company package included a car to the airport. Tamara walked out with me, down the steps to the ground floor and outside. She put on lipstick for this excursion. It was a splendid morning which hinted at the end of summer. The flowers in the beds of the estate stirred. An elderly neighbour passed us as we waited for the car to arrive. Tamara introduced us, saying, 'Sara speaks Russian badly.' The neighbour, a woman with pale-blue watery eyes, talked with enthusiasm about a trip she had made to Liverpool in the sixties.

'I remember a music group ...'

'Abba?' suggested Tamara.

'The Beatles?' I volunteered.

'Yes, the Beatles!'

*

Besides smells, Gogol was interested in tastes, undercooked macaroni notwithstanding. According to one academic there are eighty-six kinds of food in *Dead Souls*. Chichikov, after all, was progressing across the countryside from dinner to dinner. Pastries overspill the plate they are served on; a turkey, bigger than a calf, is stuffed with eggs, rice and liver; Chichikov eats a fig nestled at the bottom of a glass of milk. As I have said, Gogol burned the manuscript of the second volume. But not all of it. Some pages survived – the author must have left them on his desk or on the floor while he carried the bulk of the material to the ground-floor fireplace. The surviving pages of *Dead Souls* volume two include an ode to *kulebyaka*, the fish pie I had made at home. "'Make a four-cornered *kulebyaka*,'" says the character Petukh, a glutton.

'In one corner put the cheeks and dried spine of a sturgeon, in another put some buckwheat, and some mushrooms and onion, and some soft fish roe, and brains, and something else as well ... As for the underneath ... see that it's baked so that it's quite, well not done to the point of crumbling but so that it will melt in the mouth like snow and not make any crunching sound.'

Petukh smacked his lips as he spoke.

In 1842 Gogol published *Taras Bulba*, a much-revised version of an earlier story of the same name. The novella is a paean to the Ukrainian Cossacks of old, told through an aged Zaporozhian (they are the Cossacks who lived beyond the Dnieper falls). Bulba

was one of those characters who could only exist in that fierce fifteenth century, and in that half-nomadic corner of Europe, when the whole of Southern Russia, deserted by its princes, was laid waste and burned to the quick by pitiless troops of Mongolian robbers; when men deprived of house and home grew brave there; when, amid conflagrations, threatening neighbours, and eternal terrors, they settled down, and ... trained themselves not to know that there was such a thing as fear in the world.

Gogol often wrote of the Ukrainian dishes of his youth. Taras Bulba, whose name is the Ukrainian for potato, has an appetite for life which equals his appetite for food. When his two sons, Ostap and Andrei, return home from their Kiev seminary, Bulba tells his wife to prepare a 'proper' meal: 'We don't want dumplings, honey-cakes, poppy-cakes, or any other such messes: give us a whole sheep, a goat, mead forty years old, and as much corn-brandy as possible not with raisins and all sorts of stuff, but plain scorching corn-brandy, which foams and hisses like mad.'

The young men and their father set off for the Dnieper to fight Poles, the youths wearing red morocco boots with silver heels, golden girdles and trousers 'wide as the Black Sea'. There is more Gogolian gusto in this book than in any other, the prose singing with Wagnerian flourishes and 'the enchanting music of blades and bullets'. Chapter five has a description of a sleeping Cossack camp: 'It seemed as though the trees could be heard hissing as they stood wrapped in smoke; and when the fire burst forth, it suddenly lighted up the ripe plums with a phosphoric lilac-coloured gleam, or turned the yellowing pears here and there to pure gold.'

No wonder the book has been filmed so many times. In the 1962 movie a ponytailed Yul Brynner capers around as Bulba and Tony Curtis plays Andrei.

*

My Russian lessons at King's College London provided another tool, together with Edward and Linguaphone. Here's my diary.

1 April

We are sixteen. Annushka has a Russian grandfather but has lived all her life in England. Lynne has signed up to be a volunteer at the Sochi Olympics. Charlie works for a charity that identifies corruption in the extraction industry. I was the eldest by two decades.

Our quietly spoken teacher Irina came to Britain eighteen years ago, married an Englishman and had two daughters. She had a quick smile and I liked her immediately. She kicked off by giving us laminated cards depicting traditional items – a samovar, an *ushanka* (hat with earflaps). Nervous giggles as we went round speaking the words.

Irina has to start conversations using our minuscule vocab. 'This is as hard for me', she said, 'as it is for you.'

8 April

We covered *kto*, 'who', and *chto*, 'what' or 'that'. Cats and dogs, it turns out, had to be referred to as 'who'. I asked Irina why.

'Well,' she said, 'they are not insects.'

'No,' I said, 'but they aren't human either.' The others pursued the wrongness of referring to a cat as 'who' and a lizard as 'what'. I wondered if this was useful: was it telling us anything about Russian perceptions of consciousness? Or were we all sloshing around in an infant-school linguistic discussion?

There is something gulagy about King's, which suits the course. People wait in line for classes in the narrow corridors. The windows are frosted, the ceilings low.

One of my Russian grammar books says that *da* and *nyet* 'loosely correspond to yes and no'. But aren't those absolutes?

15 April

We did numbers today, and listened to a recording of the football results.

Regional accents come up. In the Soviet era, broadcasters trained newscasters to talk correct Russian. Irina gleefully mentions Gorbachev's plebeian southern accent, in which he put the 'wrong' emphasis on – for example – the verb *nachatsya*, 'to begin'.

22 April

Irina homes in on my filigree ring. 'Is it Russian?'

'No, it's Kosovar.'

'So it is Russian.'

'But Kosovo isn't Russia.'

'No, but, you know, it's the same tradition – Slav.'

29 April

Annushka, as we struggle in pairs with the possessive: 'My grand-father would be so ashamed.'

6 May

Made *tvorozhniki*, cottage cheese cakes, to take to class. Once I'd worked out that they needed to be heavily floured and cooked on a low heat to keep their shape they were delicious, and we ate them dipped in sugar and sour cream.

Linguaphone page forty-three. 'It is an oddity of Russian that after *dva* (two), *tri* (three), and *chetire* (four), nouns go into the genitive case singular.'

Half way through the first term. We are down from sixteen to eight.

Linguaphone page forty-five. 'The short form of the adjectives is only found in the nominative, whereas the long form declines so as to agree with nouns in all the different cases.'

10 June

I was doing some boring translating and feeling as if I weren't learning much, and suddenly Google Translate popped into my head. It was pretty good, and, critically, I knew enough to understand, for example, to change adjective endings from masculine to feminine, and also enough to insert a few mistakes. Made me wonder how schoolchildren learn these days, when they can go home to this every night. Having spent so many hundreds of hours of my youth translating Homer, Molière and Catullus, I wondered – do they just use GT now? I tried a bit of Catullus on Google Translate – Latin to Russian to English. Remember that this is one of the most famous poems from the ancient world.

> *Sparrow, the joy of my girl,*
> *the one with whom to play, which I keep on my knees,*
> *to which the tip of the finger to the first,*
> *used to bite him, and acid,*
> *When my desire to shine*
> *dear to him I do not know that he jokes pleases'm* [what?]
> *relief of her pain;*
> *I believe that a heavy passion;*
> *How could she play with*
> *and ease the sad care!*

A relief that the experiment failed.

15 June

Spent the whole afternoon in the garden yesterday trying to get three words into my head. Woke up this morning and could not call up those three words. Demoralising. The curious business of language learning is, as you might expect, linked to age. Some experts say this is due to declining dopamine levels – a known symptom of age. Dopamine is a neurotransmitter that signals pleasure in the brain and has important connections to cognitive functions. A decline in dopamine levels is partly responsible for shutting down brain plasticity in language learning.

Note that few Russian words are onomatopoeic. *Plavat*, to swim, is one of the few.

1 July

Is there such thing as a natural polyglot? Do some have what neurobiologists call 'brain plasticity'? Only in the sense that some people are better at maths than others – though perhaps that is a significant sense. The question of how the brain regulates its plasticity is a major and complex issue in neurobiology. And there is no mental gym option – you can't improve your neural hardware.

*

Mezzofanti's Gift by Michael Erard has much to say on the subject of language learning. Giuseppe Mezzofanti was an early nineteenth-century Bolognese cardinal who had the equivalent of a photographic memory in the audio department – as soon as he heard a word, he never forgot it. Byron once lost a multilingual swearing contest with him. One thinks of Mithridates, the Persian king of the second century BC, who spoke (according to Pliny) the language of each of the twenty-two territories he governed. In the first Babel Prize, held in 1987 to anoint the Polyglot of Flanders, a shy man won after speaking twenty-two languages for ten minutes each to a native speaker. When he appeared on Turkish television he received many marriage proposals. He worried that his Kyrgyz wasn't as good as it had been.

But here's the thing. Everyone said Mezzofanti was a bore in every language he spoke and never said anything interesting. One man said the cardinal reminded him of a parrot.

The internet has a plethora of sites, blogs, podcasts, classes, tutoring sessions, games and forums about language learning. New Yorker Ellen Jovin's blog, for example, is fun – she apparently learned twenty languages in seven years, largely using the Pimsleur method, a popular system devised by an American who worked in applied linguistics. Jovin also watched foreign dating shows on television. Bestselling self-help guru Tim Ferriss is a self-proclaimed language fanatic whose overpowering website promises to help you learn a new tongue.

I've learned a few languages, and the only thing that counts in the long run is thousands of hours of practice.

3 July
In class Annushka said, 'Don't sit next to me next week, I am so embarrassed that you have to help me.' She has long eyelashes.

7 July
Sitting in garden at Sabine's listening to Linguaphone. The accompanying book continually exhorts me 'not to worry about this too much at the moment', which is ominous.

9 July
Oral exam at King's. Haven't taken an oral for thirty years and it brought back the horror of it. Had to answer questions about hobbies, as if anyone with children and a full-time job could have any. Then I had to look at a pic and the examiner had a slightly different one and we had to ask one another questions. Then I had to give a presentation about my family, and invented lots of sisters (my dream). Of course I forgot everything the moment I got in. Coming out was a question if not of *esprit d'escalier*, given the vast extent of floorspace at King's, then *esprit de couloir*.

10 July
Five of us in class this week. It's a case of the last woman standing.

12 July
Irina gave an end-of-term party at home for her students and various Russian friends. We ate *sup iz krapivy* – nettle soup. Irina had picked the nettles from her garden. She held back on putting lots in, as there were so many foreigners at the party who she feared were not used to the taste. A Russian guest said, 'This is not nettle soup. It's chicken soup with nettles.' Also had my favourite Russian dish, *selyodka pod shuboi* – herring under a fur coat. 'The key thing about *borshch*', said a Russian, 'is not to kill the beetroot.' Lots of vodka shots, then sessions at the piano.

13 July
Wrote a thank-you card to Irina in Russian – my first correspondence in Cyrillic.

30 July
My late agent Gillon Aitken, who represented me in London for twenty-three years, learned Russian as part of his military service (he was in the last cohort obliged to undertake service) and went on to produce a much-admired translation of Pushkin. Over lunch one day he gave me his army vocabulary book, a painstaking list in a neat cursive hand organised alphabetically in a military exercise book. After the full-time course, the War Office posted Gillon to East Germany to spy by radio on enemy manoeuvres. A plane arrived from Cheltenham every night to pick up tapes and transcripts. Gillon filled in time by smuggling cigarettes out of East Germany in the laundry basket (the laundryman had a cut), making a sixty per cent profit per package.

1 August

I went back to the first Linguaphone CDs and realised I'd forgotten a lot of the early stuff and have to relearn it.

3 August

Displacement activity. There is more available when running a family than when a student – endless.

4 August

Got my Cyrillic running at last on my Mac after several false starts. Have a separate keyboard on which I've stickered Cyrillic characters.

7 October

First day of intermediate course at King's – Irina promoted me and David after one term of the beginner's level. We have progressed, if only to the third floor.

Fourteen students including an East End wide boy in a suit – I imagine a commodities trader – who spoke really well. He had worked in Moscow for three years. When a complicated form of a verb came up he said, 'Oh that's what you say when you ask "Do you take credit cards?"' When Irina mentioned the dative he went blank. That's the way to learn – have an active social life. (I suspect he didn't speak much Russian in the office). And you never have to go through the agony of this rote learning.

11 October

Made the Princess' hot *zakuski*, appetisers that, she considers, make or break the reputation of a Russian cook. Mushrooms in sour cream were the best, lemon juice giving the tang.

17 November

It's too late for us to sit anywhere in the classroom except our usual places. I tried to fight this, and shift seats, but couldn't beat the inexorability of habit. We are seven students. A nice man in Hush Puppies is married to a Ukrainian Russian speaker. He explained that that group constitutes one-sixth of the population of Ukraine. Pure Russians are one-sixth; four-sixths are Ukrainian-speaking Ukrainians. A half-Greek lesbian teamed up with an amiable scoutmaster in tartan trousers for the conversation segment of the class.

19 February

Heard the brilliant Edward Lucas of *The Economist* on the wireless talking about the cause of the latest Ukrainian flare-up (twenty dead yesterday). Putin caused it, according to Lucas. President Yanukovych had suggested a union with Europe. Putin paid him off.

Much later

Made the Princess' Chocolate Torte with Mocha Frosting. Had to grate cooked potatoes to go in. Sounds vile, but it worked. Delicious. Princess explains that plain cakes are called English cakes. 'But to the average Russian, cake means a fancy layer cake, and the fancier the better ... The only real native Russian cake is a tall, cylindrical yeast-raised specimen rich with eggs and shortening. This is called a *baba*, and I suppose its name derives from its shape. *Baba* is the colloquial Russian word for [old] "woman".' The king of them all is the *kulich*, a thirty-centimetre-high *baba* eaten at Easter.

Much, much later

Made beef stroganoff. After spending £9 on fillet of beef I misread the recipe and put too much butter in the sauce, then put too much flour in to counteract it, then more butter to counteract that, and so it went on. The sauce was gloopy, and not as good as it should have been. The Princess says mustard is the 'secret' to the sauce. Gets shirty about the American habit of adding tomato puree and mushrooms.

The following week I made her *kotlety* (meatballs) baked in cream. Like the stroganoff, it had a funny flavour, which I concluded was due to the consommé I was using. The latter is one of HRH's favoured ingredients. I was buggered if I was going to make my own consommé, so I went to Londis and bought the tinned kind: Baxters. Elder son said, 'Mum, stop trying so hard with the cooking.'

What would Gogol have done? Reverted to semi-cooked pasta? Everything I did in that period was half baked.

VI

We Shall Rest

In Chekhov's short story 'The Lady with the Little Dog' (*Dama s sobachkoi*) the reader doesn't know, at the end, if the two characters in failed marriages had found an acceptable solution to their unhappiness. Chekhov avoided conclusions; he wrote of people as he saw them, eschewing social commentary and parsing his material for effect: he is an impressionist. There is no Dostoyevskian message. His stories and plays deal with the essential problem of being: how to find meaning before the return to dust.

Anton Pavlovich grew up in Taganrog, a Ukrainian port on the Sea of Azov, in the Rostov region close to the restless Don. His grandfather had bought himself out of serfdom and the family progressed to the ranks of the provincial elite, though in 1887 Chekhov's father, a tyrannical grocer, lost his money. Chekhov's was a short career and a short life, though he lived under three tsars. In Russia he is best known as a short-story writer, in the West as a playwright. That must tell us something, but I don't know what it is.

He left Taganrog when he was nineteen to attend medical school in Moscow, but in his head he never really left for long. As a medic he became familiar with the corpses of children, syphilitic from birth, who had perished of cold and starvation. And from his rural childhood he knew about endemic diseases – rickets, TB and the rest. That was what he dealt with in his life, and in turn, it informed his prose.

Like Dostoyevsky, Chekhov had many dependants. Derelict brothers, needy sisters, plaintive parents, endless comings and goings between Moscow, Petersburg and Taganrog – it was Chekhov's trial. His two elder brothers were hopelessly irresponsible. They stood in his way, and he lectured them to little effect. That said, his many letters to them over the years are notably affectionate, chatty and close. He never made money as a doctor. He mostly treated peasants for free. Chekhov famously spoke of medicine as his wife and writing as his mistress, later recycling the quip to say that fiction was his wife and the theatre his mistress.

The great men and women of any field work all the time. Chekhov was no exception. In his early years as a doctor he wrote and wrote and wrote, mostly for newspapers. He was a celebrated literary man by the time he was twenty-six. This despite the fact that he suffered chronic ill health, again like Dostoyevsky. From his mid-twenties onwards, his lungs spurted blood every spring.

In 1890 Chekhov travelled thousands of kilometres across Siberia, tramping through spongy mud, swooning over 'smoky, dreamy mountains' and 'lithe' rivers, and dreaming of turbot, asparagus and *kasha*. A sausage purchased at Tyumen, he wrote home to his publisher, tasted 'like a dog's tail smeared with tar'. He crossed the taiga on the dirt *trakt*, the sole artery connecting European Russia to its Pacific hinterland. In Pokrovskaya, everyone, even the priest, was out prospecting for gold. Everything was 'hellishly expensive', but the playwright sampled the whores, finding 'Asiatic' bordellos to his taste ('no wash-basins or objects made out of rubber or portraits of generals ... you feel you are taking part in an exhibition of high-level riding skill'). On the whole he loved Siberia, though wind and rain lashed his face to 'fish scales', and he had trouble with haemorrhoids.

His goal was the penal colony on Sakhalin Island, in the Sea of Okhotsk north of Japan. Chekhov felt he had 'wasted his life on fornication' – who hasn't – and wished to write a report on the condition of the prisons and prisoners, hoping that it might do some good. It had been hard to organise the trip. The director of prisons promised that Siberia's jail gates would be open to the writer, then sent a secret telegram to ensure the opposite. To throw the authorities off the scent Chekhov pretended his aim was to conduct a census; he did go through the motions of conducting one. He was thirty. One of his brothers had TB and he had just learned that he too had the disease.

When he reached Sakhalin, he interviewed convicts and many smallpox-ravaged Gilyak families living in yurts along the river Tym and the east coast. Chekhov found the Gilyak 'clever, intelligent, cheerful and brash'. He had a humane attitude to both Gilyak and prisoners. 'Our primary concern should not be our own needs, but theirs,' he wrote of attempts to 'Russify' the Gilyak. He was preparing a travel book, but found it hard to make the leap from fiction to fact; he told his brother that when he sat down with his pen and travel notebook he felt he was wearing the wrong trousers. The main impression that emerges both from his letters and from his account of the trek, *The Island: A Journey to Sakhalin*, is how foreign he found the landscape. He wrote that he felt like a European there on the edges of the Russian empire. 'It seems to me', he said, 'that Pushkin and Gogol are not understood here.'

Sailing across the Tatar Strait on the final leg to Sakhalin (an island twice the size of Greece), Chekhov wrote, 'On my left monstrous fires were burning, above them the mountains, and beyond the mountains a red glow rose to the sky from remote conflagrations. It seemed that all of Sakhalin was on fire.' He went on to paint a picture of degradation – children sold for half a litre of alcohol, prepubescent girls prostituted, men chained to wheelbarrows. He wrote in a letter home:

> There was a convict who had murdered his wife and wore fetters on his legs. His daughter, a little girl of six, was with him. I noticed wherever the convict moved the little girl scrambled after him, holding onto his fetters. At night the child slept with the convicts and soldiers all in a heap together.

He wrote that capital punishment had been given a different form.

The book is a work of investigative journalism as well as a travel narrative. It was first published as a series of nine articles in *New Time* – a rare example of journalism as literature. There is compassion within the horror. Here he writes of an old woman called Miss Yulyana.

> Once, a very long time ago, she had killed her baby and buried it in the ground; at the trial, she said that she had not killed the child but buried it alive – she thought she would stand a better chance of being acquitted that way. The court sentenced her to twenty years. Telling me about this, Yulyana wept bitterly, but then she wiped her eyes and asked, 'Fancy buyin' a nice little bit o' pickled cabbage?'

Chekhov's Sakhalin volume conjures broken shafts of springless carriages, a pond of light cast by a tallow candle in a hovel, and the sweet call of a bittern through the darkness on a night ferry. At times, the author said, he felt his soul was made of jelly. In Nizhny Armudan he slept in a jail. The walls and ceiling were so thick with bugs and cockroaches that it seemed the surfaces 'were covered in black crepe stirring as if blown by a wind ... You could hear rustling and a loud whispering, as if the insects were hurrying off somewhere and carrying on a conversation.'

There were lights in the darkness. In the evenings Chekhov rode out along the valley 'under a glowing western sky, the dark-blue sea and a completely white moon rising over the mountains'. At one point he reflects, 'How rich Russia is in fine people.' And who can forget the cook he describes kneading sunshine into the dough?

The Sakhalin experiences seep into the fiction, but the travel book is much more than a source text. Enthralled by Chekhov's words on Siberia, I followed him there. But I went in winter.

*

Train number 80 calls at Yekaterinburg on its long journey from Moscow to the far east, and I was planning to ride the rails from there 3,371 kilometres to Irkutsk, brushing the top of Kazakhstan and dipping towards Mongolia. Chekhov stopped for three days in Yekaterinburg, knowing that he was almost at the end of the railway line, and that the cart journey ahead of him would be grim. It was to be grimmer than he imagined.

I flew from Moscow to Yekaterinburg. The low hills beyond Koltsovo airport were swaddled in grey and muted shades of blue, and bulldozers cleared the runway. In town, toddlers ran about in ski suits. I wanted to stay a few days before boarding the eastbound Trans-Siberian, so had organised a homestay.

Although a modern city, Yekaterinburg has only one skyscraper – the 187-metre Vysotsky business centre – and nobody likes it: they call it 'the beer can'. Russia's fourth largest metropolis, Yekaterinburg has long been the political capital of the Ural district, that wide stripe of mountain and plain that for many centuries formed a natural border between European Russia and its Siberian hinterland. Yeltsin was born here, and rose to become party boss of the Sverdlovsk *oblast* before elevation to Moscow.* Like the beer can, he is unpopular. When Putin insisted there should be a Boris Yeltsin Street in the city, Yekaterinburgers protested, as nobody wanted to have the former president featuring in their address. So a compromise was reached, and Yeltsin presides over a commercial street where nobody lives.

Yekaterinburgers are proud of their city's proximity to the Europe–Asia border, and a kitsch granite monument on the outskirts records the spot. I went to pay homage, and found the site underwhelming. Yekaterinburg is trafficky, but the forest soon reasserts itself when you leave town. In the straggly Ural villages nearby, gas pipes run above ground (it's cheaper than burying them). Yekaterinburgers are less proud of their city's role in the Romanov story. On 16 July 1918, a killing squad eliminated Nicholas II and his family in the basement of the mansion owned by the railway engineer Nikolai Ipatyev, and carted the bodies to flooded iron ore pits. Today, both mansion site and pits attract pilgrims. The regional government built the faux-Byzantine Church on the Blood on the site of Ipatyev's house. Monster pictures of the royal family goggle out from the railings and in that basement where they perished a red rhodonite floor symbolises blood. All low ceilings, marble and vulgar chandeliers, you could mistake the church for a hotel reception. The pit site, on the other hand (called *Ganina Yama*, Ganya's Pit, after the original owner), feels like a sacred oasis. A monastery in peaceful countryside there has seven simple wooden churches, one for each member of the royal family. A monk was shovelling snow, a mobile phone clamped to his shoulder.

* Yekaterinburg was known as Sverdlovsk between 1924 and 1991, and the surrounding *oblast* still carries that name.

At both church and pits I saw pilgrims wearing lapel buttons depicting Nicholas II. He is more popular in death than he ever was in life. After the decades of chaos that followed him, many Russians look to him as a way of revering their roots. Putin and the Church have been quick to exploit this. Putin commissioned a new set of school textbooks, allegedly intended to reduce Russians' confusion over their own history, but actually conceived as a tool to boost nationalism, and him. Around the centenary of the assassination, Putin went to some lengths to emphasise the tragedy of the murders. Although an ex-communist, he was reminding the world of the kaleidoscope of Russian history. Radio and television dutifully marked the anniversary. Putin has often, in the past, commented on the imperial family. In 1998 the authorities had beatified the dead Romanovs. They are idealised, and it was useful for Putin to focus on how Russian they were, and on the sacred and the Orthodox. Little was said about the fact that most Russians in 1917 hated Nicholas as a reactionary tsar who had not allowed the kind of co-operation between parliament and the autocracy that have might have lessened social tensions. Putin talks far less about Lenin, embalmed under his window in Red Square.

*

On the platform, young Russian soldiers, green plastic sandals hanging from rucksacks, were saying goodbye to girlfriends and mothers. Train number 80 from Moscow to Blagoveshchensk (for some reason it did not continue the few stops further to Vladivostok) was to convey me to Irkutsk, a three-night journey. I love trains.

In overheated *vagon* nine, compartment six, I found Oleg and Pavel, en route to Novosibirsk to purchase machinery for their pylon-making plant. (This railway line did not separate males from females; in time I was to find out that most lines don't.) When I entered, they were looking at photographs of pylons on a tablet. The attendant came in before we pulled out of Yekaterinburg and barked instructions. I ascertained that the lavatory closed half an hour before major stations, and that a schedule of this event was pinned on its door. She softened when I gave her a pen with LONDON on it, and took me under her wing; she said she had to, because I was the only foreigner on the train.

We watched the loamy plains of the Urals congeal into Siberian forest. By the morning, only the odd dilapidated village pierced the taiga, and bundled figures trudged from *izby* (Siberian huts) to outdoor privies. All trace of infrastructure seemed to have sunk into the frost. Ropes of freight trains passed in the opposite direction, heading west from the coal basins to the smelting plants of the Urals.

Siberia covers almost thirteen million square kilometres, which is a twelfth of the earth's landmass. In the popular imagination there is always a man in chains on the icefields. The sun never sets there – one end wakes up when the other is going to sleep. In parts it is so cold that living trees explode with a sound like gunfire and exhaled breath falls to the ground in a shower of crystals. Before the railway, the round trip to Tobolsk from Moscow could take ten weeks; to Tomsk seven months; to Yakutsk two years. The quickest way from Petersburg to Kamchatka in furthest Siberia is still often westwards via New York.

Russification took root in Siberia in the sixteenth century, when sable hunters and freebooting Cossacks began to kick up trouble in Sibir – *siberi* means 'sleeping lambs' in Tatar – then an independent khanate on the river Irtysh. In time their fortified stockades, called *ostrogi*, fanned out across the steppe, and sea otter replaced sable as the most lucrative commodity in the badlands. Cossacks and Christianity allegedly rode boldly across the land with 'civilisation' in their panniers. Trade first followed the rivers (though only in summer). Siberia became the main overland route for the export of rhubarb from China to the west, for example: in 1652 the government in Moscow declared that tasty herbaceous perennial a state monopoly. Later a post road, the *trakt*, the one Chekhov took, struggled over steppe and round mountains. Besides soldiers, prisoners (many of whom settled once released), administrators, farmers, religious dissenters and the rest travelled to Siberia to express their beliefs far from the tentacles of the Orthodox Church. Sects arrived, again in search of freedom, among them the *skoptsy*, who chopped off their testicles and breasts in an attempt to return to a state of purity. As late as the 1990s the people of the river Indigirka were in thrall to ancient superstitions and rituals (shamans and wizards were relied on for healing, for example). Siberia had become a refuge for the preservation of ideals and values, and the myth persists. There were never any serfs.

Russians who moved to Siberia in Chekhov's century were known as *Sibiryaki*. Besides those who sought to uphold unpolluted tradition far from decadent Moscow and Petersburg, others merely perceived that it was easier to rise upwards east of the Urals. A man who left Russia as a common soldier became a sergeant in Tobolsk, a captain in Yakutsk and a colonel in Kamchatka. But this was no land of milk and honey. Syphilis was rife; no true *Sibiryak*, it was said, possessed an intact nose.

Migrants from European Russia displaced indigenous peoples. More than 500 tribal groups call Siberia home, between them speaking 120 languages. They include Arctic narwhal hunters and nomadic reindeer tribes who historically milked their beasts by sucking their udders and shored up the world with a cast of evil spirits with pointed heads. Their legends bristled with young girls who shoved their fathers off cliffs and mated with an underwater penis. Young warriors downed migrating geese with balls (not their own balls) and built antler towers as seal-oil lighthouses. The Khant fished the Ob from leaf-shaped dugout canoes, the Evenk lived in the forest in bark-covered tepees and herded tens of thousands of deer. Along the eastern Arctic coast, the Chukchi hunted seal from coracles with obsidian-tipped spears. Their presence predated Russians by thousands of years. Yet they are routinely referred to as 'half-thawed humanity' and 'descendants of fish' (aren't we all?).

To tsarist Russians, the indigenous tribes were a nuisance. Some writers had an idea of what was being perpetrated against their country's ethnic minorities. Tolstoy meant Anna Karenina's husband's Native Tribes Organisation Committee as a metaphor for sterility and impotence: plump men in frock-coats sitting around tables and drafting memos, reports and summaries which nobody read. Post-tsarism, Stalin set out to destroy the non-Russian cultures. The authorities shot many hundreds of Buddhist monks or sent them to camps. When you learn what was lost in the 1930s from lamaseries on the Russian–Mongolian border it makes you weep. The Soviets imposed a committee system on the native peoples. A group of Chukchi elders told Moscow's man they didn't need a committee because they had always lived without one, and that even if they did have one, the number of walrus would not increase. These indigenous peoples, so long custodians of the land, gave the lie to the Soviet claim that the Union was a technologically advanced brotherhood.

Shamans mediated between indigenous peoples and the teeming world of the spirits. Tsarist authorities had tried to replace shamans with priests. The communists preferred to ostracise those shamans who had struggled on. They imprisoned them and threw them out of helicopters, saying that if they could fly, now was their chance.

Stalin's death ended the purges, but *ukrupneniye*, or amalgamation, followed for these benighted peoples. Russian-language schools sprouted to turn them into proper Soviets, and they were obliged to work in factories. The result was social and cultural disaster. The world is bursting with stories of ethnic destruction, but the horrors of Siberia take some beating.

National movements, fighting back, have intermittently flourished among the larger Siberian peoples. During the civil war that followed the 1917 Revolution, some groups formed partisan armies and fought for political autonomy, and sometimes for outright independence. Several Siberian cities and the parliaments of three ethnic republics adopted constitutions giving themselves the right to secede. The Sakha sought ownership of its diamond mines, the Buryat rebuilt Buddhist monasteries and the Khant protested against oil companies destroying the tundra. But the ascendant Russian nationalism today is as bad for native peoples as the communism it replaced. Putin has created a more centralised country, and a more authoritarian one. Indigenous peoples make up about 1.6 million of the total Siberian population of 32 million, and do not form a majority in any of the so-called ethnic republics except for Tuva, nestled on the Mongolian border. They are too few, and too scattered, to mount a Chechen-style war of secession. Moscow-based native rights groups are small, weak and Western-funded. And so it goes on.

*

Waking up on the Trans-Siberian, I had no idea if the train had crossed a time zone in the night. My iPhone remained loyal to local time, but it could not tell me if the time had changed, nor could the train clocks, which remain permanently on Moscow time, as does the timetable. It soon stopped mattering. I had adopted train time, and entered that unmoored state that air travel cannot match.

Oleg and Pavel had healthy bellies, and I am not a small person, which created a space issue in the compartment. It was a relief when they repaired to the dining car, which they did frequently. After a good lunch, sixty-year-old Oleg, who had one front tooth, turned loquacious. The climate in particular exercised him. 'I have lived all my life in the Urals,' he said, 'and when I was a schoolboy fifty years ago, we used to have cold winters and warm summers. I recall going to school when it was minus forty-four! We liked it – after all, there was no wind. For the past few years we have had milder winters, colder summers, and no spring or autumn *at all*. It's hard to get used to.' This was to become a theme of my visit (snow had everywhere fallen unseasonably late), as was a diatribe against Moscow's neglect of the regions. Oleg listed the high price of oil in Siberia, the bad roads, the coffers depleted by the Olympics. 'The regions suffer – look out of the window; these people have nothing.' As the sun dropped with Siberian haste, we disembarked at a station. Oleg bought a table-tennis bat of dried fish from a *babushka* on the platform, wiping his hands on the net curtains in the compartment after he had eaten it.

Often, around the (electric) carriage samovar in trains across Siberia, I heard this kind of resentment against Moscow. People feel that Siberia's rich and abundant natural resources prop up the national economy, and that *Sibiryaki*, who suffered disproportionately from post-Soviet economic transition, are neglected. I found myself sympathetic to their cause. Poverty and pollution stalk the steppe. In Norilsk, a nasty nickel city in the far north, pollution from which almost reaches the moon, life expectancy remains fifty-nine for men and seventy-three for women, compared with sixty-four for men and seventy-six for women in the federation overall.

There were two power points in each corridor, but those in *vagon* nine were, mysteriously, permanently in use, electric leads snaking under the carpet and into the next compartment to mine. It took me twenty-four hours to work out the racket: the occupants of that compartment, two bullet-headed guys in their twenties, had a bar of multiple sockets to which other passengers could buy access for 200 roubles. I paid.

During the course of the first night, someone – or something – knocked hard from below, the blows vibrating in my bunk. Had we broken down? But it was a railwayman using poles to dislodge ice on the axles. I woke for good in a station yard at Ishim, where a few people scurried, furred from crown to boot. The air was still and clear, too early and too cold for platform vendors. But a tray of hot doughnuts came on. The *provodnitsa* takes a cut. She has to supplement her wages.

The train followed the day from village to village – first lights, shovelling snow, vans beetling at noon, children walking home from some lonely school, lights going on in disintegrating *izby*. Then hundreds of kilometres of coniferous forest, the wide and monotonous sash known as the taiga, the salient ecological feature of all northern

Russia and a little-known region haunted by mythical spirits and gulag ghosts. Chekhov said that only migratory birds know where the taiga ends. I was sorry, when I disembarked at the stations, as I always did when time allowed, that I could not smell the resin of the pine needles as Chekhov did. The needles only release their scent when the sun warms them.

The *provodnitsa* brought lunch into the carriage. It was included in the ticket price. The indentations of a plastic tray held a dab of instant mashed potato, a small piece of fish, and thirteen peas. A cup of soup was billed as potato, but seemed to be sardine. Chekhov found little to eat at the *trakt* roadhouses except bread and garlic, but at the river crossings he was able to procure fish. Recuperating at Tomsk, he ate salty soup made of half-cooked duck offal which upset his stomach. At this point he was travelling in a birch-pole cart.

The smoking area between the carriages of my train was popular but unheated, so the small space achieved the feat of being both kippered and iced up. At Lyubinsky, a muffled man threw bottles of water onto a car windscreen to melt the frost. Snow covered mounds of hay. God knows how they keep animals alive in winter.

The Trans-Siberian constitutes one of the greatest engineering feats of history, and when completed in 1916 it linked the continental shores for the first time (an event already achieved in the US and Canada, though over a far shorter distance). The steaming engines transformed Siberia into a magnet for immigrants. They came in their millions once industry and agriculture developed, and the migration represented the final colonisation of Asian Russia by the imperial west. And Russia had come late to railways. In the early 1880s, it had 23,000 kilometres of rail – the same as Great Britain, which would have fitted into it ninety-four times. The battle to get the railway built involved endless committees and scenes of Gogolian government intrigue and infighting. It was Alexander III who finally sanctioned construction in 1881, and his son, Tsarevich Nicholas, who laid the first stone. Problems queued up for recognition. Paucity of labour was a big one, as was the non-existence of supplies. Felled timber was often too soft for the sleepers. Then there were the rivers, and the weather.

But they did it. Trains regularly chug onto the pages of nineteenth-century Russian literature (or probably any literature – think of Dickens or Balzac). A train opens and closes *The Cherry Orchard*. Anna Karenina hurls herself under the wheels of a train, flailing her red handbag.

Sweating on my bunk, I watched filigreed larches marching past the window. We spent half an hour in light snow at Omsk, the Whites' headquarters in the Civil War.* The grand neoclassical brick station was peppermint green, the buildings in the square beyond it pocked with corrosion. Few *babushki* prowled, owing to the season and the time, but a man was selling fur hats and boxes of sweetmeats that our *provodnitsa* picked over carefully to resell. And right by the red engine, electronic gadgets in boxes changed hands, cash stowed in a plastic bag. The train pulled out of Omsk and re-entered the taiga through a tumble of falling snow. You can only appreciate the engineering feat of the Trans-Siberian by travelling along it in winter. They might as well have laid tracks across Antarctica.

In the middle of the Siberian night, a monumental station loomed, carpeted in deep snow and brightly lit, its green paint iridescent against the black sky. The railway created Novosibirsk, the Siberian capital on the river Ob, 3,343 kilometres from Moscow and a third of the way to Vladivostok. Only 764 people lived there in 1893 – it was called Novonikolayevsk then. Once the railway came, Siberians seeking work poured in, and so did European Russians. The station is the biggest in the country, and the portion of the line I had just travelled, from Omsk, carries more freight than any railway in the world. I took my usual half-hour nostril-stinging walk along the platform.

---

* The Bolsheviks took Omsk on 14 November 1919 and found that the fleeing Whites had left for them, among other materiel, a million rifles.

Oleg and Pavel had got off. We pulled out of the station. Novosibirsk went on and on until it finally dissolved and nature resumed. Galina had boarded and entered *vagon* nine, and my compartment. She was about thirty and talked so fast I understood little, except that she was born in Altai and was headed home to Krasnoyarsk, 755 kilometres to the east. When we got to the photo-exchanging stage, she showed pictures of her examining a tree with a giant hypodermic, and she explained (I think) that this can enable her to find out the age of the tree. This was a clue that she worked in forestry. Later she instructed me on arboreal names as she ate a Bombay Bad Boy Pot Noodle with water from the samovar, advising on *Pinus silvestris* and *Betula pendula*, possibly the first time these two events have ever occurred simultaneously.

The landscape began to roll with fir trees and fenced stockholdings. The longest bridge on the line, fording the Yenisei at Krasnoyarsk, was 850 metres long and forested beneath by cranes and shipping containers. It took three years to build and at certain points more than 90,000 workers were on the job. For a European, it's tricky to fathom the size of these Siberian rivers (a Canadian would understand). Chekhov said the Yenisei was cramped by its banks.

Taishet, where the Baikal–Amur main line (*Baikalo-Amurskaya magis-tral*, known as BAM) splits off on an alternative route to the Pacific, is famous for a creosote factory described by Solzhenitsyn in *The Gulag Archipelago*. That line took workers decades to construct, requiring them to bore through or skirt seven mountain ranges and build 142 bridges; for almost half its length it ran through the perma-frost. It was among the most notorious Soviet construction projects. The environmental consequences were dire. Dreams died, as well as trees. Young communists working on the project grew disillusioned by its wasteful expense and uselessness. BAM exposed the myth of communism.

I disembarked at Irkutsk, on the west bank of the river Angara, shortly after dawn. A guide and driver met me, and we set off down the Baikal Highway. The Soviets built the road in 1961 for the Eisenhower–Khrushchev summit: a combination of poor soil, perma-frost and seismic activity added up to a major engineering challenge – and then the summit never happened because of the Gary Powers downed spy-plane episode (I had viewed a mural 'commemo-rating' that event at Yekaterinburg station). The taiga flanking the tarmac was dense with Siberian pine, cedar, larch, birch and aspen. An arc of willow ptarmigan streaked across the sky, a Naples-yellow moon still gleaming at ten in the morning. I failed to understand a word of the local news on the car radio. It turned out it was in the Buryat language. The Buryat, one of the largest ethnic groups in Russia, get half an hour of news each morning in their own tongue. Buryat once galloped south of Lake Baikal and burned camel dung inside felt yurts. Their chiefs owned tens of thousands of horses with harnesses tinkling with turquoise and silver charms.

We stopped for the driver, Sergei, to take a bathroom break in the woods. He had taken a dislike to me. 'What would you have done', he asked, 'if it were minus thirty, which it might well have been, and you were wearing those light trousers?' I said that the fabric was high-tech and I had worn the trousers in the Arctic, and showed him my merino leggings underneath, and two pairs of thermal socks. At this news he changed tack. 'Far too much for this mild weather.'

They left me in Listvyanka, where I was to spend two days alone walking the shores of the fabled Lake Baikal. Chekhov had stayed in a barn in Listvyanka while waiting for a steamer across the lake. He paid a rouble a night. Waves were breaking on the pebble beach when I arrived (Baikal does not freeze until the end of February), the snowy Hamar Daban mountains stood out sharply between an Arctic blue sky and a silver lake, and the whiff of fish drifted from the market. A woman hauled up a bucket from a public well. I was dizzy, regaining land legs after three days on a train.

Lake Baikal is an agglomeration of superlatives. It holds more water than all five American Great Lakes combined; is the deepest lake in the world (on *average* over 1,500 metres); is larger than Belgium. It is twenty-five million years old and nourishes more than 3,500 species of plants and animals, 2,600 of which can be found nowhere else. The pressure once crushed a copper bathymeter sent down to forty metres. Limnological nirvana, in the shape of a banana.

The houses around my simple hotel were not desperately poor. But Lyudmila (Lyuda), my guide, had told me they had no sanitation. From my room, an eyrie up a flight of steps from the main building, I watched the sunset. The lake was a silver triangle, and I fell asleep on my bed. The snow shoveller woke me for dinner. My amiable hotelier, Tatyana, had smoked *omul* – a white fish of the salmon family indigenous to Baikal – on a brazier in the yard. Chekhov had tried to buy meat and fish but nobody had any. They all had vodka to sell, though. 'Russians are such pigs,' he wrote home. But this was modern Russia, where nobody eats only bread and garlic and the Buryat no longer hear the timeless symphony of the forest. When we had eaten the *omul*, I sat on the sofa next to Tatyana in her living room and watched Russian *Strictly*.

The second day, snow was swirling across the beach and a sea fog had swallowed the Hamar Daban. A bear cage on the main street was empty as the beast was hibernating in a cave out back. Ducks broke trails on the lake. The post office – *Pochta Rossii* – sold tinned ham and loo cleaner. At midday it was minus nine (the day before at the same time it was plus one, revealing the vagaries of a continental climate). Three-wheeled snowmobiles scooted up and down and everyone seemed to be at it with a shovel. In an enclosed and heated bank hut containing cash machines, a man with plastic shoes lay in a corner. Schoolchildren had made bird feeders out of water bottles, and hung them on lines outside the school.

Snow blew in gusts. A couple of fishermen had set up their gear, as had three divers. I poked my head into the dive tent. Two women, one Buryat and one Russian, told me they were hobbyists, and that the water was plus five. After a slog into the wind along the shore, I turned off. The sun came out, the wind dropped, and I passed a man smoking *omul*. Kamchatka squirrels with black tails, black heads and long black ears ran in the blue firs. The snow higher up was untrodden, firs tipped white. As Chekhov wrote in 'Three Years', 'There, at sunset's end, lay reflected an eternal, unearthly something.' Then a dog started howling, and set off every dog in the valley.

When I walked back to town six hours later, the man in plastic shoes was still lying in his bank hut. People were sunbathing with their gloves on. I bought a plastic carton of *omul* caviar at the market and ate it with my fingers, sitting on the steps behind the beach. If I've ever had a more delicious meal, I can't remember it.

On the third morning, Lyuda and Sergei arrived to pick me up an hour late. As I waited, I watched television news footage of houses in England sliding into the sea during a hurricane. 'You are better off in Siberia,' said Tatyana. We exchanged goodbyes, and the three of us headed off for Irkutsk as a weak sun hovered over the lake, polishing the still headwaters of the Angara, the latter 800 metres wide as it flows from Baikal to travel 1,800 kilometres north.

Lyuda was a widow with a cat which liked classical music, especially Mozart. She spent her childhood in Yakutia. Her mother was a doctor, her father an engineer. They had no running water in those years. Her mum worked from eight until five so she sent little Lyuda to get milk. Lyuda regularly queued for three hours to buy three litres of milk. One day, after purchasing it, she slipped on ice and the milk jar smashed. 'I cried. I felt I had let my mother down.'

On the hour-long journey to Irkutsk, we discussed Putin. 'A country the size of Russia needs a tsar – someone with absolute power – and he is one,' Lyuda said. She and Sergei agreed on this point. Outside the window, pines were laced with snow and interleaved with gleaming stands of birch. It was the time when Putin's anti-gay measures were attracting protesting crusaders in the UK. Campaigner Peter Tatchell had recently stormed the stage in London when Valeri Gergiev, a keen Putin supporter, was conducting. I asked Lyuda about this. 'I have nothing against gays and have some as friends.' An inauspicious start. 'But I don't know what all the fuss is about as they only represent ten per cent of the population.' The conversation swiftly went off the rails. 'I have noticed on my travels and in my work that gay men are a higher intellectual level than average. But I have read that lesbians generally are of a lower level.' Crikey.

Forty-eight kilometres before Irkutsk, at a break in the trees, an arched iron sign announced the Taltsy Museum. Russia has five open-air museums, but I wondered, looking out at a scattering of wooden homes, a golden dome and a cluster of verdigris cupolas, if the others spoke so clearly of their time, of the loneliness of the taiga, and of the peace of those regional heartlands so many thousands of kilometres from Moscow. In the sixties and seventies, the authorities dismantled traditional buildings in outlying districts and reassembled them here, log by log. Many had been the homes of indigenous peoples – notably Buryat – and some were the work of European Russians who erected their *ostrogi* like a necklace when they penetrated Siberia in pursuit of furs. Almost all the Taltsy buildings had been abandoned as a result of floods engineered in the Soviet rush to industrialise eastern Siberia. Historians will never know how many villages were flooded during the construction of the Bratsk and Ust-Ilimsk dams.

At the museum, an oval portrait of Alexander III hung uncertainly on a larch wall in the schoolroom. Wintry sun sliced onto an abacus, a row of low smooth desks, and a blackboard inscribed with looped Cyrillic script. The silence of the Siberian forest seemed to have penetrated the room. How many decades since a child's voice had spoken there? The temperature hovered at a sprightly minus twenty – not cold for those parts – and fragments of ice and snow skittered through the air outside, where my boots crunched over deep untrodden snow, a vulgar sound in the pure silence of Taltsy. The second building I entered, pushing open a heavy door rimed with hoarfrost, was a domestic dwelling with two sleeping platforms above a stove the size of a wardrobe. Opposite, in the kitchen area, birch-bark spoons hung from a rough-hewn pole. The Buryat flourished in the region for centuries. They grew flax and cultivated wheat co-operatively, farmed cows and herded reindeer, often camping out in their yurt-like gers. When I ran my fingers over the larch walls of the Kazanskaya chapel,

I saw that the Cossacks had built them without nails. The oldest buildings had mica windows (not that different to glass, but flexible and less smooth), though a glass factory operated in the area as early as 1796, facilitated by the Angara's sandy banks. In that climate windows were always small and set deep, with ornate carved shutters.

*

By the nineteenth century the former Cossack fort at Irkutsk had grown to become the intellectual and commercial centre of eastern Russia. Chekhov declared it 'the best of the Siberian towns', perhaps not a hotly contested field. It was known as 'the Paris of Siberia'. It is not an unpleasant place – there are worse – but the French moniker has outlived its usefulness. The main square displayed traditional Russian Christmas ice sculptures, but owing to unseasonal weather, they had begun to melt, unfestively shedding arms and noses.

Chekhov stayed in Irkutsk for a week, and sold his cart there. He reported to his family, whom he said he missed, that sugar was twenty-four kopecks a pound and pine nuts six. He found the town 'totally European', and liked the way streets were paved with wood. But he did not care for the women, and missed his Moscow girlfriends. 'Siberian ladies, married or not, are frozen fish,' he wrote home. 'You'd have to be a walrus or a seal to have fun with them.' Soon after leaving Irkutsk he went to Baikal, and shortly after caught a river steamer heading east.

In a failed attempt to identify where he stayed, I walked the length of Karl Marx Street. It used to be called Bolshaya (Big) Street, and some residents still refer to it as such; they want the name changed back. The communist era has an Ozymandian aspect, sinking back into the silt from which it grew. Nearby, the white stone Church of the Saviour (*Spasskaya tserkov*) displayed an exterior fresco of priests baptising indigenous Siberians. Outside, eight schoolchildren stood guarding the eternal flame commemorating the dead of the Great

Patriotic War. 'There are two teams of pupils,' said Lyuda, who was showing me round. 'To cope with the cold, they do ten minutes on, ten minutes off.' One of the girls was wearing suede high-heeled boots. 'It is an honour for them to guard the tomb,' said Lyuda.

'Is it voluntary?' I asked.

'Yes, but it didn't used to be.'

My homestay was in the oldest part of Irkutsk. My host, Anya, handed me two keys of medieval dimensions and gave me a detailed lesson in locking and unlocking as if the key had not yet journeyed beyond Russian borders. Every surface in the tiny flat sagged with plastic dolls, trinkets, artificial flowers, furry toys, photo frames, trolls (there were lots of them, including two black ones with single dangling pearly earrings), empty M & M novelty containers and souvenir mugs. There was not a speck of dust anywhere, so cleaning was a full-time job requiring recommencement at the beginning as soon as the end was reached. The walls displayed pictures, posters, photos and more trinkets, many fixed onto self-adhesive hooks which had lost their glueable properties and wore layers of Sellotape like a palimpsest. The empty boxes of every appliance ever bought teetered atop cupboards and wardrobes. Anya had squeezed a mattress into the glassed-in balcony that protrudes from hundreds of thousands of flats all over Russia (*zasteklyonny balkon*). This was my billet.

In the morning, Anya appeared with her blond hair in dazzling shiny rolls. She had taken out her curlers but not brushed her hair. 'Minus thirteen,' she announced as I crawled from my glass box like a creature from an early stage of evolution. Everyone knew what temperature it was, all the time.

For centuries, Irkutsk was a place of banishment. From a *Spasskaya* belltower, looking out through iced lashes to the white glare of the forest beyond, I saw how far off Moscow must have seemed to an exile. Warsaw too: many Polish exiles settled in Irkutsk in the nineteenth century, and their descendants still maintain a large Catholic church.

The most famous exiles were the Decembrists. After ten years' hard labour, some were allowed to settle in and around Irkutsk. In 1838 one of them, Prince Volkonsky, a general who had fought fifty-eight battles against Napoleon, built a house (actually he built it sixty kilometres away then moved it to Irkutsk). A portrait of him in his house, now a museum, shows a handsome man with curly sideburns and epaulettes as big as his head. Lyuda and I were the only visitors at the Volkonsky Decembrist Museum. The cloakroom attendant became agitated about my reluctance to hand over my small pack. I submitted, and she gave me a large wooden token to redeem my goods at the end of our visit (penalty for loss: eighty roubles). As we strolled round, I asked Lyuda if the attendant would have to write a report about the business of my pack. 'Look,' she said. 'I worked for Intourist for years, and I know the mentality. It's tunnel vision: this is the way it's done, and doing things the correct way is the only thing that matters in the public sector. I have learned to go with it – if they say lie down, I lie down.'

More than a hundred Decembrist wives followed their husbands into exile. It took a year to get permission to go, and not much less than that to make the journey. Volkonsky's wife, Princess Maria (Pushkin's old flame), left a son behind in Moscow when she joined her husband. The infant soon died without her. The princess had three more children in Siberia. One of those perished as well, but the others survived into the twentieth century.

The exiles were not allowed to participate in city life, so Princess Volkonskaya made her house a social centre. There was a grand piano in the drawing room, and an indoor greenhouse where a gardener grew pineapples. Various Decembrists wrote about the dual aspects of Siberia: prison, and a Garden of Eden far from state authority.

*

I went home to London. Chekhov went on to Sakhalin. The gruelling experience of the journey, and the horrors he saw, marked a watershed in his life. In 1892, he bought the small country estate of Melikhovo, about sixty-five kilometres south of Moscow. It had 240 hectares of birch wood and pasture, but the main house was small and dilapidated, with no bathroom. There were outbuildings, also decaying, and three starving horses. I saw how beautifully Chekhov had restored Melikhovo when I visited, catching a train from Moscow's Kursky station and travelling for an hour and a half past factories churning out God knows what and Cheopsian pyramids of logs awaiting dispatch.

The single-storey main house, with a pale salmon exterior, was not grand. When Chekhov sat at his writing desk next to the window in his study, hares stood on snowdrifts and looked in at him. A trunk he had bought in Tomsk was in a corner of his bedroom; in his book on the Sakhalin expedition he regretted not having taken a soft bag from the outset, like other passengers on the boats and trains, as he could have used it as a pillow. He could fish in a pond from his window at Melikhovo, he wrote proudly (he had always been an angler and once caught fifty-seven carp in a day). There was a veranda in the room they call *Pushkinskaya* because Pushkin stayed there, and two stained-glass windows from Venice glinted in the pale sunlight, colours still bright. Sick peasants queued outside every day; if they were too ill to travel, Chekhov went to them, often covering long distances in his carriage. He loved the woods. 'In the forest you can feel the presence of divinity,' he wrote in a letter. In *Uncle Vanya*, which was to come, Astrov makes a fuss with his concern for the destruction of Russian forests.

Outbuildings at Melikhovo included a clapboard chalet in a cherry orchard displaying the sign 'My house, in which *The Seagull* was written'. Chekhov's parents had moved into the main house, and various siblings came and went, so he needed privacy.

In 1899 Chekhov sold Melikhovo to a timber merchant who chopped down the cherry trees. When his old dad died there in 1898 the heart went out of it. Chekhov moved to Alushta, near Yalta in Crimea, to benefit from its mild climate, eventually building a house called the White Villa there with the proceeds of *The Seagull*. The villa had an orchard where the playwright planted mulberry, almond, peach and cherry trees as well as cypress and birch. He enjoyed gardening. Rachmaninov came to stay, and played Chekhov's piano. Chekhov treated the sick in the district there too, most of them ferociously poor. He was not yet forty, but souvenir shops touted plaster busts of his image, and public bulletins were issued on his health. He once wrote 'I squandered away my faith long ago', but he kept a crucifix on his bedroom wall in Alushta. He recognised the value of religion in a person's life, as many of the stories reveal. He liked going to church.

In 1901 he married Olga Leonardovna Knipper, an actress he met at *Seagull* rehearsals. The photograph below, taken after a reading of the play, shows him in the centre and Knipper two along to the left as you look. Chekhov was forty-one when they married, Knipper thirty-three. The couple lived mainly apart, as she worked in Moscow and he was largely confined to Alushta for his health. They corresponded almost every day – she signs off her letters 'Your little dog' – pouring out love and affection. She worried about his health; she herself became ill after a miscarriage.* Chekhov whined about the visitors who interrupted his work, and when they did not come he whined that he was lonely. 'I feel I am in prison', he wrote to her, 'and I get in such a rage.' At one particularly difficult period when he missed her, he wrote to her suggesting they go to Baikal, as he had loved it so much.

* The French edition of Donald Rayfield's 1997 biography of Chekhov came out in December 2018. Since the 1997 edition, Rayfield had discovered material from a previously sealed archive from which he – an impeccably reliable source – concluded the unborn child was not Chekhov's. Rayfield suspected that the father was a director at the theatre company. Rayfield also thought Chekhov knew.

The four major plays tumbled out in a period of eight years. After a disastrous premiere of *The Seagull* in Petersburg with booing and savage reviews, the play triumphed at the Moscow Art Theatre, a venue so closely associated with Chekhov that it still carries a seagull silhouette on its programmes. Knipper played the first Arkadina. Stanislavsky directed, and played Trigorin.

Chekhov wrote *The Seagull* in 1895, *Uncle Vanya* in 1897, *Three Sisters* in 1900, and *The Cherry Orchard* in 1903. Knipper was the first Yelena in *Uncle Vanya* and the first Masha in *Three Sisters*. These plays speak for themselves, don't they? Chekhov considered all four to be comedies. He didn't see much difference between tragedy and comedy. Sonya's famous last line in *Uncle Vanya*, '*My otdokhnyom*' – 'We shall rest' – expresses Chekhov's quiet acceptance of people's misery. Their only option, after all, was acceptance. Here are the preceding lines of that epic monologue.

We shall bear patiently the burdens that fate imposes on us. We shall work without rest for others, both now and when we are old. And when our final hour comes, we shall meet it humbly, and there beyond the grave, we shall say that we have known suffering and tears, that our life was bitter. And God will pity us. Ah, then, dear, dear Uncle, we shall enter on a bright and beautiful life. We shall rejoice and look back upon our grief here. A tender smile – and – we shall rest. I have faith, Uncle, fervent, passionate faith. We shall rest. We shall rest.

Chekhov's plays are powerfully associated with this elegiac melancholy. Sometimes this vanished paradise is represented through food. Firs, the butler in *The Cherry Orchard*, remembers the cherries of yore. 'They were juicy. They were sweet. And the smell of them. They [Russians] knew what they were doing then, you see.' Chekhov did write sometimes with longing for his Taganrog childhood, for example in 'The Secret Councillor'. But he also satirises the notion of 'the good old days'. He was progressive; he did not wish for a return to the past. He looked mainly forward – campaigning actively for the poor, for example.

As I peeped through the window of the cottage at Melikhovo in which Chekhov began *The Seagull*, it was hard to imagine Trigorin conjured out of that thin air. When he planned the play, Chekhov wrote in a letter that the piece was to have 'little action and tons of love'. In *The Seagull* the lake is an offstage character, the focus of that particular Chekhovian longing that stays in the mind when one has left the theatre. 'We're sleepwalking to oblivion,' says Konstantin. Life is funny and tragic at the same time in these plays, as it really is, if you're lucky. Chekhov ushered in a modern age of theatre. Amid the boredom and languor and dashed hopes there is a poetic core to the dramas.

Tom Stoppard has said several times that you can't have enough English *Seagulls*. All four plays will go on being reinterpreted until the next ice age. I've seen three *Seagulls* over the last two years alone featuring mobile phones, laptops and spectrummy Konstantins. Life is never the same twice over, and nor is a Chekhov production. Andrei Konchalovsky recently brought *Three Sisters* and *Uncle Vanya* to Britain from the Mossovet State Academic Theatre. Both were excellent, and notably circusy – which is the way Russians perceive Chekhov's plays. Perhaps Louis Malle's 1994 film *Vanya on 42nd Street* best reveals the universality of Chekhovian drama. But who can forget Anthony Hopkins as Astrov?

David Hare has written that he greatly admires the Chekhov four-act structure – now unpopular with dramatists – and uses it himself. Here's what he said about a revival of his *Amy's View* on Broadway:

> The four-act structure is one which the modern theatre has abandoned although it's the form Chekhov, Ibsen and O'Neill all frequently favoured, and one which gives superb subtlety to the feelings of time passing. Mastery of the form involves control-ling not just what happens in each act, but also the sense of what happens between them. I had to redraft constantly. I came to

believe that the form has been abandoned because it is fiercely difficult to write a play with four principal actions. All my problems were with the second act, which did not seem to be advancing the plot. Try as I might, I was not able to make the second movement anything more than a re-statement of the first. I was in such despair that I went to see *The Cherry Orchard* in order to see how an expert handled structure. I was astonished to find that I followed exactly the same pattern that he had:

FIRST ACT: We're going to have to sell the cherry orchard
SECOND ACT: We're *really* going to have to sell the cherry orchard
THIRD ACT: We're selling the cherry orchard
FOURTH ACT: We've sold the cherry orchard.

The plays are buried in the short stories (or is it the other way round?). In 'The Lady with the Little Dog' two strangers meet in Yalta. The sea was 'the soft, warm colour of lilac and a golden strip of moonlight lay across it'. The night they become lovers, the man, Gurov, picks up a slice of watermelon in Anna Sergeyevna's hotel room and eats it unhurriedly – a characteristic Chekhovian detail. There is no message.

In Oreanda they sat on a bench near the church and looked down at the sea without saying a word. Yalta was barely visible through the morning mist; white clouds lay motionless on the mountain tops. Not one leaf stirred on the trees, cicadas chirped, and the monotonous hollow roar of the sea that reached them from below spoke of peace, of that eternal slumber that awaits us. And so it roared down below when neither Yalta nor Oreanda existed. It was roaring now and would continue its hollow, indifferent booming when we are no more. And in this permanency, in this utter indifference to the life and death of every one of us there perhaps lies hidden a pledge of our eternal salvation, of never-ceasing progress of life upon earth, of the never-ceasing march towards perfection.

Chekhov died in Badenweiler, on a cure for his TB. He was forty-four. Knipper was with him. It was terrible at the end. She said she could never go through another night like the one before her husband died. She got him home for burial. In a memoir of his friend, Maxim Gorky fretted over the fact that Anton Pavlovich's body drew into Moscow from Germany in a refrigerated railway carriage marked FRESH OYSTERS. Knipper continued to write to Chekhov after his death. She survived him by fifty-five years.

Anton Pavlovich had written to his editor on 9 December 1890 when he returned home to Moscow from Siberia: 'God's world is good. Only one thing is vile in it: ourselves.'

VII

The Lady Macbeth of Mtsensk

In October 1883, in Moscow, a friend introduced Chekhov to Nikolai Leskov, a writer twenty-nine years his senior. The younger man took Leskov on a drinking spree, and they visited the prostitutes on Sobolev Lane. Chekhov reported that an inebriated Leskov said to him, while they were in a cab that night, 'Do you know who I am?' Chekhov said he did. 'Then he [Leskov] stared at me with his rheumy eyes and prophesied, "I anoint you with oil as Samuel anointed David ... You must write."'

Chekhov admired Leskov's work, saying that the man was his favourite writer; in his story 'A Literary Table of Ranks' the narrator whimsically judges authors by the thirteen-point civil service scale, and Leskov comes seventh. (The highest place at the table, that of Actual State Councillor, is vacant. Tolstoy is seated at place number two.) Chekhov used one of Leskov's idioms, 'You stepped on my favourite corn', in *The Seagull*.

Leskov wrote in many forms. He produced novels, plays and polemical journalism, satires on Russia's inferior position in terms of progress and advancement compared with the West (which he visited as a journalist), and even a travel book describing a journey around the monastic islands of Lake Ladoga. He was a prolific scribe throughout his life. He had no gift for the theatre and his long-form prose work is patchy – don't bother with *At Daggers Drawn* (*Na nozhakh*), an 800-page doorstop. Leskov was best over the short distance: the

400-metre short story rather than the Dostoyevskian marathon. He excelled at precise observation. It is the telling detail that illuminates, not the doom-laden overview.

He was the bitterest of men. He felt, his whole long writing life, that critics did not appreciate him. He would have been bitterer still had he known of his posthumous reputation. The sole English-language biography of Leskov in the London Library Russian collection had been taken out four times in the decade before I borrowed it. (This is just as well, as it isn't very good.) Few regard Nikolai Semyonovich as a major literary figure, but at his best, he is one.

His grandfather was a priest in the village of Leski, as the old man's father and grandfather were before him. It was Nikolai Semyonovich's father who broke the line. He rose through government service, and the family eased themselves into the provincial gentry. Nikolai was the eldest of seven. He dropped out of school when he was fifteen. Always a ferocious reader and autodidact, he harboured an inferiority complex over his lack of formal education, and it fuelled the bitterness. He became a civil servant, which at the time meant largely copying documents – his biographer describes him as a human typewriter – and worked in Kiev for seven years as an assistant clerk in the army recruiting office. Leskov taught himself Czech, Polish, Ukrainian and French. He loved, all his life, reading history. For a writer, the past is all there is: the present isn't around for long enough. That's a rewarding aspect of getting old. You've got this treasure trove of material that didn't exist when you were young.

He married in 1853. The union was a disaster. The couple had a son and a daughter; the son died young of cholera. Leskov later entered into a common-law marriage, which also failed: both relationships, he confidently asserted, collapsed through the fault of the women. Of course they did. The second wife had four children when she met Leskov, then they had a son together. The boy remembered later that his father spent all his money on books.

Leskov left the civil service during the period of his first marriage to work as the agent of a Scottish businessman who had married a Leskov aunt. The Scot ran a trading and estate-management company based in Penza, 625 kilometres south-east of Moscow, and Leskov travelled all over Russia with this work, often on barges. At the outset of his story 'The Pearl Necklace' he reflects on the way travel generates writing material. 'There's simply no getting away from impressions. And they sit thick in you, like yesterday's *kasha* stewing.' He eventually moved to St Petersburg and lived there for thirty-four years, for some of that period at two separate addresses in Furshtatskaya Street, opposite an orangery in the Tauride Gardens.

As the Leskov biographer I mentioned earlier, an American scholar, wrote, however,

The true Russia was not the Petersburg of ink-pot vendettas. The real life of the country lay in the depths of those vast spaces where a peaceful population lived its age-old life of toil and repose, joy and suffering, thinking thoughts altogether different from those that agitated the deracinated literati. Leskov had never felt comfortable with intellectuals, 'that rootless and characterless herd of Petersburg scribblers'.

Leskov said that any virtue he ever saw was in ordinary people. He despised his own editors – the hands that fed him – seeing everywhere fiddlers on the proof.

Leskov fell out with everyone, and made enemies everywhere. He alienated the literary establishment and wrote vicious reviews of former friends' books. After an early flirtation with radicalism he shifted to the right, and later tacked left, forging ties then breaking them. He drowned in self-pity. He hated the regime of Alexander III and looked back to the rule of that tsar's murdered father as a progressive one that did Russia good. He swerved around in his views and managed, over time, to push everyone away.

By 1868, not yet forty, he was angry and in debt. It was a terrible year in rural Russia. The spring crops perished; in the words of Turgenev, in a letter from his own estate near Oryol,

The rye is enormous on the stalk, but the ears contain not a kernel. What a picture Russia presents now – this land everyone contends is so rich. The roofs are all uncovered, the fences are down and not a single new building is to be seen except for the taverns. The horses and the cows are dead; the people are thin – three coachmen could hardly lift my trunk between them. Dust is everywhere, like a bank of clouds; around Petersburg everything is burning up – the forests, the houses, the very land …

*

Why do we care about Leskov? Because at his best, he's (almost) among the best. The short story 'The Lady Macbeth of Mtsensk'

The Lady Macbeth of Mtsensk

('*Ledi Makbet Mtsenskogo uyezda*') appeared in 1865 (it was first called 'The Lady Macbeth of Our District'). Katerina Lvovna Izmailova is more Claire Underwood than Lady Macbeth, though she resembles both in her willingness to murder. 'She was only twenty-three years old; not tall, but shapely, with a neck as if carved from marble, rounded shoulders, a firm bosom, a fine, straight little nose, lively black eyes, a high and white brow, and very black, almost blue-black hair.' The wife of a boring old flour merchant, she engages in a passionate affair with the serf Sergei Filipych, 'a bright falcon'. Lust becomes obsessive and soon the husband is the first of the dead. The adulterous couple produce a baby, which Katerina gives away. 'Her love for the father, like the love of many all too passionate women, did not extend in the least to the child.' (I wonder what Leskov's evidence was for this assertion.) The law catches up with the murderers and Siberia beckons. Sergei betrays Katerina Lvovna with fellow convicts twice on the journey. On a ferry crossing the Volga, with snow falling, Katerina pulls her second rival into the river, which duly sweeps both of them away. Leskov sees the two women in his final sentence as fish – a strong pike finishing off a 'soft-finned little roach'.

Leskov maintains his reader's sympathy with Katerina, the adulterous murderess. This was some achievement, and one he repeated. His story 'The Amazon' concerns a brothel madam who destroys everyone close to her, emotionally at least, yet in what her creator calls her fat little heart she thinks she is a jolly good person, and one finds oneself agreeing.

Shostakovich premiered his opera *Lady Macbeth of Mtsensk* (without the article, in its English translation) in Leningrad in 1934. The Soviet culture police suppressed the work two years later on account of its scandalous modernism, and *Pravda* said it was '*sumbur vmesto muzyki*' – 'muddle instead of music'. The agonies of Shostakovich's relationship with the Soviets runs like a thread through the composer's life, and he does not always emerge a hero.

*

I had been investigating Russian song performances in London and eventually reached the *grande dame* – the distinguished Russian-music teacher Ludmilla Andrew. Known as Milla, she was born to Russian parents in Vancouver and her first language was what she calls 'kitchen Russian' learned from her grandparents. She had lived in London for half a century, translating songs and teaching at the Royal Academy of Music. One June she invited me to 'A Programme of Russian Songs and Arias' by academy students. Spring was edging into summer in Regent's Park, opposite the Nash terrace wing of the academy, and the grass shone beyond the sash windows.

In the corridors, people hurried about carrying instruments in bulbous cases, sometimes on their backs, and in the canteen students pored over sheet music. Milla softly pointed out some characters. The thin male pianists all looked like Hamlet. The young women went in and out of the Ladies, from where they emerged in performing gear. Students queued at an electronic machine at which they could book a practice room.

The programme began at two. The songs dripped with emotion – that special Russian longing was on display, married with Dostoyevskian suffering. In a break, I commented on the melancholy. 'I think it is like Welsh music,' said Milla. 'Whether Welsh composers spent too long down the mines or too long being oppressed by the English, I don't know. There is no grey in Russian music, only black and white. Take that Sviridov piece we just heard from the 1987 song-cycle *Russia Cast Adrift* – "O my homeland, O happy and eternal hour! There is nothing better than your cowlike gaze. To you, to your mists and to the sheep in the fields, I bring the sun in my arms, like a sheaf of oats." I tell my students they have to sing with emotion. They are on the whole not Russian speakers and the first phrase they learn is *"Bozhe moi!"* – "My God!" – as it comes up so often.'

Milla showed me handouts she had devised for students learning to pronounce Russian sounds. The fiendish 'ui' or ы turned out to have an English equivalent after all: 'Think of the Cockney "Daisy, Daisy".'

On 11 June we reconvened for the Ludmilla Andrew Russian Song Prize. Milla appeared carrying a multi-coloured bejewelled cane and wearing a baby-pink trouser-suit and trainers. Her fellow judge Anthony Legge, conductor and opera coach, said in his closing speech, 'Russian is the most expressive language you've ever heard – singers have to learn a new depth of sadness. But the test for the singer is not to get too sad and dragged down.'

Martyna Kasprzyk won joint first in the singing section (there was an accompanying piano prize) with 'Olga's Aria' from Tchaikovsky's *Eugene Onegin*. She shared the honour with Sarah-Jane Lewis, who sang 'Maria's Aria' from *Mazeppa* by the same composer. I spoke with Lewis afterwards, and congratulated her. Born in London of Caribbean heritage, she had a steady gaze, scarlet nails and a gentle mien. But when she opened her mouth and sang Rachmaninov's Opus 21, No. 6, 'Loneliness' – *Bozhe moi!* 'I've learned to connect with my emotions through singing in Russian', she told me, 'and expressing these huge feelings that so characterise Russian music.'

I became addicted to dropping into the RAM. Those people I saw roaming the corridors with instruments on their backs like outsize snails – they belonged to another world, that of music, and it was one to which I had no access. In the Russian classes I heard lots of Rachmaninov ('O destitute loneliness!'), and Tchaikovsky's 'None but the Lonely Heart', Opus 6, No. 6 ('Only someone who has known what it is to yearn for a meeting with a loved one can understand how I suffer'). One afternoon a brilliant countertenor with custard-coloured hair sang, over and over, 'Vanya's Aria' from Glinka's *A Life for the Tsar*.

After Glinka, in some ways a lonely pioneer in the middle of the nineteenth century when Leskov was battling it out, a circle formed around Mussorgsky, Borodin and Rimsky-Korsakov, among others. Russia had little professional musical life before 1860 – opera houses and enthusiasts were in thrall to the Italians. The rise of Slavism in literature was felt in music too – Russia was finding its cultural identity – and the Mussorgsky circle (known as *moguchaya kuchka*, which means, bizarrely, 'the mighty little heap') was at the forefront, despite the protagonists having little or no musical education. The new composers did not look to Europe.

*

Leskov was cantankerous as well as bitter, and distrusted doctors (awkward for Chekhov) to the extent that he requested an autopsy in his will to prove that his medical men had been wrong. He was keen on superstitions and provincialisms, and was the most famous deployer of *skaz*, the Russian term for a prose style using a fictitious narrator whose dialect, slang, malapropisms and so on are replicated. *Skaz* in other words makes use of the colloquial language of oral storytelling (the word comes from the verb *skazat*, to speak or tell, and *rasskazy* are short stories). Despite his fondness for superstition, Leskov's priestly ancestry and lifelong interest in the Orthodox Church emerge in many of his stories, notably the 1872 novella *Cathedral Folk* (*Soboryane*), considered a classic in Russia. In this book Leskov was writing about the wider community of Orthodox souls, not just those associated with a cathedral. Despite his interest in the Church, and his appreciation of both its social and spiritual role, he often criticised its cosy relationship with an autocratic state. How extraordinary, after the communist era, that exactly the same relationship thrives in the twenty-first century. But of course, Leskov broke with the Orthodox Church in the end.

His journey around the Ladoga islands led not just to the travel book, but also to the long short story or novella – *povest* in Russian – *The Enchanted Wanderer* (*Ocharovanny strannik*), also often translated as 'The Enchanted Pilgrim'. In this book Leskov brilliantly fused liturgical language with colloquial Russian. The work covers the life of Ivan Severyanych Flyagin, a Ladoga monk who narrates the tale in response to questions from other passengers on a ferry. Flyagin is drunk, strong, violent, intensely religious and bloodied but unbowed. Yet divine grace is at work, even in him.

*

I travelled through Leskov country with Natasha, a guide with a bouffant, and Marat, a tall, handsome driver. Neither of them stopped talking for three days. First stop was the Leskov museum in Oryol, the author's hometown, 320 kilometres south-west of Moscow. The author lived in that blue wooden house for his first eight years (he was actually born in a nearby village which no longer exists). An old woman was feeding cats outside when we drew up. The dwelling was at the end of a street, close to a gully over the river Orlik ('eaglet' – *oryol* means eagle). The curators had recreated Leskov's Petersburg study, where he worked at night fuelled by strong tea. He kept a portrait of Tolstoy on his desk, and family photographs on the walls. A ninety-year-old childless great-granddaughter was still living, in Rio. With her the line will die. She used to be a ballerina, and the museum staff had put up photographs of her in a tutu.

We had lunch in a restaurant with electronic menus under the Ariadne Hotel. Horrible music blared out. The best part of the meal was pudding – a slice of *tvorog*, served with sour cream and sugar. The music stopped for the television news, which included a feature on oligarchical bling on the streets of Moscow. Marat, a Muscovite, said life was definitely better in the Soviet Union, as 'prices stayed low and everyone was equal'. As a child Natasha lived for a decade in a communal flat. The family had a room, and shared a kitchen and bathroom with two other families, all cooking over one flame. She had been working as a tour guide for many years and was a good one. Seven years previously her husband had had a serious car accident. When she arrived at the scene, one of his eyes was on the road. She got baptised at the time. American tourists she had guided sent money for treatment.

*

'I'll beat you,' she said, 'then you beat me.' We were entering the female cabins of a Mtsensk *banya*, that national institution fabled for its health-giving benefits and the opportunity to thrash the living daylights out of oneself and others. As we draped ourselves on benches in the steam room (*parnaya*) Natasha said she had heard about Brexit on television, and asked me if I felt European. I said I did, and asked her the same question.

'Yes,' she said, as a fresh bucket of water made the wood and stones hiss. 'Though my mother's family came from Siberia, and they were Asian.'

As the bouffant began to wilt, she set to with a brutal little bouquet of twigs and began to tell the story of her mother's family. The cabin smelled of eucalyptus.

'Granny lived in western Siberia and was dark and rich and beautiful. Everyone in the village had wanted to marry her, but she chose a poor illiterate redhead with a big heart.' My skin was burning, from both the heat and the whipping. I started dreaming about the first cold-water plunge. 'My grandparents built up a big farm, with horses and sheep. Then Granny died aged thirty, leaving six kids.'

When Natasha's mother was seven, one of Stalin's footsoldiers arrived at the Siberian farm. The man gave grandpa an envelope, and ordered him to ride to town and hand it to the police. At the police station, a constable opened the envelope. 'Do you know what this letter says?' the constable asked grandpa.

'No'.

'It says we must shoot you and your children.' That particular policeman was kind, so he gave grandpa two days. The farmer galloped home. Nobody local would take the children (it was too dangerous), so he put all six on trains to destinations far and wide. Natasha's mother never saw any of her family again. Grandpa died shortly after, not from Stalin's bullet, but from a broken heart. 'I look for my relatives in crowds,' Natasha said, as sweat cascaded over her breasts and I got my own back with the crisped twigs.

And so we went on, sweating and plunging. Half way through we took chamomile tea and spoons of cloudberry jam in the resting area (*predbannik*). The *banya* reflects something immutable about Russian history, despite the cataclysm of events. When I mentioned this to Natasha, she laughed and said, 'Yes, but each cataclysm produces the same results! Nothing ever changes!' She was of course contradicting her own assertion of a halcyon Soviet era. Then she cited Viktor Chernomyrdin, prime minister during the nineties: 'We meant the best,' he said, 'but it turned out as usual.'

I often noticed this kind of fatalism, born out of historical and personal experience. It is the opposite of the American dream. Earlier in the day Natasha had told me the fairytale 'Yemelya the Simpleton' ('*Yemelya-Durachok*'), which every Russian knows. Despite the term 'simpleton' or 'fool', the character Yemelya is regarded with affection, a lazy but likeable eccentric who spends most of his time on the sleeping platform above the stove (*pech*). Until, that is, having been ordered out of the house to fetch water, he obtains magic powers through a pike he catches under a frozen river. His abilities become famous, and when the tsar summons him, Yemelya does not have to leave his cosy billet: the *pech* doubles as a means of transport. 'In this tale', said Natasha, 'Russian inertia is rewarded and fatalism is defeated. But in real life we know that never happens.'

In another existence I had written about two Russian polar missions in which amphibious trucks drove to the North Pole across many hundreds of kilometres of drift ice. The vehicles were called *Yemelya*, because the Simpleton of that name took his stove with him, as the explorers did.

As we were towelling off, Natasha told me that her mother had married her father, a military man, in Moscow, and given birth to the baby Natasha in the Khrushchev era. 'Until 1997,' she said, 'I spent my entire life queuing. I used to go by sledge to the grocery store with my mother early in the morning. We had to wait two hours outside the shop and two hours inside. Mum had to take me, as with a child in tow she could get twenty eggs not twelve, and a kilogram of butter not half a kilogram.' When Natasha was six, they went to the grocery store as usual. As her mother arrived at the store she looked round, and Natasha was not there. She had fallen off the sledge. The frenzied woman ran back and found Natasha asleep in the snow. Natasha remembered hot tears. One day, a year or so later, a shopper queuing in the same store asked Natasha and her friend if she could borrow them, so she would be able to purchase more rations. Of course, the girls didn't fancy yet more queuing. But the woman promised them a chocolate as a reward. 'A chocolate! For me!' said Natasha, the lure of that treat still sparkling in her blue eyes. 'The chocolate that woman bought us after we had queued was the tiniest thing, wrapped in yellow paper with a kitten playing on it. We were the happiest girls in the world. Last year that childhood friend came to visit me, and she said, "Natasha, have you ever eaten anything as delicious as that chocolate?" "No," I said, "nothing."'

Natasha's mother died twenty years ago. As an adult Natasha never knew anything about her maternal family except that they came from Siberia. But a cousin had recently surfaced, from Khabarovsk. This cousin came to Moscow to visit. Natasha's sister travelled to the capital for the reunion from her home outside the city, and they invited the cousin for dinner at Natasha's house. The sister went to meet the cousin at the metro.

'How will I recognise her?' she asked in advance.

'You both have mobiles,' said Natasha. But when the sister looked into the crowd surging like a wave over the top of the station steps, a face shone out 'like a torch'. 'I saw one of us,' she said.

*

Leskov chopped and changed in many departments but consistently opposed the persecution of religious minorities. Old Believers in particular feature in his fiction. He admired them for their refusal to compromise with the modern world.

Who are the Old Believers? They grew out of the reforms that split the Russian Church in the seventeenth century, an event which Solzhenitsyn claimed influenced the national destiny more than the Bolshevik Revolution. Promulgated by Patriarch Nikon, the reforms aimed to cleanse spiritual practice. But Orthodox traditions were the beating heart of old Russia, and its rituals sacrosanct to those who linked change with Greek contamination. Conservatives considered the reforms heretical, and it was they who became Old Believers (OBs). Russian Christians had always crossed themselves with two fingers, and the breakaway sect was not minded to change when Nikon introduced the three-fingered cross to bring Russia in line with the Greek Church. Some OBs hacked off their index fingers; hundreds walled themselves up in their churches and immolated themselves; thousands settled in wayside chapels (*chasovni*), and no God-fearing man would ever pass one without a prayer to the solitary icon that kept a freezing vigil.

Though Leskov quarrelled with his Church, he never wavered from the view that understanding Orthodoxy held the key to understanding Russia. He developed a fascination with icon painting (the traditional, old-fashioned sort, not the slapped-on commercial tatteries of contemporary Moscow) and befriended an icon painter and restorer, an OB who lived in a shabby district of Petersburg and used a brush with three hairs. As OBs do not appoint priests and bishops, icons represent a vital contact with the true faith. It was in this icon painter's workshop that Leskov wrote *The Sealed Angel* (*Zapechatlenny angel*), a dazzling story about men working on a Kiev suspension bridge in the 1850s. Leskov had seen the construction of the Nikolayevsky chain bridge over the Dnieper when he was living in Kiev. It was the first multi-span suspension bridge in Europe, and the longest in the world. The English engineers employed a team of OB masons, stonecutters and labourers. This crew carried their icons from site to site in a cart at their own expense. 'We had two icons in particular,' says the narrator,

> one copied from the Greek by old Moscow court masters: our most holy lady praying in the garden, with all the cypresses and olive trees bowing to the ground before her; and the other a guardian angel, Stroganov work. It's impossible to express what art there was in these two holy images. You look at Our Lady, how the inanimate trees bow down before her purity, and your heart melts and trembles ...

The novella begins in a Ukrainian inn during a blizzard. Many have taken shelter. The atmosphere is steamy, the room packed. A man begins to tell a story.

*

Why isn't Leskov better known outside Russia? The translator and scholar Robert Chandler maintains:

We English have always expected our Russian writers to be unambiguously serious. We want to be shown a character's spiritual development; we want to be given truths to live by. But what Leskov gives us is something else: story matters more than character, and all we get by way of metaphysical insight is a sense that life's horrors and beauties are so intermingled as to be beyond all understanding.

A Russian literary critic captured the quality of this difference when he wrote, 'If Turgenev's or Chekhov's world may be compared to a landscape by Corot, Leskov's is a picture by Brueghel the Elder.'

*

Natasha, Marat and I proceeded forty-nine kilometres north-east from Oryol to Mtsensk, the thousand-year-old town on the river Zusha where Leskov's Lady Macbeth unsexed herself. Ziggurats of watermelons lined the roads. We drove around for some time, past dusty bus stations and flyblown alleys, looking for poor old Afanasy Fet's memorial. Everyone directed us to a golden statue of Turgenev, where a man was scything the grass just as he would have in the days of Ivan Sergeyevich. We eventually found the white Fet memorial bust surrounded by parched flowerbeds and scorched earth. I wondered if anyone had visited it for fifty years.

The semi-forgotten poet Afanasy Afanasyevich Fet (pronounced 'Fyet') was born in Mtsensk in 1820, making him eleven years older than his (relative) neighbour Leskov. His verse was small scale. Think of Emily Dickinson. Few would disagree that he became the outstanding lyrical poet in nineteenth-century Russia. Here he is describing dawn:

> *A whisper, a breath, a shiver,*
> *The trills of the nightingale,*
> *A silver light and a quiver*
> *And a sunlit trail.*

As one critic observed, Fet's work 'lives in the borderland between words and music', and Fet himself wrote of 'the indeterminate sphere of music', influenced, no doubt, by the new Mussorgsky circle. Calm, light and airy nature drew him, thematically, as did spring and dewy gardens. He writes in delicate half-tones, conjuring moods, Vaughan Williams rather than Wagner, and Wordsworth rather than Marlowe: a poet of evocation, not ideas. He sat on the political sidelines and was a natural reactionary, which went down poorly with the intellectual radicals of the 1860s, who thought writers should be socially committed (presumably the reason poetry was marginalised at that time, prose being considered a more effective vehicle for political expression).

He had an odd childhood: at the age of forty-four, his adoptive father, a Mtsensk landlord named Shenshin, had met a pregnant 22-year-old while visiting Germany. During his visit the young woman divorced her husband, had the baby and married the Russian, whereupon all three fled to Mtsensk, but the union was not legal in Russia, so the baby Fet was technically illegitimate. When he was fourteen and at boarding school, he received a letter informing him that he was obliged to take the surname of his German biological father (actually Foeth). He felt, he said, like a dog that had lost its master. He studied law and philology at Moscow University and began writing poetry when he was twenty, the year Lermontov published his final poetry collection, so another case of the baton passing. He lived in a gloomy flat in Malaya Polyanka Street in which his bedroom overlooked a birch, inspiring his poem 'The Sad Birch Tree by My Window'. After serving as an army officer, including a stint in Crimea, Fet returned to Mtsensk and bought a smallholding. His literary peers admired him, notably Tolstoy, his friend for many decades. Fet's work did not sell well in his lifetime, but subsequently teachers throughout Russia introduced his poetry to the classroom – Fet was often the first poet a Soviet schoolchild read.

When Fet was fifty-four, the tsar granted him permission to revert to the name of Shenshin: this allowed the poet to take up the privileges of the nobility, including, crucially, the right of inheritance. Fet increased his landholding, and wintered every year in Moscow. He was bitter, like Leskov, perhaps because of his original status as a non-nobleman, which he fought against for years, and he was a gloomy man – a characteristic at odds with the dreamy evocations of his verses.

> *I have come to you to greet you,*
> *To tell you that the sun is up,*
> *The sun's hot light now waits to greet you*
> *And trembles through the leaves and sap;*

> *To tell you that the forest is awake,*
> *Ferociously awake, every branch is budding,*
> *Each bird awake*
> *And full of spring;*

To tell you that I come again
(I do not know what I shall sing)
With yesterday's same passion,
To serve you – a happy song is ripening.

He wrote some of his most delicate love poetry when he was seventy, a period when his work was fashionable. Around that time he bought a property in Moscow's Plyushchikha Street.

*

Natasha had selected Zushka for lunch, a restaurant on the ground floor of a Khrushchev-era block. It was a plain, high-ceilinged institutional space with strip lighting, the tubes of which were black with the corpses of expired flies. Five workers from the Mtsensk bakery, an employer of 200, had taken the day off to celebrate a birthday. They were already well stuck in. When the three of us appeared, the bakers spotted a foreigner (you can't hide it) and clamoured for me to join their table. I accepted their hospitality. Igor, the baker's general manager, was first out of the stocks. 'Ebraica name?' he asked. One-eyed Vasily, an engineer, said little, but smiled a wide smile that took up almost all the space under his nose. Two middle-aged Larisas and the birthday girl, Yelena (forty-seven that day), made up the jolly group. We ate *solyanka*, salty beef and vegetable soup, and drank many vodka shots. 'Happy Birthday' rang out in cod English. We danced. They were keen adulterers: Igor and one of the Larisas groped, and Vasily couldn't take his hands off Yelena's tits, though she was too drunk to respond. When we left, the bakers came out to wave us off. I found them charming. They appeared undignified in many ways but they were Leskovian characters, sailing nobly into the future with no hope of money, or decent healthcare provision, or ushering their children into better lives than the ones they had lived.

The three of us headed north across undulating land dotted with sloping-roofed houses and crumbling cottages set in fields of purple and gold. Natasha's phone trilled regularly, as it was her fourteen-year-old daughter's name day, and all her friends called to congratulate her. She had got into the car that morning with a stash of plastic bags in which to stow *griby* (mushrooms), sold at roadside stalls. Natasha and Marat talked non-stop about the potential varieties on offer, and grew overexcited when the first fungi hove into view. When we stopped, a man was selling bottles of unpasteurised milk on top of his Zhiguli, from which he had removed the back seats.*

After an hour stopping and starting Marat said, 'Right. I'm not pulling over again.' We were heading to Moscow in a hurry – the real one, not the one for which the three sisters longed. I had a train to catch, and squeezed into the back of the car amid multiple plastic

---

* The lovable Zhigulis remain ubiquitous in Russia, even though they are no longer manufactured. They enjoy a lively presence on social media, notably in the form of the exported Lada versions.

sacks of fresh mushrooms and a large glass jar of dried ones I had bought, caught up in my friends' enthusiasm.

Harlequins of wheat and rye and bright green beetroot fields chequered the wide open spaces of the Oryol *oblast*, punctuated by wild-flower meadows, birch forests, smallholdings and larger farms, but no agribusiness. My companions had bought, along with their *griby*, blackcurrants and raspberries to eat in the car. Berry juice stained the pages of my notebook that afternoon. I tried to keep up with the non-stop chatter from the front seats, which was hard, as Marat could only speak at one speed. He lived in a small apartment with his 23-year-old daughter who worked in a bank and his former wife, from whom he was divorced. A succession of subsequent relationships had foundered on the rocks of his domestic situation. 'Did you really love any of them?' Natasha asked.

'No,' he replied.

'So,' she said, 'you are holding out for true love.'

We drove to Tula and had lunch in an old tram run by an Armenian – wonderful in every way, except for the heavy metal belting out of the television. We ate a spicy meat dish and *Russkaya krasavitsa* salad – Russian beauty – with eggs, cabbage, mayonnaise, tomatoes and cucumbers, the whole dish shaped alarmingly into a smooth dome (I don't want my food to look like half a football). Over the meal I asked Marat if he had been to Pskov. But the question came out as, 'Did you ever beat dogs?' The pair of them found this hilarious. I considered using 'Did You Ever Beat Dogs?' as the title of this book.

In the capital, I was taking the night train north. Marat was off to drink vodka at a friend's dacha, Natasha to pilot twenty-three Americans round the Kremlin. On a Friday afternoon, as usual, titanic traffic jams paralysed the streets as people headed out of town to their own dachas. As we crawled along the six-lane boulevard running alongside the coffee-coloured river Moskva, the jam brought on another round of lamentation over the demise of Soviet life. 'We had no cars!' said Natasha. 'We could never have imagined this.'

*

As for Leskov, in late middle age he became even more cantankerous than he had been in his youth. By then he hated the Church, the state and the literary establishment. His work had become didactic and tiresome. But on 20 April 1887, when he was fifty-six, he met Tolstoy, with whom he had long corresponded, and that changed everything.

He was in thrall to the self-appointed sage intellectually, and had dallied with Tolstoyan ideas and ideals of spirituality. The authorities had banned Tolstoy's work by then, and it was hard to obtain illegal copies. Leskov wanted to be a professional holy man, as Tolstoy (intermittently) did. He disagreed with Lev Nikolayevich on some points. But after the pair met, Leskov became a fully fledged disciple rather than a critical supporter, and Tolstoy's role as his guide was secure until the end. The meeting took place at Tolstoy's Moscow house. Leskov seemed to have found what he was looking for: someone to follow, to whom he could offer up unconditional devotion. Biographers say it was a father-substitute issue. Nikolai Semyonovich said Tolstoy was 'sincere to the point of sanctity'. It was mostly a question of religious devotion. Leskov had for a long time rejected the official Orthodox Church (while still respecting the Old Believers), embracing instead a more earthy Christianity which he believed could lead people to live better lives. The two men only met once more. It was as if Tolstoy gave Leskov the confidence to be himself. The accession of the repressive Alexander III had further liberated Leskov's thinking: the country was going backwards, and a writer had to take a stand.

VIII

The Poetry of Procrastination

7 January

Orthodox Christmas Day. Visited Kalinka and Samovar, a shop and restaurant in west London's Bayswater. No windows in Samovar. A Christmas tree stood looking sorry for itself and flatscreen televisions spewed images of icescapes, cats and babies. Waitress a middle-aged blonde, and I could have kissed her for not speaking English. Cheap wood, plastic tables and an area in the corner marked VIP displaying a black and silver upholstered banquette, surely redundant, as no VIP would come to this hole. The art on the wall, for sale, was bejewelled and psychedelic. The meatless *borshch* was good, the *bliny* warmed up and horrid. Nobody else came in. Both places 'units' in a 'market' off the arse end of Queensway. Other units included a mosque (shoes queuing outside), a Russian hairdressing salon, and several souvenir stalls – though who was ever going to appear here to buy souvenirs remained a mystery. A cover for something else. Kalinka was a horrible food shop with a few withered once-fresh items and the full range of processed gunk one finds in Russian stores: crisps, jars of gherkins and tinned everything. The place advertised itself on the internet as a bookshop. Three shelves at the back held a selection of airport thrillers.

Next to Samovar a Russian film shop, again windowless, sold DVDs, all of the violent variety. This grubby corner of Bayswater represents the Russian community in London. Oligarchs are a minuscule minority. Here is the seedy reality, V. S. Pritchett's London brought up to date.

4 February

Heard veteran hack Ann Leslie on the radio talking about how amazing it is that Putin is so popular, as he is short and doesn't drink, two characteristics Russians hate.

6 February

Edward introduces the instrumental case. 'It's the last one,' he says, with an exhausted expression. I sense that we have arrived at the end of one battle in the war.

Last week E brought up the topic of Russian words that have entered the English language. It seemed to me that he didn't have many – *troika* and *sputnik* aren't really considered English terms. He also nominated *ballet*. I looked this up before the next lesson, and found that the *OED* disqualifies that etymology. Tackled on the subject, he said that he had warned me before not to believe a word he said.

The plane trees were bare when Edward introduced what he called a 'vital word': *Oblomov*. It means 'a lazy, sluggish person, possibly suffering existential angst'. All literate Russians are familiar with this word (abuse followed from Edward about national levels of functional literacy). 'And you must also know *oblomovshchina*,' he said, 'which denotes inertia.'

I had read Ivan Goncharov's 1859 novel *Oblomov*. But I didn't realise to what extent the name had entered the language.

It's a long book. Ilya Ilyich Oblomov (the stress is on the second O) is a likeable nobleman who spends most of his time in his bed in a multi-occupancy home on Gorokhovaya Street, a major Petersburg artery ('in one of those big houses on Gorokhovaya Street, which could have accommodated the whole population of a country town').

A move to the armchair is a major achievement. One morning he drinks his tea in bed and almost manages to get up: 'In fact, glancing at his slippers, he even began to extend a foot in their direction, but presently withdrew it.' He wears a *khalat*, a kind of oriental dressing gown with sleeves wide at the cuffs.* *Khalatnost*, sloppiness, negligence or dressing gown-ness, is a handy Russian word denoting the ability to spend most or all of the day in that garment and slippers.†

In his thirties and in good health, Oblomov is long retired from his civil service post. He lives off the income from his family estate 1,600 kilometres away, which he has never visited as an adult (can't be bothered). His servant Zakhar, a bald old man with a long beard, attends to him, shuffling about in a grey suit with brass buttons. Flies settle on plates of uncovered food. The newspaper on the desk is a year old. Oblomov finally gets dressed at the beginning of Part II of Goncharov's novel, but only because a visiting friend insists on it.

It's not a novel about crime, punishment, war or peace. This is the poetry of procrastination. Early on in the story, Oblomov recalls his spoiled and idyllic childhood in a kind of dream sequence or flashback. He remembers the daily routine at Oblomovka (the estate) and a sense of an immutable rural world.

> The river burbles merrily and playfully along, widening in spots into a pool and then, narrowing into a swift thread of a current, pauses for reflection and just trickles over the rocks, branching

---

* 'A bathrobe! What is it with these old men and their bathrobes? It's insane,' Tina Brown said in an interview with the *Guardian* in 2017 at the height of the sexual-abuse-in-Hollywood revelations. But Harvey Weinstein was not Oblomov, and Brown isn't Goncharov.

† Note that Russians don't have the monopoly on this kind of compressed language. Consider the Finnish verb *kalsarikännit*, 'to get drunk at home in your underwear with no intention of doing anything else'. Or a verb from the extinct Yaghan people of the canals of Tierra del Fuego which means 'to unexpectedly come upon something hard when eating something soft' (they lived off shellfish).

into frisky rivulets whose babbling lulls the surrounding countryside into a sweet slumber … There are no robberies, murders
or other calamitous events; their [the people's] tranquillity is never
broken by strong passions or ambitious enterprises.

Goncharov describes a 'lethargy, simplicity of manner, quiet, and
passivity' dictated by the seasons and the church calendar, and the
hero's father is portrayed as a lovable figure in a 'wadded, cinnamon-
coloured coat'. Oblomov grew up, he says, 'like a plant in a greenhouse',
his nurse reciting Leskovian folk tales of wood goblins. After lunch
everyone retires for a long nap in heat-induced torpor. There might
be a sneeze in the hayloft, or a bark, until the estate slowly comes
back to life.

Oblomov is physically lazy, but he thinks a lot, an advocate for the
contemplative life as opposed to the life of action. At one point in
the novel he protests that he hadn't been asleep; he had been thinking.
'Isn't everybody looking for the same thing as me? After all, surely
the purpose of this hustle and bustle of yours, all these passions, wars,
trade and politics is to achieve precisely this very peace and quiet, to
strive for this ideal of paradise lost?'

He doesn't gamble or visit prostitutes or drink excessively, and he can't
concentrate on reading. He eats, gluttonously, mushroom stews and other
old-fashioned Russian food, and he dozes. A journalist friend visits –
Oblomov of course supine in bed – and talks about his trade. After the
man has left, Oblomov reflects on the horrors of the scribbling life.
'Yes,' he imagines, 'to think of being forced to go on writing, writing,
like the wheel of a machine – writing tomorrow, writing the day after,
writing though the summer is approaching and holidays keep passing
one by! Does he never stop to draw breath, the poor wretch?' He receives
a letter from the manager of his estate explaining that the financial situation is deteriorating and that Oblomov must visit to make some
decisions. Zakhar attempts to persuade him to do so. His master demurs.
'Nay, but you ought to wash, and then to write that letter,' urges Zakhar.

'Yes, I suppose I ought. I will do so presently. Just now I am engaged in thought.' As a matter of fact, he did read a page of the book which was lying open – a page which had turned yellow with a month's exposure. That done, he laid it down and yawned. 'How it all wearies me!' he whispered, stretching, and then drawing up his legs. Glancing at the ceiling as once more he relapsed into a voluptuous state of coma, he said to himself with momentary sternness: 'No – business first.' Then he rolled over, and clasped his hands behind his head.

His schoolfriend Stoltz introduces Oblomov to a young woman, Olga Ilyinskaya, and the two fall in love. 'Yet,' Goncharov records, 'the ultimate direction, the inmost significance of his life still remained confined to the sphere of good intentions.' In other words, Oblomov can't raise the energy to get on with wedding plans, and Olga realises she must leave him. She marries Stoltz. In the meantime, and inevitably, the managers of the estate steal Oblomov's money. He has been drafting that letter to them for years, urging reform, but is always defeated by worries about grammar after the first sentence.

Finally Oblomov has a child with his widowed landlady, Agafya Pshenitsyna, whom he marries – so he does manage to do something. Goncharov writes lovingly of the food Agafya cooked for Oblomov: buns smelling of cinnamon and vanilla, hot white rolls and steaming pies.

What is the book about? Partly it is a satire on the pointless existence of the Russian nobility of the period and the sclerosis of the civil service – a large house is 'heated, and lighted at the public expense' for a councillor – but it is more than that: it conjures the ennui of a Hamlet or a Kafka. The novel was a notable success when it appeared. Tolstoy wrote, '*Oblomov* is a truly great work, the likes of which one has not seen for a long, long time. I am in raptures over *Oblomov* and keep re-reading it.' Chekhov said Goncharov was 'ten heads above me in talent'. Somewhat later, on the other hand, Lenin – born in Goncharov's hometown of Simbirsk (now Ulyanovsk), a city on the

Volga 900 kilometres east of Moscow – saw Oblomov as a symbol of everything that was wrong with Russia. If social progress were to be made, then Russians must cleanse their Oblomovian tendencies, announced the Great Leader. Anyone who failed to put his or her back to the socialist plough was an Oblomov. It was that simple. Later still, Nabokov revealed that Goncharov was 'a stupefying bore'.

*

Who was Ivan Alexandrovich Goncharov? He was born into more or less noble stock two years before Lermontov and three years after Gogol. He was nine years older than Dostoyevsky. His childhood home in Ulyanovsk is a charming late eighteenth-century, three-storey red-and-white brick building, a wealthy merchant's house really, which the Russian state has preserved. When the author was growing up peacocks pecked in the courtyard and canaries flapped around the drawing room. Goncharov went to Moscow University and worked as a civil servant, translator and tutor, living mainly in Petersburg where he complained about the bleak and overcast skies. He was large and ungainly.

The Poetry of Procrastination

He travelled to Alaska – then a Russian outpost – and Japan on a trade mission led by an admiral. The leaky frigate *Pallada* set sail from Kronstadt, the Russian naval base on the Gulf of Finland; her mission was to open up the hitherto isolationist Japan. Moscow suspected that the US was trying to prise open Japan for trade, so wanted to get its own oar in. While *Pallada* was at sea, the Crimean War erupted. The frigate bellied across a stormy North Sea and put in at Portsmouth, from where Goncharov visited London, admiring Englishwomen's legs as they hitched their skirts to cross the road and observing the Duke of Wellington's funeral. Thence onward to South Africa, Singapore, Japan and China. The author left the mission in Siberia and made his way overland to Irkutsk, then home – a journey of 11,000 kilometres. His book about the journey, *The Frigate Pallada*, is bland (nothing is said about the appalling relations between admiral, captain and everyone else, documented in both archival and published sources), but it is redeemed by quotidian detail, the comic presence of the author's servant, Fadeyev, who treated his master like a child, and amusing cultural clashes: in Japan the delegation from *Pallada* to the Nagasaki governor's mansion, unwilling to sit on tatami mats, carried chairs from the ship, with the result that their hosts had to erect platforms in order to sit at the same height as their guests. Goncharov writes a lot about what he ate and drank. He revelled in Singapore's cheap pineapples (they were exotic at home), and enjoyed hot sake after a meal in Japan – though he was against the Japanese habit of putting a clove at the bottom of a teacup. He also disliked the new fad in Shanghai for canned food.

A good idea, but what is it, really? It turns out that some of these preserves really cannot be eaten; the dealers take advantage of the trust of the buyers; one cannot check what is inside. One cannot open each tin, tightly sealed with lead. Later on, at sea, it turns out that the beef tastes like veal, the veal like fish, the fish like eggs, and everything like God knows what. Often it looks and smells uniformly the same.

The Frigate Pallada outsold *Oblomov* by a wide margin. It's an odd book, reiterating many of the prejudices of the era, including anti-Semitism and the notion that only European civilisation engendered progress. Goncharov was keen to demonstrate the success of Russia's colonising mission in Siberia. For that reason, the Tsarist regime considered *The Frigate Pallada* essential reading, and now the Putin era promotes the book, as it embarks on its own expansionist mission. It is a book for all seasons. A replica vessel sails around the world today, the first Russian ship to have its own iconostasis, the wall of icons that demarcates the holiest space in an Orthodox church. As a leading academic in the field writes, 'The symbolic meanings attached to the new *Pallada*'s transoceanic cruises glorify the Russian tradition of exploration and colonisation, the projection of Russian naval and state power, Russia's role in the global world order, and Russian nationalism, in which Orthodox Christianity again begins to play an important role.'

*

Goncharov lived for nearly thirty years in a bleak flat overlooking a courtyard in Mokhovaya Street, and worked for a time as literary censor for Alexander III. He went slightly mad in his last years and lashed out at other Russian writers, notably Turgenev, for impeding his literary reputation abroad, and for plagiarising his work. He even accused Flaubert of stealing his characters. He died of pneumonia in Petersburg in 1891, so famous, on account of *Oblomov*, that crowds gathered outside the gloomy flat to mourn. In 1956 the Soviets moved his ashes to the Volkovo cemetery in that city.

At the end of the book, a literary acquaintance asks Stoltz what happened to the now-deceased Oblomov.

'He came to rack and ruin – though for no apparent reason.' As he spoke Stoltz sighed heavily. Then he added: 'His intellect was equal to that of his fellows, his soul was as clear and as bright as glass, his disposition was kindly, and he was a gentleman to the core. Yet he – he fell.'

'Wherefore? What was the cause?'

'The cause?' re-echoed Stoltz. 'The cause was – the disease of Oblomovka.'

'The disease of Oblomovka?' queried the literary gentleman in some perplexity. 'What is that?'

'Some day I will tell you. For the moment leave me to my thoughts and memories. Hereafter you shall write them down, for they might prove of value to someone.' In time Stoltz related to his friend what herein is to be found recorded.

Writers have adapted *Oblomov* many times, in Russian, English and other languages, for the big screen, for television, for the radio and even for the theatre. *Son of Oblomov* opened at the Lyric Theatre, Hammersmith, London in 1964 and transferred to the Comedy Theatre in the West End the same year. It ran for a long time, starring Spike Milligan, who used less and less of the original script until eventually the entire piece consisted of improvised farce.

*

I examined my travels to see if I could identify any Oblomovs. My friendly landlords in Anadyr in the Russian Far East some years ago certainly barely did anything except watch television. I had arranged homestay bed-and-breakfast accommodation through the regional tourist agency, an otherwise purposeless organisation, since Anadyr and the whole Chukotka region was essentially closed to foreigners. (As for the possibility of internal tourism – no Russian wanted to go to Anadyr.) When I arrived at their small, two-bedroom apartment on the second floor, Marina and her husband Sasha welcomed me warmly and we began the first of many 'conversations' in which we battered our heads against linguistic brick walls (I had not yet started to learn Russian). When I hung my parka in the hall, the wall-mounted coat rack crashed to the floor. Neither of my hosts took the slightest notice. The flat was dangerously hot – throughout the Russian Arctic, coal-fired heating is centrally controlled – and Marina and Sasha, both in their sixties, did not wear dressing gowns; they wore shorts and vests, basking in the last rays of the dying star of Soviet munificence. Oblomovism rather suits the Soviet reality: why do anything when you don't have to? In my room a tin can shaded a bulb that dangled over a Formica table, beaming a tube of light onto the table, and leaving the corners of the room in darkness.

*

A Transaero 747 had conveyed me to Anadyr from a distant runway of Moscow's Domodedovo airport. After an eight-hour flight, when the doors returned to manual and laboured arthritically open, cold air whooshed down the aisles. A squad of armed military personnel stomped on board, planting themselves at the front of each cabin to check documents. To arrange entry into Chukotka I had spent eighteen months engaged in a process too labyrinthine to warrant transcription here, eventually inserting myself as an artistically inclined scientist onto the books of the Chukotka Science Support Group. As my papers had not emerged from the catacombs of bureaucratic inertia until the tail end of the Arctic summer, I set off at the last possible moment before the Big Freeze. When my turn came to submit my documents to scrutiny on the plane, a woman sergeant peered at them before stretching across the middle row of seats to hand them to a colleague. The sergeant was slight, with downy cheeks. But her stiff peaked cap made up for it, and so did her gun. People coughed and stamped their feet in the invading cold. Mobile phones leapt to life. Then the second officer waved me through. At the time, it seemed like a minor Old Testament miracle.

I knew, though, that only the first hurdle was behind me. Getting into town from the airport was the next: one had to cross a bay which in late September might or might not be frozen. To reach the covered barge that made the crossing, I followed other passengers to a bus of a type familiar from footage of the Korean War. The road followed an automated rail track trundling wagons of coal across the tundra to a rusting military shipyard. When we decanted from the bus, everyone squinted across the bay at a vessel breasting the water. Platelets of ice turned slowly in the shallows. The barge docked and people began pushing to get on. I joined in and found a seat in a large cabin in which brown frilly curtains heavy with grime hung from windows smeared with salted grease. But the water, an embayment of the Bering Sea, sparkled with cold sunlight, and three beluga fluked between us and the diminutive buildings of Anadyr on the far shore. On the white cliffs to the north-east, the blades of a zig-zagging formation of wind turbines lolloped through endless rotations.

Unlike Oblomov, who had choices, the 7,000 residents of Anadyr have few. There is little work, and the average monthly wage hovers just above $200, so there is little disposable income either. The town doesn't even have any kiosks, those functional stalwarts of the land-scape elsewhere in the Federation. Everything has to come in by ship in summer, plane in winter. The supermarket was the only one in a region the size of France. In it I paid $11 for five bananas and $7 for three apples (I also saw Arctic roll in the freezer, flown in from a factory south of Petersburg). A resident had stuck a flyer on a telegraph pole advertising his flat in exchange for a one-way air ticket to Moscow. Unemployment runs at seventy per cent in the surrounding villages. There is a lot of talk in Europe of Russia's emerging middle class, but it doesn't exist in Chukotka.

The Soviet period was a disaster, not least because supply lines were so long and so corrupt that little was left by the time goods reached the Russian Far East except things nobody wanted, such as the fabled ten thousand left-foot gumboots. (On that occasion, transport planning failed to the extent that the 10,000 left boots went in the opposite direction to the same number of right boots, heading nobody knew where.) Every single good social indicator fell and all the bad ones leapt, suicide and murder rates among them. Whenever it looked like it could never get worse, it did.

The indifference of a market economy turned out to be as disastrous as Sovietisation had been. Jobs disappeared along with the old regime, and reindeer herds, the staple of the rural areas, reached a level dangerously near unsustainability. These days Anadyr, capital of a region in excess of 735,000 square kilometres, has many features of urban development, such as a dozen sets of traffic lights, many of which work, yet it gives one the sense of a being only half evolved – out of the water, but short of the dunes. The old Russia had gone, but the new one had yet to arrive to replace it. One was in addition unable to shake off the image of a police state. When one day I bought *pirozhki* and sat on the steps of the telephone exchange eating them before going in to look at emails at one of the public terminals, a policeman approached me and began barking. When I stammered that I didn't speak Russian, he shouted 'No eat!' and waved me off angrily with a thumb.

I was always hungry by lunchtime: the underemployed tourist bureau advertised their accommodation as B&B, but one B would have been enough, as no breakfast ever made an appearance at Marina and Sasha's.

On successive days I worked my way through the fare at Restaurant Anadyr, devouring cabbage soup, pickled herring, liver stroganoff with watery mashed potatoes, pork dumplings and doughy *pelmeni* packets. To reach the Anadyr one entered a large, anonymous building and mounted a flight of swerving wooden stairs, entering the restaurant, on the first floor, through a pair of saloon swing doors inlaid with frosted glass. The cavernous room featured improbably high ceilings, strip lighting and, at the far end, a low stage equipped with a drum kit and two standing mikes. A pair of mini-skirted elderly waitresses with dyed hair sat around doing nothing. A tower of white bread teetered on every linen cloth, and alongside the prices the menus displayed the weight in grams of each portion – a relic of the communist years. The teaspoons had holes punched in them so they would not be stolen. Was it the stigma that made them unstealable, or their unsuitability for certain teaspoon-orientated tasks such as ... but I couldn't think of a single one, except melting rocks of crack cocaine.

I had planned to explore the area. But I had not reckoned on an absence of roads. Anadyr was a prison and I was an inmate, along with the rest of the population. I did manage a short hike across the tundra. Sunlight bounced off the mosses of the plain, lingering on the water pooled in swampy hollows. Only the faintest breath of wind moved the blades of sedge, and silence hung heavily, except for the 'whee-hee' of Aleutian terns. The oceanic surface of the earth puckered with low growths of cottongrass, stands of alders, or a bilberry bush. When I turned away from its bitter grandeur, the castellations of Anadyr's housing blocks rose, self-contained as a medieval citadel. That day the smoke from the central heating plant went up straight, like a plumb line.

On Saturday the sun had vanished, and white horses played on the bay. In the shortening days, you felt winter shouldering in: cold air tickled the nostrils, and distant vistas shivered in advance of their swaddling snow. The bunting-washing hung stiff as salt cod. To take our minds off incarceration, a brass band played stirring tunes on the steps of the House of Culture, a central-casting Soviet monster with a swooping metal roof and a façade that said 'Don't come in here'. On the gritty shore behind, a group of men lit a barbecue with a blowtorch.

It was already owl light when I hurried up the wooden steps of the cathedral for the five o'clock Saturday service, and the taffeta sheen of the golden domes had flattened. The whole building, appropriately scaled up from the modest local churches, was made of weathered aspen boards: a magnificent chalet of a cathedral. Inside, candlelight flickered over painted faces, the tidal drone of a male choir rose and fell and ponytailed young monks strode around noiselessly, following the muttered instructions of the priest, a tall, broad figure whose stomach swelled tight against the black fabric of his robe. Puffs of incense smoke trailed woozily among the dozen worshippers, who shifted from foot to foot, touching their headscarves. Here were the obedient servants of the eastern Church quietly commemorating their martyrs, their lilting low prayers echoing back to a time before oligarchs and collectivisation, though not before reindeer. Here too, coming down on us few, was an abiding spiritual calm that the Soviets failed to obliterate.

Or was it? The peace of the cloisters was not the one that passed all understanding. Father Agafangel, the officiating priest, was at that time embroiled in a fight with his bishop, and the dispute had made the national press amid a hailstorm of denunciations. The bishop, a known nationalist renegade and arch-conservative, had himself publicly denounced the patriarch for his support of democracy and mobile phones. (A week after my return from Chukotka, the patriarch dismissed the bishop.)

The next morning, gangs of workers filed into the park outside my window soon after sunrise, picking up rubbish and stuffing it into hemp sacks. Another gang was repainting zebra crossings. I asked Marina about this unusual and un-Oblomovian activity. Eventually, via pictograms, she explained that preparation was under way for a long-discussed one-day presidential visit: the first time any head of state had ever visited Chukotka, going back to the earliest recorded days. I knew straightaway what Dmitry Medvedev was coming for: to strengthen Russia's claim to offshore hydrocarbons.

I heard on the wireless that the president had arrived at ten in the morning and vanished into meetings at the Chukotka Hotel. Anadyr was tense all day, unfamiliar figures in dark glasses patrolling its streets and federal choppers buzzing across the sky. At six, several hundred Russians swarmed around the entrance of the supermarket, which was opposite the hotel, hoping for a glimpse of the dwarfish big man. People tugged at their collars as the chill of a leafless polar autumn gusted in from the bay. I wedged myself alongside a group of women on the platform at the top of the supermarket steps, looking down at the crowd, and at the police line holding it back. Security vans blocked both ends of the road. Despite the menace of the vans, and of the stocky men who stood smoking by the hotel entrance, the night had a fairground ambience. A pair of schoolboys wrestled, parents rocked prams, and mobile phones, held aloft, captured pictures of a Black Maria backed up tight to the double doors of the hotel.

At 8.20 p.m., three men in suits hurried out of the hotel lobby. A murmur rippled through the crowd. Two more men appeared, carrying silver metal cases. Then it was him. A thrill swelled among the people, they clapped and whistled and their cameras flashed. It was really him!

We had assumed Medvedev would bundle straight into the back of the Black Maria, avoiding the crowd and the sniper's bullet. But he didn't. He strolled to the side of the vehicle, acknowledging the cheers by raising both arms and smiling. He was wearing a thigh-length leather jacket. Then he got into the van through the sliding side door, a small fleet of limousines appeared, and the cortège drew away. The flushed crowd dispersed in a thrum of chatter.

I followed him to Moscow the next day. Beluga were swimming in the bay again. In the shallows, ivory shards of porcelain ice washed in and out with the ragged edges of the waves from the barge. As the horn of our vessel lowed, I looked back for the last time at the central heating plant puffing out its dark grey steeples, dogs scavenging on the docks. Around the town, the sky reached down to the tundra.

*

Oblomov lives on. Samuel Beckett – an unexpected figure to appear on the scene – working in Paris in the thirties, became involved with Peggy Guggenheim, who nicknamed him Oblomov. How odd that an intellectual titan like Beckett should be coupled with a character defined by never doing anything. It wasn't Guggenheim's idea, though: Beckett had used Oblomov as a pen name, insisting that we are all, as he observed in *Waiting for Godot*, born of those who 'give birth astride of a grave'. (Or, as another genius with the initials S.B., Saul Bellow, noted, there is always 'the continual muddy suck of the grave underfoot'.) Perhaps Guggenheim's usage of the name reveals that genius can go unnoticed in the gravelly detail of daily life.

*

My first publication was a translation, not something I wrote myself. It was an essay in Greek about the poet Cavafy for a literary anthology of that kind of thing. Before taking up Modern Greek I had spent thousands of hours of my youth translating Homer for my studies – probably too many hours, when I should have been doing something else. I am not very good at written translation, and have a tremendous respect for those who carry it off. Having a smaller vocabulary than English, Russian in particular requires the translator to wrestle constantly with nuance. (*Dusha*, for example, means 'soul', and also 'heart' in a figurative sense. The word appears more than a hundred times in *War and Peace*.)

The one I hold dear to my own *dusha*, as a woman, and as a translator, is Constance Garnett, the first to turn *Oblomov* into English. Born in Brighton in 1861, Garnett translated seventy volumes from Russian, including all Dostoyevsky's baggy monsters. She was an indefatigable worker who moved through the literary and political circles of a troubled time and emerged as a heroine, always on the side of the poor and oppressed, fighting in a man's world. She was the opposite of a Little Englander, determined to see things from an international point of view.

Fair-haired, short-sighted and in poor health all her life, Garnett had a pinched childhood. When she went up to Newnham College, Cambridge as a scholar at seventeen, she had never before left Sussex. She read classics and maths, both of which provided rigorous training in the art of translation and the expression of precise meanings. She began learning Russian just before she turned thirty when she fell in with a gang of fiery exiles. She lectured a little, taught, moved to London, and associated with the Fabians – a movement which she later joined, and later still left. She was friends with George Bernard Shaw, who claimed he would have liked to marry her had he been richer. Garnett worked at the People's Palace, a library designed to improve the education of working people in London's East End. She married Edward Garnett, a publisher's reader and would-be novelist who started a newspaper for cats (motto '*Cave Canem*') which included a food column. His family had always been sympathetic to political refugees, and the newlyweds embarked on married life with an altruistic sense of purpose. For her part Connie befriended many Russian Jews who had fled persecution after the assassination of Alexander II. The couple set up home in Surrey in a cottage where Constance once picked twenty-seven quarts of blackberries in a day and found a mouse preserved in a jar of treacle.

In 1905 the Garnetts took a flat in Hampstead. Edward's father lived nearby in Tanza Road, and to get there Constance had to walk past the butcher's shop which is now my house – perhaps she bought lamb chops in the very room where I am writing these pages.

She began translating from the Russian with Turgenev, with whom she felt a deep affinity. Her work rate was astonishing. Her friend D. H. Lawrence described her sitting in the garden accumulating a tottering pillar of sheets on the grass alongside her. Of her Turgenev, Joseph Conrad, another friend, wrote, 'She is in that work what a great musician is to a great composer – with something more, something greater. It is as if the interpreter had looked into the very mind of the Master and had a share in his inspiration.' Her husband meanwhile became one of the most distinguished editors of his generation, nurturing the careers of such giants as Conrad, and as a result he wielded influence. He too was committed to Russian literature, and championed Russian writers all his life, once declaring, 'The Russians have widened the scope and aim of the novel.'

Constance went to Russia twice. The first visit was in winter, and she described 'shaggy ponies so prettily harnessed and everywhere the delicious sound of metal on the frost like the clink of skates'. People wore such voluminous clothes that she found it hard to tell a man from a woman. She saw great poverty – 'the white weak faces' – and later wrote to *The Times* asking what could be done to help starving Russians. She read Russian much better than she spoke it and could only have a basic conversation.

When she took on Chekhov he was barely known outside his own country despite his fame at home. Garnett had tried to get someone to publish Chekhov in English and nobody would – imagine that her typescript of *The Cherry Orchard* languished in the drawer of her settle for many years. Characteristically, she kept at it until she achieved success. During the war years she translated seven volumes of Dostoyevsky. The man had been dead for a quarter of a century and many Russian intellectuals considered him their greatest novelist, but again, virtually nobody had heard of him in the English-speaking world. Garnett made Dostoyevsky a household name, and he did the same for her. Ernest Hemingway was one of many who admired her Dostoyevskys, as well as her Tolstoys. 'I remember', he told a friend, 'how many times I tried to read *War and Peace* until I got the Constance Garnett translation.' Not everyone shared his opinion. One critic described her Chekhov as a Victorian death rattle. Nabokov jumped in to damn her versions. But compare his translation of Gogol's sleighbells in *Dead Souls* to Garnett's. *Chudnym zvonom zalivayetsya kolokolchik* becomes:

Garnett: 'The ringing of the bells melts into music.'
Nabokov: 'The middle bell trills out in a dream its liquid soliloquy.'

Who, do you think, has the tin ear?

Like many sickly children, she carried on for decades – in her case until she was eighty-five, long outlasting her healthier siblings. Her work has stood the test of time. I love her, and I love her stuff. She had been weaned on the great English Victorian novelists, and she has their ear for language. Equally at home with the playful and the serious, Garnett always seems to strike the right note. 'Groholsky embraced Liza,' she begins Chekhov's short story 'A Living Chattel', 'kept kissing one after another all her little fingers with their bitten pink nails, and laid her on the couch covered with cheap velvet.' She certainly worked too fast and there are mistakes, but it must be the spirit that counts. When I read Garnett's translations I feel I am responding to paragraphs penned by Turgenev and Tolstoy themselves, not to someone else's version of them. Her work gives the lie to Cervantes' assertion that reading a translation is like looking at a Flemish tapestry from the wrong side: although the figures are visible, they are obscured by bits of thread.

Garnett lives on, of course; like all writers she speaks from beyond the grave. In the early 1970s she featured as the main character in the satirical play *The Idiots Karamazov*, which was premiered at the Yale Repertory Theatre. A young actor called Meryl Streep played Garnett. It was a piece about the pitfalls and complexities of translation: the Russian for 'hysterical homosexual', according to the fictionalised Garnett, was 'Tchaikovsky'.

*

What is the nature of translation? Is it fidelity to words on a page? Or fidelity to tone? Both, but the translator must serve the interest of the reader first and foremost, rather than working as a slave for the writer. It is sometimes said that in order to convey atmosphere a translation must be redone for each generation. But I like Louise and Aylmer Maude's 1930s versions of Tolstoy because they are period pieces in themselves. Take this from 'The Death of Ivan Ilyich':

> At the entrance stood a carriage and two cabs. Leaning against the wall in the hall downstairs near the cloakstand was a coffin-lid covered with cloth of gold, ornamented with gold cord and tassels, that had been polished up with metal powder. Two ladies in black were taking off their fur cloaks.

Compare this with a modern translation:

> At the entrance to Ivan Ilyich's apartments stood a carriage and two cabs. Downstairs, in the front hall by the coatrack, leaning against the wall, was a silk-brocaded coffin-lid with tassels and freshly polished gold braid. Two ladies in black were taking off their fur coats.

This version loses the old-fashioned 'cloakstand' in favour of 'coatrack', 'cloth of gold' in favour of 'silk-brocaded', and 'metal powder' goes altogether. Of course, nobody knows what metal powder is these days, but the mention of it conjures a lost world, one in which parlourmaids knelt for hours polishing coffin lids. And while we know what fur coats are, fur cloaks better convey us to Tolstoy's Russia. The modern translation is, like the Maudes' version, a collaborative effort, in this case by Richard Pevear and Larissa Volokhonsky. This pair were and are the subject of the great Russian-to-English translation punch-up of our time. Pevear, an American poet, writer and translator from various European languages, was living in Manhattan in the 1980s with his wife Volokhonsky, a Russian émigrée. Pevear began reading a translation of *The Brothers Karamazov*. Looking over his shoulder,

Volokhonsky criticised what she knew to be errors. So they set about making their own *Karamazov*. A collaboration began, back and forth between the two of them, and a domestic industry was born. They won prizes. They appeared on *Oprah* (seriously) after the star selected their *Anna Karenina* for her bookclub. Sales soared. But what a fuss. Correspondence raged in the pages of literary journals, academics and other suspects accusing Pevear and Volokhonsky of a 'deplorable' return to the translations of old which relied too literally on the text (glossism – 'the practice of enforcing word-for-word translations of English idioms on Russian prose'), with nastiness all round. An article in *Commentary* magazine was entitled 'The Pevearsion of Russian Literature'. You can sometimes see what the critics mean. Compare the following lines from *Anna Karenina*:

> Garnett: 'All his efforts to draw her into open discussion she confronted with a barrier that he could not penetrate, made up of a sort of amused perplexity.'
>
> Pevear and Volokhonsky: 'To all his attempts at drawing her into an explanation she opposed the impenetrable wall of some cheerful perplexity.'

Virginia Woolf worked in the same collaborative way with a native speaker, in her case S. S. Koteliansky – their names appear alongside one another on the title pages of their books. Samuel Solomonovich, known as Kot, had met Woolf and others in the ghastly Bloomsbury set in 1917. Five years later Woolf published her third novel, *Jacob's Room*. It was a turning point in her career. But three weeks previously she had published, with Kot, a translation of suppressed sections of Dostoyevsky's *Demons* as well as other Dostoyevskiana. It was the first of three Russian translations Woolf published. She knew little Russian. 'I scarcely like to claim that I "translated" the Russian books claimed to me,' she told a student planning a book on her own oeuvre. 'I merely revised the English of a version made by S. Koteliansky.' In his obituary of Kot, Leonard Woolf, who also collaborated with the Russian, described how Kot 'would write out the translation in his own strange English and leave a large space between the lines in which I then turned his English into my English'.

*

Alexander Herzen was born, like Goncharov, in 1812 (1812!). He wrote like an angel and should be better known to English-speaking readers. I first came across him when walking to the British Library: he has a blue plaque nearby.

Herzen played a major role within the cultural elite under both Nicholas I and Alexander II. He was the son of a Russian nobleman and his common-law German wife, and as a child slept with his serf nanny on the floor beside him. The family spent their summers at an idyllic country estate south-west of Moscow where the boy gazed at endless cornfields ruffled by the breeze. He went on to study maths and natural sciences at Moscow University: he always believed that evolutionary theory was essential to an understanding of history.

(Lermontov was his classmate at college.) From the start he had robust political views, supporting the Decembrists, and in 1834 he was arrested, exiled and imprisoned for eight years for injudicious speech and writings. By the time he returned to Moscow in 1842 he was a prominent intellectual. Herzen inherited a fortune five years later and beetled off to the West, as they all did. He expeditiously got his money out of Russia just in time, and never set foot in Moscow again.

He had a high forehead and wore his dark hair long at the back in later years, and did not stint on the facial hair. His wife had an affair with a German poet before dying of pleurisy. Herzen himself had children by his best friend's wife. His mother and youngest son drowned during a shipwreck in France. Much later, a daughter committed suicide. In 1852 Herzen moved to London. He participated in the debates that preoccupied the Russian intelligentsia from the 1840s to the 1860s, notably those concerning the notion of Russia's historical destiny, its relationship with the West, and generally zeitgeisty issues about what was to be done, and he developed ideas about Russian socialism. He had been in Paris in 1848, and realised that his revolutionary zeal had been overtaken by events: in other words, he was out of date. While in Paris, he saw Turgenev every day. He wrote stories, and a novel. Herzen was always busy, and always well dressed.

Herzen set up the Free Russian Press in London; its output included two journals, and he published articles and pamphlets that were banned in his homeland, giving a voice to dissidents abroad. The secret police were on his case, and he was engaged in a permanent rearguard action to get his publications through. The liberation of the serfs in 1861 clouded Herzen's skies: a real thing had happened, but Alexander II was certainly not altogether on the right side. Herzen had hated Alexander's father, Nicholas I, with all his heart and mind, but he was also disillusioned with Western politics, having initially been a Westerniser, but finding no easy solution in his adopted homeland. He now went for the Dostoyevskian notion of the fallen West in need of redemption.

My Past and Thoughts (which begins, 'Vera Artamonovna, come tell me once more how the French came to Moscow') dilates, as the title suggests, on personalities and on the issues of the day. It is a tour de force (and Constance Garnett translated it). In homage, Tom Stoppard features its author as the main character in his 2002 trilogy *The Coast of Utopia*. Herzen was a great writer, or almost great. He opposed the bad guys and spoke from abroad to keep the idea of freedom alive in his native land. He was inconsistent – everyone's right – so it's hard to get a handle on him. But his most famous book will stand the test of time.

IX

Deep-Sea Fish

An elderly countess steps down from a railway carriage, assisted by a man and a woman. She is wearing a dark coat with a white fur trim and a black hat. The sky is aspirin white, but there is no snow on the platform. Puffs of cetacean smoke rise above the engine. The flickering sepia footage blacks out for a second. Then it comes back. The three walk slowly towards an isolated station house. The countess draws on gloves. As they approach the building, a slim, bearded figure in the doorway sees them, and then slams the door.

Sofya Andreyevna had been married to Lev Nikolayevich Tolstoy for forty-eight years, and had given birth to thirteen of his children. He was the most famous man in Russia, after the tsar. At four in the morning on 28 October 1910, Tolstoy had carried a candle into his live-in doctor's bedroom on the first floor of the ancestral home and woken him, telling the man that they had to leave. Tolstoy said, 'Don't wake Sofya.' He was eighty-two, and wished to renounce the world, and his wife was of the world. The two men rode to the nearest station in a carriage, wrapped up against the cold, as winter was already seeping in from the north. They bought third-class tickets to Kozelsk and headed to the Optina Pustyn monastery, thence on to visit Tolstoy's sister in her convent. After that they set off for the Caucasus. But Tolstoy fell ill, and was obliged to get off the train at Astapovo (a station now called Lev Tolstoy). They put him in a small iron-framed bed in the stationmaster's house, a mortal body poised to rejoin the minerals.

Tolstoy had left a note at home for Sofya Andreyevna saying, 'I can no longer live in the luxurious conditions in which I have lived until now.' He continued, 'I know that my going away will grieve you, and I am sorry for it; but please believe and understand that there was nothing else for me to do. My position in the house is becoming, and has become, unbearable.' Sofya threw herself into the pond, but it was shallow. After changing her clothes she chartered a train to Astapovo, but when she got there her husband's acolytes wouldn't let her into the stationmaster's house until Lev Nikolayevich had lost consciousness. The footage shows her pressing her face against the window.

They had been saying for years that Sofya Andreyevna was hysterical. Who wouldn't have been? Lev Nikolayevich was one of the most egotistical men to have lived. Which is why he was able to give us the impregnable masterpieces *War and Peace* and *Anna Karenina*.

News of the count's illness percolated, and soon hundreds pressed around the platform, sixty army officers among them. A Pathé man, stills photographers and reporters crowded round the little station-master's house alongside hordes of villagers.

He died at 6.05 in the morning on 7 November, before the sun's first full rays had cast shadows on the fields. A square pool of icy moonlight shone through the window of his room onto the bare wooden floor. The count had often written about the moment of death. He must have known, as he lay in the iron bed, that it was his turn. It was appropriate that he had expired at a station, as his fiction associates the railway with death, not progress. Anna Karenina perishes under a train and throughout the eponymous novel the railway represents the ugly threat of modernity, adultery, nightmare.

Students across the land demonstrated when they heard he was gone, expressing their sorrow that such an influential critic of the government had fallen silent. When the body travelled back to the ancestral home, thousands followed the cortège and sang hymns, others kneeling in the weak sunshine when the bier passed. They buried him and raised an unmarked mound over the grave which they sowed with grass seed.

When I visited his grave, an oriole was pulling at a worm on the mound. The bird and I were alone among shafts of midsummer light filtering through a stand of ash trees. Beyond clumps of bluebells and hollyhocks, yolky lily blooms patterned the surface of the shallow pond where Sofya Andreyevna had hurled herself. A small sign at the edge of the grave ordered, in Russian, 'Silent Zone'. The chirruping oriole had not read that sign.

*

The name of Tolstoy's estate, Yasnaya Polyana, means Bright Glade (and, on the subject of language, the emphasis is on the second 'o' in 'Tolstoy'). In his diaries Lev Nikolayevich describes candlelight burnishing the icons in a corner of his grandmother's bedroom, and a serf orchestra playing as he, a small boy, walked down the alley of beech trees leading to the main house. His son Lev Lvovich said that Yasnaya Polyana was an organic part of his father.

Notwithstanding this affection, Tolstoy lost the main house at a game of faro with fellow officers while fighting in the Russo-Turkish war in the Caucasus ('I'm so disgusted with myself that I'd like to forget my existence'). It was typical of his contradictory self. He had inherited Yasnaya Polyana, in the Tula region 200 kilometres south of Moscow, in 1847 when his father died. He was nineteen. After he gambled it away, serfs took it down brick by brick and rebuilt it on a neighbouring estate. From then on, Lev and the family lived in the two wings that had been added to the original manor. A single stone remains of the main house, engraved with the words that Tolstoy was born at that place.

I was there in early summer. A willow stooped over the central alley where the serf orchestra had once played Haydn, and butterflies danced in the roses beneath. In May 1897, Tolstoy wrote to Sofya, 'The extraordinary beauty of spring in the countryside this year would wake the dead.'

A dwelling called Yasnaya Polyana had existed from at least the seventeenth century. At that time the property was on the southern border of the Moscow principality. Tolstoy's grandfather Prince Nikolai Volkonsky inherited the estate and built the north-east wing where Lev grew up. A distant relative of the Decembrist Sergei Volkonsky who settled in Irkutsk, he was the prototype for Prince Andrei Bolkonsky in *War and Peace*, and Bald Hills, the Bolkonsky estate, bears many similarities to Yasnaya Polyana (though it is not in the same place).

The author's branch of the family were country cousins. Sprigs bloomed in court circles. Lev Nikolayevich's father went to the bad in ways nobody knows in detail, but his troubles involved sex and drink. Tolstoy inherited the title 'count', but in the sclerotic Russian hierarchy he was not considered a proper noble. He did not remember his mother, as she died before he was two. As an old man he revealed that he had often prayed to her soul. He developed an ancestor cult.

Tolstoy was twenty-nine years younger than Pushkin and thirty-two years older than Chekhov. The year 1828, when he was born, was a bleak time, even by Russian standards. Nicholas I ran a police state. He had begun his feculent reign by suppressing the Decembrist uprising, and his regime had grown increasingly repressive and reactionary. In April of the year of Tolstoy's birth Russia declared war on Turkey to support Greek independence. Two weeks before baby Lev appeared, a Russian army defeated the Turks at the Battle of Akhaltsikhe, despite being outnumbered by more than three to one. Tolstoy's parents must have felt they lived in a permanent state of war. And the Caucasus and Crimea were waiting in the wings.

In 1847, when he came into his inheritance, Tolstoy dropped out of Kazan University. He and his three siblings had lived in the town on the Volga after their father died, guests of a wealthy aunt and uncle. Lev was a pleasant-looking young man, with a high forehead and hair the colour of dark sherry. He stood five foot eleven (180 centimetres). After his attempt at university, Lev went to Moscow for a few months in 1850, staying first in the Hotel Chevalier and then in a small flat on Sivtsev-Vrazhek Lane in the Arbat. He was twenty-two, and started writing in that flat. It appears in *War and Peace* when Nikolai Rostov and his mother move in after the French invasion. One glimpses Tolstoy's youthful spontaneity in his diaries of that period. On 25 January 1851 he wrote, 'I've fallen in love, or imagine that I have; went to a party and lost my head. Bought a horse which I don't need at all.' He was human, but he didn't show it much in later years, except in his novels and stories. Fiction never lies. Tolstoy was obsessed with truth, as a writer must be, but he only told it when he was writing. Later, when he preached celibacy, he was still exercising his *droit de seigneur*.

In 1851 Tolstoy joined the army and served as an artillery officer in the Caucasus, for a period in Pyatigorsk, the spa town in the forest where Lermontov took his bullet. Tolstoy wrote about visits to a local STD clinic. He had already suffered a dose while a student at Kazan. Much later, editors expunged references to any of that from the multi-volume Russian official work, which included diaries and letters, because great Russian writers don't contract those kinds of things. Tolstoy's first sexual experience was with a prostitute, and afterwards he knelt at the side of the bed and wept. Of course he did. Or rather, of course he said he did.

He transferred to Crimea, and saw the horror of war. Those experiences marked him for life, and infiltrated much of the work to come. He transposed his thoughts on the battlefield back to the 1812 conflict. In *War and Peace*, Nikolai Rostov grasps the reality of what had seemed a heroic venture when he and his fellow officers had galloped off in their brocaded uniforms, batmen going ahead with the luggage. *I'm a nice person*, he thinks when the fighting begins, *and they are trying to shoot me!* As an officer Tolstoy saw, as if for the first time, the gap between his own class and the peasantry, and he rejected, as a result, both the officers' brotherhood that bound the army together, and the crude nationalism of his era. (It was not as crude, however, as today's variety.) A century on, the same heroic ideals that dispatched so many Russians to Borodino perished in the trenches of what we still call the Great War, though the outbreak of that catastrophe did not generate anything like as much enthusiasm in Russia as it did in Germany and Britain.

Again, as a writer must, Tolstoy put it all down on the page. He had already published a successful book *Childhood* (*Detstvo*), but his *Sevastopol Stories* (*Sevastopolskiye rasskazy*) elevated him to the top rank. He lived in Petersburg for a period after leaving the military, more or less as a literary boulevardier. In 1855 the despot Nicholas I expired. Alexander acceded, and relaxed the censorship rules. He emancipated the serfs in 1861. There was hope.

*

Tolstoy married Sofya Andreyevna, sometimes known as Sonya, in 1862. He was thirty-four, she eighteen. He was an hour late for the wedding, as his servant couldn't find any clean clothes. Not long after their marriage, Tolstoy insisted that the couple read one another's diaries (he had even made her read some of his before the wedding, detailing his sexual adventures), and they carried on doing so for decades, inevitably provoking emotional agony all round. What a poor idea this was. Lev Nikolayevich recorded accounts of monkey business with serf girls. At least a dozen illegitimate Tolstoys grew up at Yasnaya Polyana.

He became a magistrate shortly before his marriage and tried to improve the peasants' lot. Indulging a fantasy of living like a *muzhik* himself, at one point Tolstoy started making his own shoes, toiling at menial tasks on the estate and eating only porridge. After years soldiering with 'ordinary people', he wanted so much to turn his back on the privilege he had inherited. But it was embarrassing. Much later he embodied his ideal in the character Levin, named after his creator, in *Anna Karenina* and wrote the famous scene about him blissfully scything and sweating.

*

The main house, originally one of the wings, was white with green iron roofs, and accreted with extensions and verandas with carved balustrades. It smelled of polished wood, with notes of musk and must, and the part where the servants lived displayed objects including a whistle with which Sofya Andreyevna checked whether the night watchman was awake. They had put out Tolstoy's chess set. He sometimes played with Turgenev, but was no match for the gentle giant. And his rifle was there, taller than him. On the master's passport – a sheet of paper then, with a description rather than a photograph – under 'reason for travel', he had written 'for treatment', which is what they all put. His leather travel box held, in buttoned straps, three crystal bottles for eau de cologne. Just as his experiences in the army taught him about class inequality, Tolstoy's months in Switzerland and Germany revealed the comparatively low level of education in his native land. As a result, in 1859 he opened a serf school on his estate and taught there himself. Illiteracy in Russia ran at over ninety per cent at that time. The school didn't last very long.

The mail arrived every day from the railway station at Kozlova Zaseka (now called Yasnaya Polyana) brought in a black leather bag still hanging in the hall. In front of it, a cathedral shadow fell on the beech floor. The large, light dining room off the hall featured a sixteen-leg table with a samovar at one end. It was a living room as well, with sofas and a round mahogany table with a lamp shaded by pleated paper. The family sat in that corner for many hours over the decades, playing balalaikas and mandolins, taking turns at one of two grand pianos or setting records on the gramophone. The famous

Kramskoi portrait of Tolstoy stared down unhappily from the wall. The artist painted two; the other is in the Tretyakov Gallery in Moscow. Tolstoy included Kramskoi in *Anna Karenina*, disguised as the artist Mikhailov (who paints Anna's portrait – Levin notes that the picture is more beautiful than the real Anna, but that flesh and blood always triumphs over art in the end). It was an equitable bargain: a painter painted a writer and a writer wrote about a painter. Repin's even more famous portrait also hung there. A student of Kramskoi, Repin painted Lev Nikolayevich in 1887. There was a portrait of Sofya's father, a man so grand that he sent his shirts to Holland to be laundered.

Off the dining room, in the little living room, known in the family as Sofya's study, she copied out 180,000 pages of her husband's work. Though it is a myth that she wrote out *War and Peace* seven times.

Tolstoy had a Shavian fondness for gadgets, and in the house a 1908 Thomas Edison recording device (which had been sent by Edison himself) played, for visitors, a crackly reel Lev Nikolayevich had made,

his own voice instructing the children to be good and kind and to carry on being so after he died. It was like hearing the cat speak.

On the first-floor landing, a turreted 200-year-old English grandfather clock displayed the correct time. Tolstoy used to pass it on the way to his study at night, his passage lit by kerosene lamps. The desk in his secretary's room on the first floor stabled an American typewriter in a metal case with 'Remington' written on it in Cyrillic. There was a screw-down copying machine like a flower press which could produce ten copies at a time.

Next door, Tolstoy's library held 10,000 volumes in glassed birchwood cases. Hundreds were in languages other than Russian: Tolstoy learned many tongues, to various degrees of fluency. When he was reading the *Iliad* he had a go at Ancient Greek and wrote to Afanasy Fet to say he was speaking the language in his sleep.

The veranda off Tolstoy's south-facing study looked out onto beech trees and bougainvillea. The three-drawered writing desk in Persian walnut in the study had a baize top, and the padded green sofa on which his mother had given birth to him was in the corner. Many of Tolstoy's own progeny popped out on it too. The piece appears in many of the novels. Sometimes he got his servants to move his desk and this leather sofa from room to room, following the sun. He wrote *Anna Karenina* in the guest room, underneath a pair of antlers which duly found their way onto the page.

In Tolstoy's bedroom they had preserved his dumbbells. The type of tunic hanging above his bed, worn with a belt, came later to be known in all Russia as a *tolstovka*. (The word appears on internet sites selling hoodies.) He had a wooden box for stiff white collars, but the single bed was spartan.

Yasnaya Polyana, still owned by the family, has its own restaurant and hotel. I had lunch at the Prospekt with Sasha, a Tulak guide with eyes as blue as gas jets, and two others whose identities I never established. There were only four tables, rugs on the wall, and a set menu of salad, *borshch* and potatoes with cream, cheese, meat and mushrooms served in an earthenware pot. Sasha, à propos of nothing, launched into the standard speech about how everyone used to be friendly and take one another as they were, but now it's all about money, and what can you do for me? It was a conversation I often heard in provincial Russia, and it always included the trope 'In the old days we all earned *more or less the same*.' Sasha was curious about the outside world. 'Is it true', she asked me over the meatless borshch, 'that in Britain you can't go up to a bunch of strangers in a bar and join in?'

After eating, we strolled round Sofya Andreyevna's orchard, where Tolstoy had learned to ride a bike. French apple trees were still flourishing, as well as blackcurrant, redcurrant and gooseberry bushes.

*

The estate hotel was a crumbling Soviet relic a kilometre from the main house. The management billeted me in a cavernous VIP suite which turned out to have nothing but space and mice (not even drinking water or a bedside light). Dinner, as lunch, arrived without me ordering it – salad, *golubtsy* (stuffed cabbage with sour cream) and a raisin strudel, all served with ferocious haste. I kept curtains and windows open at night to watch the moon and breathe in the scent of eucalyptus and moist earth. It was not hard, in the granular darkness, to imagine a bearded figure slipping by, crunching lime leaves underfoot and discussing typescripts and shoe making with his friend Fet before heading off to make trouble, more often than not with a winsome serf girl.

The next morning I forgot something in my room, and when I popped back five minutes after leaving, two maids were in there checking, according to my guide, that I hadn't stolen anything. Though what was there to steal?

*

In *The Cossacks* (*Kazaki*) Tolstoy's gift for conjuring a scene surpassed anything he had written before. 'It was one of those wonderful evenings that occur only in the Caucasus,' he wrote in chapter five.

> The sun had sunk behind the mountains but it was still light. The evening glow had spread over a third of the sky, and against its brilliancy the dull white immensity of the mountains was sharply defined. The air was rarefied, motionless, and full of sound. The shadow of the mountains reached for several miles over the steppe … An old Cossack, returning home from fishing with his trousers tucked up and his hairy grey chest uncovered, has a net across his shoulder containing silvery fish that are still struggling; and to take a short cut climbs over his neighbour's broken fence and gives a tug to his coat which has caught on the fence.

In chapter thirteen, clouds of golden dust mass as the herd lows at the gates.

> The girls and the women hurried through the streets and yards, turning in their cattle. The sun had quite hidden itself behind the distant snowy peaks. One pale bluish shadow spread over land and sky. Above the darkened gardens stars were kindling, and the sounds were gradually hushed in the village.

The older Cossacks, including protagonist Daddy Yeroshka, who doesn't know his age, think the young are fops who do nothing but admire their boots.

*

In 1863, a year after his wedding, Tolstoy went by carriage to Tula, the ancient town near his estate where he had served as a magistrate, to buy a panama hat. On the way home he sketched out a plan for

War and Peace on the back of the receipt for the hat; receipts were A4 size then, but still. Five hundred and thirty nine characters populate the novel, of whom 200 are historical. How did he keep it all in his panama'd head, let alone on his panama receipt?

He published the novel in instalments. When he started, the book was about a Decembrist returning with his family from exile. Tolstoy admired the progressive Decembrists, and revered his ancestral links to those putative revolutionaries. But as he rewrote and reworked, 1812 supplanted 1825. By the summer of 1869 *War and Peace* had engrossed all literate Russia. The book appeared in one volume that year. In the novel, the war has a powerful effect on the officer class: it brings them close to the peasant ways of the old Russia and draws them away from the influence of French culture that had dominated their youth. Tolstoy returned to the theme again and again. Early in *War and Peace* he satirises the pretension of the Russian elite. Anna Pavlovna has a cough, and she says it is *la grippe*, a fashionable new term. Almost all the writers in *Mud and Stars* addressed this theme. It was too big to ignore. As a counterpoint, Tolstoy zooms in on the detail. Who can forget the pickled mushrooms and buttermilk rye cakes in the wooden cabin of the man bright-eyed Natasha calls 'Uncle'? There is no such thing as a national culture, but Tolstoy comes close to conjuring one. Besides his grand themes, he records the soft tissue of history: the perishable bits.

The Russian title of the book is *Voina i mir*. To modern Russians *mir* means 'world' as well as 'peace', but this has only been the case since the spelling reforms after the Revolution: in the nineteenth century the two *mir*s were spelled differently. Tolstoy did not mean to express universality in his title, only peace. Yet his canvas is as broad as Russia itself. The story follows five aristocratic families over fifteen years. And who are we Russians? the author asks.

The film to watch, of the many versions of *War and Peace* made either for the big screen or for television, is Sergei Bondarchuk's 1960s four-parter. The director cast himself as the clumsy, myopic protagonist

Pierre Bezukhov, and wore a white rabbit hat. The budget ran to 13,000 extras, and the eighteen-day Battle of Borodino (stressed on the final syllable) must be among the best fighting scenes ever filmed. Like Tolstoy, Bondarchuk alternates between the close-up shot and the bird's-eye view. In pale morning light, waves of infantry crash over the plains. The camera pans, then switches to an officer loading a cannon, a French infantryman cleaning a bayonet, a man darning a sock. And Napoleon himself, standing on a grassy knoll receiving messages from saluting officers as hooves thunder and smoke and dust obscure the action. It was the era of epic Soviet cinema, but this was an epic of epics. No wonder Bondarchuk had two heart attacks towards the end of filming, during the second of which he was clinically dead for four minutes.*

*

Besides gadgets, Tolstoy and Shaw both loved cars, practised vegetarianism (in Lev Nikolayevich's case only later in life), became pacifists (Gandhi acknowledged Tolstoy as the founder of the pacifist idea), and campaigned to improve the social conditions of the poor. Both, as old men, played vatic roles in their homelands. And, of course, the beards. Shaw is the more irritating of the two, besides being the lesser writer. But the Russian had none of the feminism of GBS. In fact, Tolstoy didn't like women very much – though you could say he didn't like anyone. In his novella *The Kreutzer Sonata* (*Kreitzerova sonata*), published in 1889, his ignorance of women's appetite for sex is embarrassing. It is a cruel and bleak and wonderful work, and one of pathological misogyny. Sex is an appalling business in *Kreutzer*; it's curious, in the light of that, that Tolstoy had so much of it. In the story, a man on a night train tells his fellow travellers that he has murdered his wife, as he believed she was betraying him with a violinist.

* If you're short of time, on the other hand, listen to 'War and Peace in Five Minutes' (available on the BBC website), written by John Crace and read by Simon Callow.

'I heard, and I remember, the momentary resistance of her corset and something else, and then the knife sinking into something soft.' The allegedly adulterous pair had played Beethoven's 'Kreutzer' Sonata together. The murderer rants about the evils of contraception – a hobbyhorse of Tolstoy's at the time – and asserts that women are partly to blame for general licentiousness and for wearing seductive clothes. Sex and violence are united, revealing, in the author's mind, that nobody should ever have sex at all (except him). The authorities in both Russia and the US banned the novella. I don't know why the *Lady Chatterley* case a century later is so much more famous.

Tolstoy wrote *The Kreutzer Sonata* around the time of his twenty-fifth wedding anniversary. Sofya transcribed it, and persuaded her husband to tone down the scenes of marital violence. 'I know in my heart', she wrote, 'that this story is directed against me. It has done me a great wrong, humiliated me in the eyes of the world and destroyed the last vestiges of love between us.' In her diary she wrote that *Kreutzer* 'is untrue in everything relating to a young woman's experiences'.

There is, however, confusion here. Tolstoy put many of his own views into the mouth of the murderer, Pozdnyshev. But the character is not Tolstoy. Pozdnyshev is a raving madman, and the author was not. Much ink has been spilt on the sexual commentary in *The Kreutzer Sonata*. Some feminist scholars have argued cogently that the old man wasn't a rebarbative misogynist. In his fine biography of the count, A. N. Wilson points out that the advocacy of celibacy is found in the New Testament and is therefore not out of keeping with Christian teaching (and therefore, presumably, not simply evidence of Tolstoy being bonkers). Wilson also suggests that as venereal disease was rife in rural Russia in the 1880s, causing much misery including among babies and children, so Tolstoy – and anyone who could – had a duty of sorts to preach against the evils of licentiousness. The question is not as straightforward as commentators have suggested. In addition, as a sinning Christian myself, I know that one can believe one thing and do another. Most people are aware that marriage can be hell, and

Tolstoy makes the point often: in *Ivan Ilyich*, for example, and of course in *Anna Karenina*. When I read the *Kreutzer* novella for the third time, I came round to the view that readers have misinterpreted the story. But I still have sympathy for Sofya Andreyevna.

In 2013 Russia's children's ombudsman refused to allow the reintroduction of sex education into schools (the Orthodox Church had banned it), defending his decision with the statement that children could learn all they need to know by reading Russian classics, and he cited Tolstoy. Yes, ten-year-old Ivan and Tatyana, have a look at *The Kreutzer Sonata* and *Anna Karenina* to learn all you need to know about carnal relations. Russia has the fastest-growing rate of HIV infection in the world, yet this ombudsman, Pavel Astakhov, who reports directly to Putin, said on national television, 'The best sex education that exists is Russian literature … I am against any kind of sex education among children. It is unacceptable to allow things that could corrupt children.'

As for the genesis of *Kreutzer*, Tolstoy was himself a gifted composer. His son Sergei wrote, 'Never in my life have I met anyone who felt music so intensely as my father.' Sergei reported that in the 1870s his father played the piano for three or four hours a day. Before writing his story, Tolstoy had often listened to Beethoven's 'Kreutzer' Sonata (No. 9, in A major, for piano and violin). 'I had the illusion that I was discovering entirely new emotions,' says Pozdnyshev when he hears the music.

Beethoven at first named the piece after the black violinist and conductor George Bridgetower. The composer conducted and played the piano at the first performance, with Bridgetower on violin. They worked by sight, with no rehearsal. At the end, Beethoven leapt off the podium to embrace Bridgetower as he was so moved by his virtuosity: all agree it is a fiendishly hard piece to play. But later that night the pair had a fight over a woman's reputation, and Beethoven renamed the sonata after Rodolphe Kreutzer, the most famous violinist of the era. Kreutzer never played it, though, because it was too difficult.

Chekhov, so much more likeable than Tolstoy and, crucially, able to laugh at himself, read *The Kreutzer Sonata* while travelling through

Siberia on his way to Sakhalin, and wrote home to say how much he admired it. But after three months in the penal colony he said, look, can we really afford the luxury of this stuff?

Five years after the appearance of *The Sonata Kreutzer*, Constance Garnett visited the Tolstoys at their Moscow town house. She fell for the old man, but not for Sofya Andreyevna, whom she described as 'a Philistine, admirably qualified to be the wife of the Mayor of Brighton'. This was mean. Of course Sofya's life was absorbed in domesticity, servants notwithstanding, and in slavishly typing up her husband's work, orchestrating its publication and nursing him when he was ill, not to mention giving birth thirteen times. She made all her husband's shirts (using the same sewing machine for forty-five years) because he said that he didn't like having his clothes made elsewhere. But Sonya published poems and a book of children's stories. Her handwritten cookery book includes recipes for partridge in herring sauce (frequently prepared in the years before Lev Nikolayevich embraced vegetarianism) and Anke cake, named after a friend of German descent. There are no instructions, only a list of ingredients:

One pound of flour
Half a pound of butter
A quarter of a pound of caster sugar
Three egg yolks
One glass of water
(The butter should come straight from the cellar, it needs to be on the cold side).

Sounds horrible.

After *War and Peace* Tolstoy wrote a *Children's ABC*, then planned a book on the six-foot-eight monster Peter the Great. He read the historical volumes prodigiously, and tried to start the novel thirty-three times before abandoning the project and ushering *Anna Karenina* into the world.

When all is said and done, I wonder if the greatest of Tolstoy's talents are his psychological insight and his ability to portray it on a page. Or at least, those gifts equal his ability to draw a landscape in words. When Vronsky looks at his lover Anna all dressed up for him, Tolstoy writes,

He liked it all, but how often had he liked it already.

I don't know if I have ever read anything more crushing. When I looked at *Anna Karenina* for the first time, I thought, 'He knows all about me. He wrote this specially for me.' Tolstoy is an incomparable interpreter of the often unconscious motives behind human behaviour. What are motives but deep-sea fish, gilling in the murky waters of the human mind? Tolstoy wants the reader to like Anna, because she desires to live truthfully, as he did. Is there happiness, the novel asks, without self-deception?

In 1878, after finishing *Anna Karenina*, Tolstoy went to Petersburg to stay with his mother-in-law on Chekhov Street. He had not been to the city for seventeen years. He was still fidgeting with research about the Decembrists. Tolstoy went through various spiritual crises and conversions in his life, turning towards and away from Orthodoxy, confecting his own brand of religious thinking and at one point deciding that he wanted to be a *strannik*, or wanderer. His faith was always of the mystical variety, and for a long time he identified as a *yurodivy*, Russia's special brand of holy fool. After a turbulent period of introspection he wrote the novella *The Death of Ivan Ilyich* (*Smert Ivana Ilyicha*) about the consequences of living without meaning and the quest for identity. In the book he returns to a central theme of *War and Peace* – how should we live?

In 1888, two years after *Ivan Ilyich*, Sofya gave birth to their last child and their first grandchild was born. Five of their thirteen had died, three in infancy.

Around the time Nicholas II ascended the throne, in 1894, Tolstoy began supporting persecuted sectarian groups. (Like many intellectuals who went in for that kind of thing, he cultivated high ideas about humanity in general, but didn't like individuals much. One thinks of Bertrand Russell or H. G. Wells.* Whereas Shaw really was a fugleman for the oppressed.) The authorities duly accused him of 'spreading a terrible infection of anarchy and atheism throughout the whole of Russia'. Lev Nikolayevich's standing with the government reached its nadir after he appealed on behalf of the Dukhobors, a religious sect who, like the master, advocated chastity, pacifism (Dukhobors refused to serve in the army) and communal sharing of goods. Tolstoy published a manifesto on their behalf donated royalties, and contributed funds towards the group's emigration. He wrote a letter about them to *The Times* in London, and on 23 October 1895 the editor published it along with its enclosure, a long report on the persecuted Dukhobors. 'In Russia', Tolstoy wrote in his letter, 'this article would not be allowed by the censor. Therefore I address myself to you, asking you to publish it in your journal.' He had also criticised the Orthodox Church for its unwillingness to stand up to the abuses of a cruel and dictatorial regime. One wonders what he would have made of the Russian Church's supine role today. The Church decided the cure for this virus was to remove its source, and in 1901 it excommunicated Tolstoy. The authorities snooped on him all the time, and exiled his most loyal followers. The man got so far into the doghouse that by the end he could not publish anything officially in Russia.

The world spun away from Lev Nikolayevich. By 1896 he said that he could not bear the luxury in which he lived. This was hard for his family. They were not sybarites, but they did not want to wander the

---

* And indeed Linus, the philosopher in Charles Schulz's Peanuts cartoon strip. 'Humanity,' he once exclaimed. 'I love humanity. It's people I can't stand.'

land as paupers. The senescent Tolstoy said that he hated himself and his life.

The 1905 war with Japan humiliated Russia, and the country was not modernising at the same pace as its rivals. Ukraine was causing trouble. As an old man, Tolstoy turned away from the world and embraced his own form of Orthodoxy, despite his excommunication. He attracted a growing band of acolytes, known as Tolstoyans, many of whom pitched up at Yasnaya Polyana, and many of whom were bonkers. They followed the bearded saint as if he were a guru. Most of them became vegetarians like him, and one promoted a diet of grass and hay. Sofya wrote in her diary that there was 'not one normal person' among his followers.

The Tolstoyans were determined to cut Sofya out of her husband's life, but it was the bald aristocrat Vladimir Chertkov who succeeded in replacing her as the chief object of the great man's affections. A former guards officer twenty-six years Tolstoy's junior, Chertkov was an editor and a publisher as well as an intelligent reader, and he ended up controlling much of Tolstoy's income, as well as establishing himself as his literary executor. Commentators are divided on Chertkov's role: critics often portray him as a villain, but he did some good things. He assisted, for example, in obtaining permission for thousands of Dukhobors to emigrate to Canada (and wrote to *The Times* on their behalf, as Tolstoy had). Some outside the circle valued Chertkov's advice – that bitter curmudgeon Leskov did. Chekhov was grateful to Chertkov for publishing some of his stories. (Bizarrely, Chertkov's grandfather was the serf owner who had sold Chekhov's grandfather the family's freedom.)

Nicholas II remained unimpressed by the Tolstoyan championship of outliers. The tsar confined Lev Nikolayevich to Yasnaya Polyana – no hardship – and sent Chertkov off to the Baltic provinces. Tolstoy was too visible an institution now for them to imprison or shoot him, so the authorities left him more or less alone and punished his acolytes. Chertkov subsequently fled to the south of England, where he settled in a large Victorian house in Tuckton near Bournemouth, a place brimming with Russian revolutionaries, political émigrés, Tolstoyans and assorted crackpots. There he set up the Free Age Press in order to publish cheap editions of Tolstoy's work in English and Russian. Chertkov kept Tolstoy's manuscripts in the Tuckton cellar under twenty-four-hour guard. He and his cronies converted a nearby disused waterworks into a printing press with Cyrillic hot-metal type and smuggled Tolstoy's works back into Russia. Chertkov probably got a million copies to the author's homeland. This was a tremendous achievement. Meanwhile, Tolstoy was posting typed copies of his diaries to Tuckton. Many of those in the Tolstoyan English circle, however, distrusted Chertkov. One was among the earliest and distinguished, if slightly wooden, of Tolstoy's translators and biographers, Aylmer Maude. Far from sharing Tolstoy's belief that marital love was 'bestial', the sprightly Maude was enjoying an affair with his landlady, the family-planning pioneer Marie Stopes, who was in a celibate marriage herself. (I know, it's hard to keep up.)

Other Tolstoyan colonies sprang up in the UK, all more or less running out of steam within a generation. One in the Cotswolds, Whiteway, founded in 1898, staggered on for many years and still bears the name, but there is nothing Tolstoyan about it. In 1931 a thousand Tolstoyans established a commune in Siberia. But those were hard years to believe in anything in Russia.

After more than nine years in England, Chertkov was able to return to Russia, and to Sofya's horror, he settled close to Yasnaya Polyana. He was something of a spiritual martinet, and told Tolstoy that he must cease bicycling on the grounds that it was un-Christian. Was he a destructive force in the Tolstoy marriage? I think he probably was, but if it hadn't been him it would have been someone else.

*

Towards the end of his life Tolstoy accepted inevitability, at least to a certain extent – he was a restless egomaniac, and it wasn't really in his nature to accept anything. Born under a tsar who was essentially a medieval ruler, in his long life Tolstoy rode in a car, used a typewriter, and talked to Chekhov on the telephone. What a call that must have been. Two years before Tolstoy's death, Sergei Prokudin-Gorsky printed a photograph of him in colour. Some say it was the first colour print in Russia. In 1908 Alexander Drankov turned up at Yasnaya Polyana and made a film for the count's eightieth birthday. You can view it on YouTube.

*

Sasha came with me as far as Tula, founded the same year as Moscow. It was the place where Tolstoy bought a panama hat and sketched the plot of *War and Peace* on the back of the receipt. We crossed the river

Upa and passed the golden onion domes of the Tula kremlin and a still-functioning weapon-manufacturing plant founded by Peter the Great. Tula's workshops have always produced samovars, hence the Russian saying 'You don't take a samovar to Tula', coined by Chekhov and still in use. Another aphorism has it that when a man and his wife go to a health spa and he looks at other women, you say to him, 'Why bring your own samovar to Tula?'

Sasha was visiting her mother, who was moving to a new apartment in town. Bulldozers had razed the mother's Khrushchev-era block. She was glad, as the jerry-built flat had impossibly thin walls – her next-door neighbour often chipped in on conversations. The earlier apartments, built under Stalin, had thick walls. 'Say what you like about Stalin,' Sasha said, 'but he kept us warm and private.' I remained silent, hoping that the topic would be dropped. But it wasn't. 'Stalin took us from the plough to the nuclear bomb,' Sasha continued. I looked out of the car window. 'If we hadn't had Stalin we wouldn't have won the Great Patriotic War. My mother always says, not only did he stabilise prices, he lowered them.' Two statues of Stalin had recently reappeared in the capital. Putin loves Stalin. The president had also brought back the Soviet national anthem, which lasts hours.

The family had just raised $5,000 to get Sasha's brother out of military service (which used to be three years, then changed to one for the army and eighteen months for the navy). This, understandably, was another cause of bitterness. 'And then', Sasha said, embarked now on a full-scale litany of horrors, 'there are the *vory*.' I knew about Russia's super-mafia. 'They operate in Tula, you know,' she said, 'it's not just in Moscow and Petersburg.' The *vory v zakone* (sort of translatable as 'thieves-in-law') have survived, like some prehistoric creature which has never evolved, no matter what the Russian system lobs into the water. This fearful Russian *cosa nostra* probably originated in the gulags; like the Japanese *yakuza*, the criminals identify their membership of the tribe with tattoos. The oligarchs rather like the *vory*'s efficient organised criminal methods, often being criminals themselves. I am not sure the *vory* are as brutal as the Calabrian 'Ndrangheta – but I wouldn't bet against it.

Before moving to Yasnaya Polyana to be close to her mother in Tula, Sasha had worked as a tour guide in Moscow. She regularly conducted groups around Stalin's grave (Khrushchev had the body removed from Lenin's mausoleum). 'I remember', she told me, 'taking an old woman round. She recounted that she used to work in a thread factory, and stole some thread to make clothes for her brothers and sisters. For this crime she went to the gulag for seven years. "But", this old woman said, "it taught me not to steal, so that was a good thing."' It was difficult to know what to take from this anecdote. Sasha was like a machine which, once set in motion, lost control of its brakes. 'We all hate Gorbachev,' she said. 'He split up a great strong country. Why? It's true that we have a better life in Russia now than they do in Georgia and the Stans, but that means all the people from those places come here to get work.' Flat central Asian faces were certainly everywhere on the streets of Moscow. 'Before,' Sasha said, 'we were one big happy family.' Except the ones who died, presumably.

I butted in with a spurious question about that troublesome 'ui' sound. I was persisting with 'Daisy, Daisy' but it was not yielding results, and I was still hopeless at speaking Russian. 'Lower jaw forward,' urged Sasha, before clearing her throat to continue on the track she was determined to follow. She had seen Lady Thatcher's funeral on television, and observed the public mourning in the UK, but she had also viewed dancing in the streets as people celebrated the former leader's demise. She was baffled, and asked my opinion of Thatcher. I gave it. 'But she made Britain great,' countered Sasha, as if she were prepared for my answer, it not being the one she wanted. 'She raised the status of Britain in the world.' Fortunately we stopped at that point to buy a bag of *pryaniki*, filled cakey gingerbread, a not very nice speciality of Tula.

Sasha was still not willing to let her skew-whiff nationalism drop. With a mouthful of *pryanik*, she said, 'Britain and America always seem to do better than us, and I don't think that's fair.' This was a reiteration of the same old national inferiority complex of Tolstoy's novels. While fretting about Western advancement in science and technology, however, the writer believed in the superiority of the Russian soul over the soulless materialistic West. Russians were uncertain about their place in Europe (and still are, but increasingly less so, and the current regime would have no qualms about abandoning the West, its ideals and its culture altogether). Russia is of course not unique in this regard. When I lived in Greece for a couple of years, it took me a while to work out why Greeks viscerally hated Americans. It was because they, the Greeks, thought that in a world with its wits about it, it was they who would be the superpower. I detected an ambivalence in Sasha's attitude to the current regime. While harking back to a Soviet paradise, she also admired Putin's attempts to recover an idealised version of the past by forging a national identity. A Russian scholar has defined it as 'restorative nostalgia'.

Why, I wondered after Sasha had dropped me at the train station, were Russian leaders, one after the other, constitutionally unable to enact meaningful reform which might, in improving the general Russian lot, reduce the confounded tension and ambiguity which fostered nationalism? Catherine the Great hadn't, the tsars of the Golden Age hadn't, and certainly nobody has since.

*

The closing years of Tolstoy's life were pathetic, in the true sense of the word. Battles between Sofya and the disciple Chertkov intensified. Everyone argued, and Tolstoy chopped and changed over ownership of copyright, ownership of manuscripts, and over his will. The damned diaries again came to the fore: Tolstoy wanted Chertkov both to read them and to have them. Sofya was adamant that they belonged to her.

A note of farce entered proceedings when Lev Nikolayevich instructed a new secretary (appointed by Chertkov) to begin writing up daily proceedings at Yasnaya Polyana in invisible ink, and then send the carbon copy underneath to Chertkov. Sofya wrote in her diary that Chertkov was 'the embodiment of the devil'. She found a gun and fired at a picture of him on the wall. Everyone said and still says – even her most sympathetic biographers – that she had become mentally ill. If she had, it was her husband's fault. After he left the house for the last time he wrote to one of their children to say, 'Let her know that I desire only one thing – freedom from her.'

Even when Tolstoy fled Yasnaya Polyana, he couldn't rid himself of his love of self-dramatisation and his addictive need to take centre stage. On the train to Astapovo he revealed himself to other passengers, riding his hobby horses. When he was dying in the station house he sent for Chertkov. Accusations stormed to and fro, before and after Lev Nikolayevich expired. Almost everyone involved in the drama that had played itself out in the family home kept records, and many published them, with the result that the whole ghastly saga is in the public domain. Those accounts read like a fugue in many voices. Scholars and others have picked over it all. Tolstoy's son Lev Lvovich publicly blamed Chertkov, responding in a book of his own to a volume written by Chertkov in which the latter claimed he had nothing to do with the crumbled marriage. Chertkov edited the official ninety-volume Jubilee edition of Tolstoy's writings (the 928 letters Tolstoy wrote to Chertkov himself fill five volumes). In the Soviet era another batch of commentators leapt in, accusing Sofya of – the ultimate crime – bourgeois values. As in every other matter, the Soviet position on Tolstoy shifted with the wind. Lenin had hated Tolstoy because if people had followed him, there would have been a peaceful revolution. After the Second World War, the count's star rose again. It turned out that he hadn't been a toff after all, and was at one with the workers. So that was all right.

Deep-Sea Fish

By the time Tolstoy died, Nicholas II had come to believe that the writer had destabilised the Romanov dynasty. Tolstoy possibly did play a role in what only in hindsight looks inevitable. The tsar abdicated seven years after Tolstoy's death. In 1941 the German army moved in to Yasnaya Polyana. When they left, they tried to burn it down, along with its 200-year-old ash trees.

Envoi

Vengeance is mine; I will repay

Tolstoy uses this quotation from the Book of Romans as an epigraph to *Anna Karenina* (using the Church Slavonic version). St Paul was citing a passage from Deuteronomy. But what does it signify? Tolstoy can't have meant God was punishing Anna Arkadyevna for her adultery. He didn't believe in that kind of simplistic theology, and he makes Anna so likeable (she became more likeable as each draft progressed, as if he, her creator, was falling for his heroine). At any rate, I leave it here, because much of the time none of us knows what anything means. And because – this is one thing I do know – writing is the best way of taking vengeance on life itself.

Acknowledgements

Thanks as always to my editor at Cape, Dan Franklin – *Mud and Stars* is our seventh book together. Also to my agent Lisa Baker, my editor at Pantheon in New York, LuAnn Walther, and my US agent Kathy Robbins.

Others to whom I owe gratitude include Ludmilla Andrew and Richard Shaw at the Royal Academy of Music, Rosamund Bartlett, Darren Bennett for the maps, Nell Butler, Robert Chandler, Susannah Clapp, Adam Fergus, Irina Forbes, Edward Gurvich, Sophie Harris for the jacket, Phil Kolvin, Douglas Matthews for the index, Vesna Popovski, Canon Simon Stephens, Colin Thubron and Daisy Watt at Cape.

The Society of Authors awarded me a grant to enable me to keep going – thank you – and Linguaphone donated a really useful language-learning course. Editors who commissioned pieces to assist me on my travels included Jessamy Calkin at the *Telegraph Magazine*, Jackie Holland at Telegraph Supplements, Polly Hope at BBC Radio 4, Victoria Mather at *Vanity Fair*, Nick Trend at the *Telegraph* travel desk and Samantha Weinberg at *The Economist*. Several theatres cooperated with the project by getting me to performances of Russian plays and operas, including the Arcola (possibly my favourite theatre in London), the Royal Opera House and the St James Theatre.

I benefited from so much wisdom and advice both in Russia and in the UK (and the US). Still, all errors, regrettably, are my own.

List of Illustrations

All photographs taken by the author unless otherwise indicated.

p. 2 Alexander Pushkin, portrait by Vasily Tropinin, Pushkin State Museum of Fine Arts, Moscow (Getty Images)

p. 4 Trigorskoye

p. 8 Pushkin. Postage stamp issued 1949

p. 13 Abram Gannibal, portrait by unknown artist, Russian State Library, Moscow. Some historians dispute it really is his portrait (Getty Images)

p. 16 The author at Pushkin's grave at the Svyatogorsky Monastery

p. 22 Pskov

p. 31 Fyodor Dostoyevsky, Staraya Russa

p. 34 Dostoyevsky's house, Staraya Russa

p. 35 Fyodor Dostoyevsky, portrait by Vasily Perov, Tretyakov Gallery, Moscow (Getty Images)

p. 36 Dostoyevsky's notes for chapter five of *The Brothers Karamazov*, The Picture Art Collection (Alamy)

p. 37 Anna Dostoyevskaya, portrait by N. A. Lorenkovich, Pushkin State Museum of Fine Arts, Moscow (Getty Images)

p. 45 Dostoyevsky. Postage stamp issued 1956

p. 49 Church of the Transfiguration, Kizhi Island

p. 59 Nastya and Raban

List of Illustrations

Notes

All books published in London, unless otherwise indicated

Abbreviations

AC Anton Pavlovich Chekhov
AF Afanasy Afanasyevich Fet
AH Alexander Ivanovich Herzen
AP Alexander Sergeyevich Pushkin
FD Fyodor Mikhailovich Dostoyevsky
IG Ivan Alexandrovich Goncharov
IT Ivan Sergeyevich Turgenev
LT Lev Nikolayevich Tolstoy
ML Mikhail Yuryevich Lermontov
NG Nikolai Vasilyevich Gogol
NL Nikolai Semyonovich Leskov

Chapter 1: The People Stay Silent

'Listened to Pushkin at': quoted in David Magarshack, *Pushkin: A Biography*, 1967, pp. 118–19.
'My friends, this brotherhood': AP, '19 October', trans. Henry Jones, in Robert Chandler, *Alexander Pushkin*, 2009, p. 13.
'[Pushkin] is finishing the': quoted in Chandler, *Pushkin*, p. 21.
'dreadful side whiskers, dishevelled': quoted ibid., p. 58.

'our immortal bard, who': quoted in Magarshack, *Pushkin*, p. 139.

'In alien lands I': AP, *Collected Narrative and Lyrical Poetry*, trans. Walter Arndt, Ann Arbor, MI, 1981, p. 51.

'On the shore of': AP, *The Bronze Horseman*, trans. T. J. Binyon, in Binyon, *Pushkin: A Biography*, 2002, p. 434.

'"I am in love"': AP, *Eugene Onegin*, trans. Stanley Mitchell, 2008, p. 63.

'The iambic tetrameter is' (in footnote): ibid., p. xli.

'Applause all round. Onegin': ibid., p. 15.

'Through sleeping streets, past': ibid., p. 18.

'At least three hours': ibid., p. 17.

'Naught touched Onegin to': ibid., p. 24.

'with hatred blazing': ibid., p. 126.

'A certain general of': ibid., p. 168.

'"But I am someone"': ibid., p. 195.

'That moment comes to': AP, 'To …', trans. Antony Wood, in Chandler, *Alexander Pushkin*, p. 39.

'Moscow is a city': quoted in Magarshack, *Pushkin*, p. 250.

'At work everyone was': *New Yorker*, 27 February 2012.

'My friend in days': AP, 'To My Nanny', in *Selected Lyric Poetry*, trans. James E. Falen, Evanston, IL, 2009, p. 107.

'We all know there': quoted in Peter Pomerantsev, *Nothing Is True and Everything Is Possible: Adventures in Modern Russia*, 2015, p. 6.

'It was television through': ibid., pp. 6–7.

'What's Crimea to him?': quoted in Peter Conradi, *Who Lost Russia? How the World Entered a New Cold War*, 2017, p. 333.

'When Putin returned to': *New Yorker*, 6 March 2017.

'Though written in a': quoted in Magarshack, *Pushkin*, p. 192.

'Russians are nice people': Alexandra Kropotkin, *The Best of Russian Cooking*, New York, [1947] 1993, p. viii.

'Not enough different kinds': ibid., p. ix.

'I must warn you': ibid., p. 20.

Chapter 2: A Heart's Journey

'The sun shone bright': quoted in Joseph Frank, *Dostoevsky: A Writer in His Time*, Woodstock, England, 2012 (abridged one-vol. ed.), p. 620.

'filth on the floors': quoted ibid., p. 189.

'**Two hundred men in**': FD, *The House of the Dead*, trans. Constance Garnett, [1915] 2004, pp. 99–100.

'**I learned [there] that**': quoted in Frank, *Dostoevsky*, p. 244.

'**For real Russians, the**': FD, *The Brothers Karamazov*, trans. Richard Pevear and Larissa Volokhonsky, 1992, p. 234.

'**Time and again he**': Frank, *Dostoevsky*, p. 244.

'**boundless vanity and overweening**': ibid., p. 96.

'**hunched, emaciated, with a**': quoted ibid., p. 912.

'**I love you to**': quoted ibid., p. 729.

'**The science of this**': *The Brothers Karamazov*, p. 171.

'**In the enlightened world**': ibid., pp. 313–14.

'**We possess the genius**': quoted in Frank, *Dostoevsky*, p. 785.

'**the new ideas, because**': *The Brothers Karamazov*, p. 663.

'**This is the age**': ibid., p. 90.

'**The most basic spiritual**': quoted in Frank, *Dostoevsky*, pp. 692–3.

'**Raskolnikov, student of nonsense**': *The Oldie*, September 2014.

'**He will get stuck**': *The Brothers Karamazov*, p. xv.

'**wastelands of literary platitudes**': Vladimir Nabokov, *Lectures on Russian Literature*, New York, 1981, p. 98.

'**with a haemorrhoidal face**': *The Brothers Karamazov*, p. 659.

'**fragments of thought flashed**': ibid., p. 359.

'**Ivan wanted to rush**': ibid., p. 650.

'**They reached Liteyny Avenue**': FD, *The Idiot*, trans. David Magarshack, 1955, pp. 157–8.

'**He found the book**': Frank, *Dostoevsky*, p. 700.

'**Just as the highest**': quoted ibid., p. 932.

'**Clark Gable tried to**': Alexandra Kropotkin, *The Best of Russian Cooking*, New York, [1947] 1993, p. 116.

'**Yes, we'll help Fyodor**': *Guardian*, 6 April 2013.

'**I am a sick**': FD, *Notes from Underground*, trans. Richard Pevear and Larissa Volokhonsky, 1993, p. 3.

'**Dostoevsky was tormented by**': programme notes, *Notes from Underground*, Print Room at the Coronet, London, October 2014.

Chapter 3: The Heart within the Tomb

'**I went to see him**': quoted in V. S. Pritchett, *The Gentle Barbarian: The Life and Work of Turgenev*, 1977, p. 232.

'**Do you not think**': IT, *Fathers and Children*, trans. Avril Pyman and W. R. S. Ralston, 1962, p. 225.

'**Nikolai Petrovich, however, continued**': ibid., p. 4.

'**English washstands represent progress**': ibid., p. 21.

'**Times in those days**': quoted in Leonard Schapiro, *Turgenev, His Life and Times*, Cambridge, MA, 1982, p. 38.

'**There is nothing in**': quoted in Eva Kagan-Kans, *Hamlet and Don Quixote: Turgenev's Ambivalent Vision*, The Hague, 1975, p. 19.

'**She never regarded me**': quoted in Elisa Z. Posell, *Russian Authors*, Boston, 1970, p. 76.

'**I have considered you**': Barbara Beaumont (ed.), *Flaubert and Turgenev: A Friendship in Letters – The Complete Correspondence*, New York, 1985, pp. 38–9.

'**There's only one man**': ibid., p. 69.

'"**Well, Peter? Cannot you**"': *Fathers and Children*, p. 1.

'**because his style is**': quoted in Richard Garnett, *Constance Garnett: A Heroic Life*, 1991, p. 183.

'**like all women who**': *Fathers and Children*, p. 121.

'**yesterday's loaf**': ibid., p. 120.

'**are not good or**': quoted in D. S. Mirsky, *A History of Russian Literature*, 1949, p. 170.

'**Bazarov rose. The lamp**': *Fathers and Children*, p. 132.

'**In a remote corner**': ibid., p. 275.

'**No, no and a**': ibid., p. 276.

'**His large nature overflowed**': quoted in Fred Kaplan, *Henry James: The Imagination of Genius – A Biography*, New York, 1992, p. 269.

'**I agree with no**': *Fathers and Children*, p. 94.

'**My son, fear the**': IT, *First Love*, in *The Novels of Ivan Turgenev, Vol. XI*, trans. Constance Garnett, 1897, p. 349.

'**Rakitin is myself. I**': quoted in Schapiro, *Turgenev*, p. 75.

'**Old age, my dear**': quoted in Beaumont, *Flaubert and Turgenev*, p. 64.

'**to say how glad**': quoted in A. N. Wilson, *Tolstoy*, 1988, p. 336.

'**The sour cream in**': Anya von Bremzen, *Mastering the Art of Soviet Cooking: A Memoir of Love and Longing*, New York, 2013, p. 297.

'**thoroughly gentrified Moscow Jews**': ibid., p. 45.

'**steeped and saturated history**': ibid., p. 222.

'**as a time machine**': ibid., p. 6.

'He cleared minefields by': ibid., p. 96.

'Liza, teach the children': ibid., p. 97.

'Your average *Homo sovieticus*': ibid., p. 133.

'in just a bony': ibid., p. 20.

'a story about Soviet': ibid., p. 2.

'with an ivory palette': ibid., p. 158.

'kitschy, mayonnaise-happy seventies': ibid., p.173.

'could be a metaphor': ibid., p. 174.

'The "disaster" Tobias had': Sara Wheeler, *The Magnetic North: Travels in the Arctic*, 2009, p. 54.

'At the root of': *Vanity Fair*, 2 March 2012.

Chapter 4: I Am Yours in Heart

'Hunching his shoulders and': quoted in Laurence Kelly, *Lermontov: Tragedy in the Caucasus*, 1977, p. 107.

'When he laughed, his': quoted ibid., p. 107.

'Haven't you heard of': Peter France and Robyn Marsack (eds), *After Lermontov: Translations for the Bicentenary*, Manchester, 2014, p. 45.

'was like an errant': quoted in Kelly, *Lermontov*, p. 133.

'Far off, with wild': ML, 'The Battle of the Valerik', trans. C. E. L'Ami and Alexander Welikony, in Kelly, *Lermontov*, p. 130.

'I am yours in': ML, 'Izmail Bey' (1832), trans. Laurence Kelly and cited in *Tragedy in the Caucasus*, p. 45.

'Wildly beautiful is the': Alexander Bestuzhev, 'Ammalat Bek', trans. T. Shaw, *Blackwood's Edinburgh Magazine*, April 1843.

'Yesterday I arrived in': ML, *A Hero of Our Time*, trans. Philip Longworth, New York, 1962, pp. 109–10.

'From the forest and': Vasily Grossman, *Life and Fate*, trans. Robert Chandler, 1985, pp. 142–3.

'Gambling, wine and fighting': quoted in Kelly, *Lermontov*, p. 165.

'I have a congenital': ML, *A Hero of Our Time*, trans. Natasha Randall, 2009, p. 82.

'I remember, at this': ibid., p. 141.

'The head of the': quoted in Kelly, *Lermontov*, p. 179.

'smoked like an extinguished': *A Hero of Our Time*, trans. Randall, p. 93.

'It is Byron I': quoted in Peter Cochran, 'Byron's Influence on European Romanticism', in Michael Ferber (ed.), *A Companion to European Romanticism*, Oxford, 2001, p. 71.

'For three whole days': quoted in Kelly, *Lermontov*, p. 199.

'Pushkin's Onegin stretches himself': Vladimir Nabokov, 'The Lermontov Mirage', *Russian Review*, November 1941, pp. 31–9.

'I run through the': *A Hero of Our Time*, trans. Randall, p. 138.

'Britain is so fascinating': Olga Fedina, *What Every Russian Knows (and You Don't)*, 2013, p. 111.

Chapter 5: We All Come out from under Gogol's Overcoat

'We all come out': attributed to Dostoyevsky, origin unknown.

'Far off I saw': quoted in Charles Johnston, *Talk about the Last Poet*, 1981, p. 57.

'behind his laughter you': John Cournos, introduction to *Dead Souls*, in *The Collected Works of Nicolai Gogol*, 2009, Kindle location 4059.

'the greatest play ever': Vladimir Nabokov, *Nikolai Gogol*, New York, 1959, pp. 35–6.

'poetry in action, and': ibid., p. 55.

'his own peculiar smell': NG, *Dead Souls*, trans. Donald Rayfield, 2008, p. 6.

'God, what a sad': quoted in William Lyon Phelps, *Essays on Russian Novelists*, New York, 1911, p. 54.

'of showing themselves in': NG, *Dead Souls*, in *The Collected Works of Nicolai Gogol*, Kindle location 4330.

'The landlady ... returned with': ibid., Kindle location 5127.

'The united tops of': quoted in Nabokov, *Nikolai Gogol*, pp. 87–8.

'I am reminded ... of': *Los Angeles Times*, 2 June 1988.

'Soon there spread before': NG, 'The Overcoat', in *The Collected Works of Nicolai Gogol*, place and date of publication unknown, Kindle location 2283.

'became the greatest artist': Vladimir Nabokov, *Lectures on Russian Literature*, New York, 1981, p. 54.

'Jesus Christ will help': quoted in Nabokov, *Nikolai Gogol*, p.125.

'Russia, are you not': *Dead Souls*, trans. Rayfield, p. 267.

'gowned, whey-faced officials ... laboured': Catherine Merridale, *Red Fortress: The Secret Heart of Russia's History*, 2013, p. 83.

'"Make a four-cornered *kulebyaka*"': quoted in Anya von Bremzen, *Mastering the Art of Soviet Cooking: A Memoir of Love and Longing*, New York, 2013, p. 13.

'was one of those': NG, *Taras Bulba*, in *The Collected Works of Nicolai Gogol*, Kindle location 76.

'We don't want dumplings': ibid., Kindle location 36.

'wide as the Black': ibid., Kindle location 150.

'the enchanting music of': ibid., Kindle location 605.

'It seemed as though': ibid., Kindle location 654.

'But to the average': Alexandra Kropotkin, *The Best of Russian Cooking*, New York, [1947] 1993, p. 232.

Chapter 6: We Shall Rest

'smoky, dreamy mountains ... lithe': quoted in Rosamund Bartlett (ed.), *Anton Chekhov: A Life in Letters*, 2004, p. 227.

'like a dog's tail': quoted ibid., p. 219.

'hellishly expensive': quoted ibid., p. 228.

'no washbasins or objects': quoted ibid., pp. 243–4.

'fish scales': quoted ibid., p. 222.

'wasted his life on': quoted in Ivan Bunin, *About Chekhov: The Unfinished Symphony*, trans. Thomas Gaiton Marullo, Evanston, IL, 2007, p. xix.

'clever, intelligent, cheerful and': AC, *The Island: A Journey to Sakhalin*, trans. Luba Terpak and Michael Terpak, in *A Journey to the End of the Russian Empire*, 2007, p. 85.

'Our primary concern should': ibid., p. 88.

'It seems to me': AC, *A Journey to Sakhalin*, trans. Brian Reeve, Cambridge, 1993, p. 43.

'On my left monstrous': *The Island*, trans. Terpak and Terpak, p. 16.

'There was a convict': AC, *Letters of Anton Chekhov to his Family and Friends*, trans. Constance Garnett, New York, 1920, p. 227.

'Once, a very long': quoted in *New Yorker*, 2 February 2015.

'were covered in black': *The Island*, trans. Terpak and Terpak, p. 60.

'under a glowing western': ibid., p. 50.

'How rich Russia is': *A Journey to Sakhalin*, trans. Reeve, p. 486.

'**Russians are such pigs**': quoted in Bartlett (ed.), *Anton Chekhov*, p. 230.

'**There, at sunset's end**': AC, 'Three Years', in *The Princess and other Stories*, trans. Ronald Hingley, Oxford, 1990, p. 129.

'**the best of the**': quoted in Bartlett (ed.), *Anton Chekhov*, p. 225.

'**totally European**': quoted ibid., p. 229.

'**Siberian ladies, married or**': quoted in Donald Rayfield, *Anton Chekhov: A Life*, 1997, p. 227.

'**In the forest you**': quoted in Rosamund Bartlett, *Chekhov: Scenes from a Life*, 2004, p. 201.

'**I squandered away my**': letter to Sergei Diaghilev, quoted in Janet Malcolm, *Reading Chekhov: A Critical Journey*, New York, 2001, p. 84.

'**I feel I am**': quoted in Jean Benedetti (ed.), *Dear Writer, Dear Actress: The Love Letters of Olga Knipper and Anton Chekhov*, 1996, p. 26.

'**We shall bear patiently**': AC, *Uncle Vanya*, in *Moscow Art Theatre Plays*, trans. Jenny Covan, New York, 1922.

'**They were juicy. They**': AC, *The Cherry Orchard*, trans. Simon Stephens, 2014, p. 14.

'**little action and tons**': quoted in Geoffrey Borny, 'The Seagull: From Disaster to Triumph', in *Interpreting Chekhov*, Canberra, 2006, p. 141.

'**We're sleepwalking to oblivion**': AC, *The Seagull*, trans. John Donnelly, 2013, p. 18.

'**The four-act structure is**': David Hare, *Acting Up: A Diary*, 1999, p. 169.

'**The soft, warm colour**': AC, *The Lady with the Little Dog and Other Stories*, trans. Ronald Wilks, 2002, p. 225.

'**In Oreanda they sat**': ibid., p. 229

'**God's world is good**': quoted in Bartlett, *Anton Chekhov*, p. 253.

Chapter 7: The Lady Macbeth of Mtsensk

'**Do you know who**': quoted in Donald Rayfield, *Anton Chekhov: A Life*, 1997, p. 102.

'**There's simply no getting**': NL, *The Enchanted Wanderer and Other Stories*, trans. Richard Pevear and Larissa Volokhonsky, 2013, p. 433.

'**The true Russia was**': Hugh McLean, *Nikolai Leskov: The Man and His Art*, Cambridge, MA, 1977, p. 173.

'**The rye is enormous**': quoted in V. S. Pritchett, *The Gentle Barbarian: The Life and Work of Turgenev*, 1977, p. 241.

Notes

'She was only twenty-three': *The Enchanted Wanderer and Other Stories*, p. 1.

'a bright falcon': ibid., p. 10.

'Her love for the': ibid., p. 44.

'soft-finned little roach': ibid., p. 44.

'*sumbur vmesto muzyki*': *Pravda*, 28 January 1936.

'We had two icons': *The Enchanted Wanderer and Other Stories*, pp. 48–9.

'We English have always': *Spectator*, 4 May 2013.

'If Turgenev's or Chekhov's': D. S. Mirsky, *A History of Russian Literature*, 1949, p. 316.

'A whisper, a breath': quoted in Maurice Baring, *An Outline of Russian Literature*, 1915, p. 233.

'lives in the borderland': ibid., p. 232.

'the indeterminate sphere of': AF, *I Have Come to You to Greet You: Selected Poems*, trans. James Greene, 1982, p. 68.

'I have come to': *I Have Come to You to Greet You*, p. 24.

'sincere to the point': McLean, *Nikolai Leskov*, p. 517.

Chapter 8: The Poetry of Procrastination

'In one of those': IG, *Oblomov*, trans. Stephen Pearl, New York, 2006, p. 1.

'In fact, glancing at': IG, *Oblomov*, trans. C. J. Hogarth, 1915, p. 4.

'A bathrobe! What is': *Guardian*, 18 December 2017.

'The river burbles merrily': *Oblomov*, trans. Pearl, pp. 83–6.

'lethargy, simplicity of manner': ibid., p. 100.

'wadded, cinnamon-coloured coat': *Oblomov*, trans. Hogarth, p. 70.

'like a plant in': ibid., p. 87.

'"Isn't everybody looking for"': *Oblomov*, trans. Pearl, p. 157.

'"Yes, to think of"': *Oblomov*, trans. Hogarth, p. 23.

'"Nay, but you ought"': ibid., pp. 35–6.

'Yet, the ultimate direction': ibid., p. 23.

'heated, and lighted at': ibid., p. 16.

'*Oblomov* is a truly': quoted in *Oblomov*, trans. Pearl, p. xxi.

'ten heads above me': ibid., p. xv.

'a stupefying bore': quoted in Galia Diment, 'The Precocious Talent of Ivan Goncharov', in Galia Diment (ed.), *Goncharov's Oblomov: A Critical Companion*, Evanston, IL, 2008, p. 3.

'A good idea, but': IG, *The Frigate Pallada*, trans. Klaus Goetze, 1987, quoted in *New York Review of Books*, 3 March 1988.

'The symbolic meanings attached': Edyta M. Bojanowska, *A World of Empires: The Russian Voyage of the Frigate Pallada*, Cambridge, MA, 2018, p. 293.

'"He came to rack"': *Oblomov*, trans. Hogarth, p. 194.

'give birth astride of': Samuel Beckett, *Waiting for Godot*, 1956, p. 89.

'the continual muddy suck': Saul Bellow, *Mr Sammler's Planet*, 1970, p. 215.

'She is in that': quoted in Richard Garnett, *Constance Garnett: A Heroic Life*, 1991, p. 185.

'The Russians have widened': quoted in Helen Smith, *The Uncommon Reader: A Life of Edward Garnett*, 2017, p. 36.

'shaggy ponies so prettily': quoted in Garnett, *Constance Garnett*, p. 117.

'the white weak faces': quoted ibid., p. 261.

'I remember how many': quoted ibid., p. 266.

'The ringing of the': quoted ibid., p. 318.

'Groholsky embraced Liza, kept': AC, 'A Living Chattel', in *The Complete Short Stories*, trans. Constance Garnett, Hastings, 2017, Kindle location 444.

'At the entrance stood': LT, *The Death of Ivan Ilyich*, trans. Louise and Aylmer Maude, 1935, p. 6.

'At the entrance to': LT, *The Death of Ivan Ilyich and Other Stories*, trans. Richard Pevear and Larissa Volokhonsky, 2009, p. 41.

'deplorable': quoted in a letter in the *Literary Review*, October 2013.

'the practice of enforcing': ibid.

'The Pevearsion of Russian', *Commentary*, July/August 2010.

'All his efforts to': quoted in Janet Malcolm, 'Socks', *New York Review of Books*, 23 June 2016.

'To all his attempts': quoted ibid.

'I scarcely like to': quoted in Rebecca Beasley, 'In Violet Ink', *Times Literary Supplement*, 1 February 2013.

'would write out the': quoted ibid.

'Vera Artamonovna, come tell': AH, *My Past and Thoughts*, trans. Constance Garnett, 1924, vol. 1, p. 3.

Chapter 9: Deep-Sea Fish

'I can no longer': quoted in Derrick Leon, *Tolstoy: His Life and Works*, 1944, p. 351.

'I know that my': quoted ibid., p. 351.

'I'm so disgusted with': quoted in A. N. Wilson, *Tolstoy*, 1988, p. 109.

'The extraordinary beauty of': Rosamund Bartlett, *Tolstoy: A Russian Life*, 2010, p. 11.

'I've fallen in love': quoted in Irene and Alan Taylor (eds), *The Assassin's Cloak: An Anthology of the World's Greatest Diarists*, Edinburgh, 2000, p. 54.

'It was one of': LT, *The Cossacks*, trans. Louise and Aylmer Maude, 1916, p. 17.

'The girls and the': ibid., p. 53.

'I heard, and I': LT, *The Kreutzer Sonata*, in *The Death of Ivan Ilyich and Other Stories*, trans. Richard Pevear and Larissa Volokhonsky, 2010, p. 159.

'I know in my': quoted in the *Guardian*, 31 October 2014.

'is untrue in everything': quoted ibid.

'The best sex education': quoted in the *Guardian*, 20 September 2013.

'Never in my life': Sergei Tolstoy, 'Music in Tolstoy's Life', trans. Aylmer Maude, *Musical Times*, 1 June 1926.

'I had the illusion': quoted in Angus Watson, *Beethoven's Chamber Music in Context*, Woodbridge, Suffolk, 2010, p. 134.

'a Philistine, admirably qualified': quoted in Richard Garnett, *Constance Garnett: A Heroic Life*, 1991, p. 128.

'One pound of flour': quoted in Bartlett, *Tolstoy*, p. 321.

'He liked it all': LT, *Anna Karenina*, trans. Joel Carmichael, New York, 1960, p. 711.

'In Russia this article': *The Times*, 23 October 1895.

'not one normal person': quoted in Bartlett, *Tolstoy*, p. 350.

'the embodiment of the': *The Diaries of Sofia Tolstaya*, trans. Cathy Porter, 1985, p. 356.

'Let her know that': quoted in Wilson, *Tolstoy*, p. 511.

Select Bibliography

All books published in London, unless otherwise indicated.

Ascherson, Neal, *The Black Sea*, 1995

Baring, Maurice, *An Outline of Russian Literature*, 1915

Bartlett, Rosamund, *Chekhov: Scenes from a Life*, 2004
  Anton Chekhov: A Life in Letters, 2004
  Tolstoy: A Russian Life, 2010 (ed.)

Benedetti, Jean (ed.), *Dear Writer, Dear Actress: The Love Letters of Olga Knipper and Anton Chekhov*, 1996

Binyon, T. J., *Pushkin: A Biography*, 2002

Bojanowska, Edyta M., *A World of Empires: The Russian Voyage of the Frigate Pallada*, Cambridge, MA, 2018

Chandler, Robert, *Alexander Pushkin*, 2009

Fedina, Olga, *What Every Russian Knows (and You Don't)*, 2013

Figes, Orlando, *Natasha's Dance: A Cultural History of Russia*, 2002

Frank, Joseph, *Dostoevsky: A Writer in His Time*, Woodstock, England, 2012 (abridged one-vol. ed.)

Garnett, Richard, *Constance Garnett: A Heroic Life*, new ed., 2009

Haywood, A. J., *Siberia: A Cultural History*, Oxford, 2010

Hosking, Geoffrey, *Russia and the Russians: A History*, 2001

Kelly, Catriona, *St Petersburg: Shadows of the Past*, 2014

Kelly, Laurence, *Lermontov: Tragedy in the Caucasus*, 1977

Kropotkin, Alexandra, *The Best of Russian Cooking*, New York, 1947

McLean, Hugh, *Nikolai Leskov: The Man and His Art*, Cambridge, MA, 1977

Magarshack, David, *Pushkin: A Biography*, 1967

Malcolm, Janet, *Reading Chekhov: A Critical Journey*, New York, 2001

Maude, Aylmer, *The Life of Tolstoy*, 2 vols, 1908–10

Merridale, Catherine, *Red Fortress: The Secret Heart of Russia's History*, 2013

Mirsky, D. S., *A History of Russian Literature*, 1949

Nabokov, Vladimir, *Nikolai Gogol*, 1959

    Lectures on Russian Literature, New York, 1981

Pomerantsev, Peter, *Nothing Is True and Everything Is Possible: Adventures in Modern Russia*, 2015

Pritchett, V. S., *The Gentle Barbarian: The Life and Work of Turgenev*, 1977

Rayfield, Donald, *Anton Chekhov: A Life*, 1997

Reid, Anna, *The Shaman's Coat: A Native History of Siberia*, 2002

Smith, Helen, *The Uncommon Reader: A Life of Edward Garnett*, 2017

Von Bremzen, Anya, *Mastering the Art of Soviet Cooking: A Memoir of Love and Longing*, New York, 2013

Williams, Rowan, *Dostoevsky: Language, Faith and Fiction*, 2008

Wolmar, Christian, *To the Edge of the World*, 2013

Index

Index

Index

Index

St Petersburg: author avoids, xiii; author resists robbery attempt in metro, 54; Chekhov's family in, 148; Chekhov's *Seagull* booed in, 174; citizens visit Pyatigorsk, 101; Dostoyevsky and, 30–1, 33, 35–6, 43, 47, 51; Dostoyevsky's death in, 46; founded by Peter the Great, 2; Gogol in, 122; in Gogol's writings, 122, 126; Goncharov lives and dies in, 206, 208; and journey to Kamchatka, 155; Ladozhsky railway station, 54; and Lermontov's service in Caucasus, 92, 94; Leskov moves to, 181, 187, 192; and Nicholas II's handwriting, 22; Oblomov in, 202; Onegin in, 12; Pushkin returns to from exile, 23; Pushkin's friends in, 3, 9; river cruise to Moscow, 47–8; settlers in Siberia, 156; site, 7, 96; and succession to Alexander I, 9; supplies supermarket in Anadyr, 212; time zone, 8; tobogganing, 15; Tolstoy in, 233, 246; train journey to Spasskoye-Lutovinovo, 72; Turgenev exiled from, 71; Turgenev meets Lermontov in, 91; in Turgenev's *Fathers and Sons*, 73; Turgenev's tomb in, 68; *vory* (criminal gangs) in, 251

Sakha people, 157
Sakhalin Island, 149–51
Salomineya, 58–9
Samovar (London restaurant), 201
Sasha (of Anadyr), 210, 212
Sasha (Tulak guide), 238–9, 250–3
Schulz, Charles: Peanuts cartoon, 247n
serfs: freed, 70–1, 224, 233; on Turgenev estate, 68–9; in Turgenev's stories, 70
Sergei (driver), 21, 29, 38, 163, 166
Sergei (of Petrozavodsk), 55, 57, 61–2
Seto people, 29
shamans, 156–7
Shaw, George Bernard, 218, 242, 247
shchi (cabbage soup), 50–1
Shenderovich, Viktor Anatolievich, 120
Shenshin (Mtsensk landlord), 194
Sheremetev family, 133
Shostakovich, Dmitri Dmitriyevich: *Lady Macbeth of Mtsensk* (opera), 184

Siberia: Chekhov in, 148–9, 151, 155; flooding, 167; immigrants, 160; and Putin's nationalism, 158; resentment of Moscow, 159; Russification and exploitation, 155–8; self-esteem and consciousness, 252–3; Soviet repression in, 157; tribal people and lifestyle, 156–8
Sinclair, Clive, 86n
skoptsy (religious fanatics), 156
Slavism, 185
Slezkine, Yuri (grandfather and grandson), 83
Sochi, 86, 94–9, 109, 117–20; *see also* Olympic Games
Solovki islands, White Sea, 60
Solovyov, Vladimir Sergeyevich, 46
Solzhenitsyn, Alexander Isayevich: on Old Believers, 191; *The Gulag Archipelago*, 163
Spasskoye-Lutovinovo estate, xi, 66–71, 74–5, 77–8
Stalin, Josef V.: dynamites Kremlin churches, 132; grave, 252; oversees famine, 94n; persecutes writers, 5; policy in Siberia, 157; praised by Sasha, 251; and siege of Leningrad, 88; terror and purges, 82, 86
Staraya Russa, 30, 34, 37, 38
Stopes, Marie, 249
Stoppard, Tom, 175; *The Coast of Utopia*, 225
Streep, Meryl, 220
Suslova, Apollinaria Prokofyevna ('Polina'), 33n
Suslova, Nadezhda Prokofyevna, 33n
Sviridov, Georgy Vasilyevich: *Russia Cast Adrift* (song-cycle), 184
Sweeney, John: 'The Truth about Putin's Games' (TV programme), 118–19

Taganrog, 147–8
taiga, 160, 163, 167
Taishet, 163
Taltsy Museum, 167
Tamara (host at Grint Institute), 129, 133–4
Tanya (Tatanya; guide), 111–12, 114, 116
Tatchell, Peter, 109n, 166

Index

penguin.co.uk/vintage